STEPS TO
SPIRITUAL PERFECTION

The Newman Press
SIGNIFICANT SCHOLARLY STUDIES

The Newman Press imprint offers scholarly studies in historical theology. It provides a forum for professional academics to address significant issues in the areas of biblical interpretation, patristics, and medieval and modern theology. This imprint also includes commentaries on major classical works in these fields, such as the acclaimed Ancient Christian Writers series, in order to contribute to a better understanding of critical questions raised in writings of enduring importance.

STEPS TO SPIRITUAL PERFECTION

*Studies on Spiritual Progress
in Evagrius Ponticus*

Jeremy Driscoll, OSB

THE NEWMAN PRESS
NEW YORK/MAHWAH, N.J.

Cover design by Cindy Dunne
Book design by The HK Scriptorium

Library of Congress Cataloging-in-Publication Data

Driscoll, Jeremy, 1951–
    Steps to spiritual perfection : studies on spiritual progress in
Evagrius Ponticus / Jeremy Driscoll.
        p. cm.
    Includes bibliographical references (p.   ) and index.
    ISBN 0-8091-4264-3 (alk. paper)
        1. Evagrius, Ponticus, 345?-399. 2. Spiritual
life—Christianity—History of doctrines—Early church, ca. 30-600. 3.
Monastic and religious life—History—Early church, ca. 30-600. I.
Title.
    BR195.C5D75 2005
    248'.092—dc22

                                                2005017817

Published by
THE NEWMAN PRESS
An imprint of Paulist Press
997 Macarthur Boulevard
Mahwah, New Jersey 07430

www.paulistpress.com

Printed and bound in the
United States of America

CONTENTS

Introduction
WHY READ EVAGRIUS

We seek after virtues for the sake of the reasons of created things, and from these we pass on to contemplation of the Logos who gives them their being. And the Logos is accustomed to manifest himself in the state of prayer.

The state of prayer is the condition of passionlessness, which by a supreme love snatches up on high the mind in love with wisdom, the spiritual mind.

—Evagrius Ponticus, *Chapters on Prayer*, 52, 53

What mysterious and attractive texts! And indeed, they are typical of Evagrius. They seize our attention; we understand in part; and yet we are drawn elsewhere by them, into a realm whose presence we have at best but sensed and yet within which we do not yet know how to navigate or maneuver with the poorly developed tools of our inner life. We want to enter this realm and move gracefully within it, and yet we know we have need of a guide. Where shall we find one? Who knows the map that has charted the rugged journey, filled with pitfalls, which my mind would undertake so that at last, freed from its vices and thousands of lies, it may be snatched up on high in its love for wisdom? Who can show me that way?

Well, the fact is, others have gone that way and have spoken of it. If we too truly would make similar spiritual progress, we should do well to listen to them. That is to say, there is a tradition about these things. It extends back thousands of years and has always been called simply what it is: *philosophy,* love of wisdom. For Christians, the coming of the divine Logos in the flesh is a definitive revelation of the true path to wisdom. Nonetheless, they continued to call their journey *philosophy,* and the achievements of the ancients were not lost to them.

Evagrius Ponticus is virtually an emblem of this remarkably fruitful encounter between the treasures of ancient philosophy and the definitive Christian revelation of that for which the philosopher seeks. As an instance, let us come again to the texts with which we began. There are so many themes—tightly condensed, memorably phrased—in no more than just a

1

few lines. Any ancient philosopher would recognize this style and know what to do with it. It would be memorized and then pondered at length in a repetitive whispering aloud of its phrases. The ancient would recognize as well its traditional themes, its inherited vocabulary.

"Seeking after virtues"—every ancient philosopher would know that one must begin with this issue and struggle during a lifetime to establish firmly the virtues within. Yet Evagrius—master guide!—knows that virtues really are not an end in themselves but rather a precondition for understanding the world rightly. And so enters another theme dear to the wisdom-seeking tradition: the meaning of the world around us. Thus, "We seek after virtues for the sake of the reasons of created things." Not just vaguely to know created things but more: to know their reasons; in Greek, their *logoi,* that is, the intricate and ordered ways in which the myriad beautiful details of the created order, the cosmos, come from a single and overarching Logos and tend again toward that original source.

Yet Evagrius is a Christian sage, and he is guiding Christian disciples. If he knows how naturally to speak the vocabulary of his culture that formulates the deepest longings of the Greek soul, he knows also how to inflect his speech with the progressively emerging insights of those who were seeking and finding wisdom in Christ. So here, he indicates Christ with the title Logos—at once thoroughly Greek and biblical. If virtues are not an end in themselves, then neither is knowledge of the created order. The created order leads to contemplation of its architect, the divine Logos, the Christ. The encounter with the Logos is not merely of this created order. It is a peering through it, a contemplation, a manifestation, a divine appearing. It has a Christian name: prayer. "And the Logos is accustomed to manifest himself in the state of prayer."

How can we come into such a place of prayer? How do we learn it, reach it, arrive there, stay there? "The state of prayer is the condition of passionlessness." Passionlessness—still another word from the ancient tradition. But what does it mean? For our ears it may seem a strange word and not an especially attractive one. Yet whenever we react like that to ancient texts, more often than not it is because something of the meaning escapes us. The context here suggests that we are dealing with a highly desirable something, something closely connected to a "supreme love." Passionlessness in this ancient culture did not mean being without feelings, verve, or personality. Quite the contrary, it meant having all one's inner energies in order in such a way as not to be pushed around by them. Those energies out of control were called passions. So, again, how can we come into the place of prayer where the Logos manifests himself? Our inner energies must come into line. Our passions must be tamed. This creates a *condition* (yet another technical term of the spiritual geography) in which our strongest inner energy—love—can carry us upward toward that for which we most long;

thus, a "condition of passionlessness, which by a supreme love snatches up on high the mind in love with wisdom, the spiritual mind."

Who was this Evagrius who crafted such mysterious and attractive texts, and thousands more like the two we have just examined here? Could he be a steersman for spiritual seekers today? Under his guidance could I really come to wisdom and to a place of prayer, prayer in which the divine persons manifest themselves to me?

Evagrius was a desert father who lived in the Egyptian monastic semi-eremetical communities of Nitria and Cells from 386 to 399. He was the first of the desert monks to share through extensive writing the already developed monastic wisdom from the Egyptian milieu. Once trained by his own spiritual fathers, he soon became a much appreciated father to others. He passed on what he had received; and, as happens often in this sort of exchange, what he had received became more in him. He contributes to the growing tradition. Much of the desert tradition was passed on orally, in conversations among the monks about every conceivable dimension of their spiritual journey, in intimate encounters between a master and a disciple, where the more personal dimensions of the matter could be discussed. The fathers gave to their disciples what were called simply "words," that is, a few memorable phrases worth repeating again and again that address some dimension or other of the spiritual quest. Evagrius, like the other fathers, guided many in oral exchanges. He also wrote his "words." The two texts with which this introduction opened are simply written "words." They pass on the desert wisdom, and the desert wisdom passes through him, with his unique contribution. Evagrius wrote for disciples who were too far distant from him to enjoy the advantages of the oral encounter. This necessity was a boon for subsequent generations. Those to whom he wrote were stunned by the care with which he formulated his words. They realized that they had a treasure in hand. They copied his words and shared them with others.

We too are far removed from the possibility of an oral encounter with Evagrius, and yet this much at least might attract the attention of anyone today who is on the lookout for a challenging guide to spiritual growth. In Evagrius's own lifetime many people found guidance in his writings and came thereby to wisdom and the place of prayer. Subsequent generations also did. The writings were passed on, and they are available to us. So, why not look at what others have considered a special treasure? Are we so different from others who have set out in search of wisdom? In some ways, of course, there is a difference between ourselves and the ancients, but in fact the gap can be bridged. Then wisdom from the past works again for us today, and so we escape the previously unnoticed limitations of our contemporary paradigms.

This collection of studies attempts to cross the gap of difference between ourselves and another time; it wants to build a bridge to a treasure from the past. I started this work twenty years ago when I first encountered what I have called mysterious and attractive texts. I struggled with them; I understood only in part. But by my struggle I made progress, and I came to see what others had seen before me; namely, that these texts were treasures. Indeed, they were in fact a spiritual guide. They were for me what they were from the start: a way of receiving words from one of the desert masters too far distant for a live encounter. His words awakened in me new spiritual desires. He defined for me and thus helped me to understand what previously were but inchoate movements of my interior life. He uttered many warnings and laid down challenging conditions that were requirements for what he had taught me to so long for—namely, knowledge of the Holy Trinity in a luminous place of prayer.

After about ten years I began to set down in writing what I was learning. I conceived of my writing about Evagrius as no more than the passing on of his "words." Nonetheless, the difference in time and culture between Evagrius and ourselves seemed to require more than merely citing the ancient texts that carried his wisdom. Explanation was needed: a way past the strangeness and a passage through to the mystery. But in the end, it was only the word of Evagrius that I hoped to let stand. I wanted to share with my reader how I had learned to come under his guidance. Once I had finished the preliminary labor required to hear him, I found that what he said was of immediate relevance to my own growth in the spiritual life.

In 1991, I published a large study in which I attempted to let stand what Evagrius said in a text known by the title *Ad Monachos*. In 2003, Paulist Press reissued this study, updated and rearranged, in its *Ancient Christian Writers* series. This present volume collects together eight other review-length studies that I have published in scattered places between 1994 and 2003. They have been reedited for inclusion in a single volume that can act as a companion volume to *Ad Monachos* in the *Ancient Christian Writers* series.

Evagrius may be considered a classic of fourth-century Egyptian monasticism. There is an art to reading any classical text from any period different from our own. The classic calls to me from another time. It provokes and challenges my point of view. If I am to read it fairly and accurately, I must risk its point of view. It tells me: Change your life, learn to think differently, see things otherwise; you have not yet imagined what you will find here.

A crucial insight in my learning to risk Evagrius's point of view was given to me by the scholar of ancient philosophy Pierre Hadot.[1] It could be said

---

[1] P. Hadot, *Exercices spirituels et philosophie antique* (Paris, 1987); idem, *Philosophy as a Way of Life, Edited and with an Introduction by Arnold I. Davidson* (Oxford: Blackwell, 1996). See my own work for a lengthier description of how Hadot helps to read Evagrius: *Evagrius Ponticus: Ad Monachos*, translation and commentary by Jeremy Driscoll, OSB, Ancient Christian Writers, vol. 59 (New York/Mahwah, NJ: The Newman Press, 2003), 196–214; hereafter referred to as ACW *Ad Monachos*. What follows here is a brief summary of that material.

that Hadot's lifelong project as a scholar has been to open up the contemporary relevance of ancient Greek and Roman philosophy by means of one principal hermeneutical key. Ancient philosophy, he insists again and again, was a way of life. It was not some form of arcane talk or thought. Insofar as it talked and thought, it was with a view of promoting a "mode of existing-in-the-world, which had to be practiced at each instant, and the goal of which was to transform the whole of the individual's life."[2]

Monasticism too was and is a way of life. It is not possible to interpret correctly any texts of value that emerge from the monastic environment without reference to the concrete way of life that the written words are meant to promote. It is useful to distinguish, as Hadot does in explaining ancient philosophy, between *forms of discourse* and *forms of life*. Forms of discourse are the philosophical or monastic language that reoriented the adept toward a new form of living. Discourse pointed the way toward conversion, a change in the way of seeing things that led to a change in the way of living. So philosophy in the ancient world was never what it can often seem to be now; namely, a form of abstract thinking practiced by a small group of academic professionals. Philosophy was fundamentally a way of living; a form of discourse accompanied it.

Something similar is true for the monasticism represented by Evagrius. It was fundamentally a way of life, and there was a discourse that accompanied it. But Evagrius is not understood if the reader stays only within the world of discourse. As a closed circle, Evagrius's monastic discourse can seem to the contemporary reader like so much theoretical speculation, and one wonders where it is all going. Some few find the closed circle oddly fascinating, but most are inclined to pass on to something whose relevance is more immediately apparent. Yet there is literally a breakthrough for the reader who understands that the discourse really makes sense only in reference to practicing the way of life that the discourse is indicating.

When Evagrius came to the desert to make himself the disciple of the masters who had already lived there long before him, he came already formed by the Greek philosophical tradition. In him, the desert tradition, different from the Greek tradition, was able to fit itself into the philosophical tradition in which he had been formed. A most fruitful synthesis was slowly stitched together. Such a synthesis is usually not a consciously intended project. It happens. One does not say, "I'm Greek in my culture, and now I'm meeting another culture, and so I will form a synthesis." No, one person meets another and comes under the other's influence. Besides, no person is a pure product of a single culture. Plenty of "Greek" was already in the Egyptian air, even if the air there was different from what Evagrius had breathed in his formative youth. Moreover, the synthesis of

---

[2] Hadot, *Philosophy as a Way of Life*, 265.

which Evagrius is such a fine example was happening everywhere in the ancient world. Christianity had long presented itself to its contemporaries of the Greco-Roman culture as the true philosophy, the true *way of life*. This was natural, for Christians were not culturally innocent. They were a part of the Greco-Roman culture, and with its forms they advanced in their understanding of the mystery of Christ.

So when the time comes for the monk Evagrius to be a spiritual guide for others and to offer them words that would form them in the monastic way of life, he instinctively begins to shape his discourse into categories defined by the philosophical tradition, all the while adding to that tradition a specifically Christian content and the unique inflection of this latter that was given it by the desert tradition. Here are riches coming together from many directions. They can still nourish today any Christian who seeks to grow in the spiritual life.

Evagrius's discourse forms a coherent system, beautifully complex; but—again!—the system does not exist for itself; it promotes a way of life. Nonetheless, grasping the coherence of the discourse is how it becomes useful in life. What coheres in the theory is meant to indicate the manner in which the different dimensions of our life, both interior and exterior, cohere and flow together into an order that tends toward a goal. If they do not cohere, there is no moving toward the goal.

We become more alert to the coherence of Evagrius's system when we notice that a good many of his words are concerned with three major areas of life, areas identified also by the philosophical tradition. In Greek these were called *topoi,* master themes that required treatment. For example, among the Stoics there were three master themes that formed the major parts of their philosophy: ethics, physics, and logic. Evagrius's teaching falls within these categories, even while also going beyond such themes. But Evagrius's "words" can be described as concerned with thinking correctly about doing the good (ethics), thinking correctly about the world (physics), and thinking correctly about thinking itself (logic). Yet we must note well: this division of themes was a pedagogical arrangement on the part of both Evagrius and the philosophical masters. It was suited to *discourse.* But the *way of life* itself was not divided into parts. This was a unitary act that involved *living* the insights of the various themes all at once.

So, *discourse* leads to a way of *living.* Evagrius learned the neat order of ethics, physics, and logic from the Greeks and utilized some of their best insights in his teaching. Nonetheless, as I have already said, the content and emphasis of his teaching are fundamentally Christian, and they are played in the key of the desert monastic tradition. He is a master of the delivery of his teaching; in his mouth and hand the tradition receives a unique cast. With Evagrius, thinking correctly about doing the good is very concretely articulated. It will involve, of course, establishing the correct measure of food and drink, arriving at sexual continence, living simply, and helping the poor. But above all it will have to do with controlling one's irascible energies in relations with others. What the monk does with food, drink, sex, and poverty all have ultimately to do with the forming of a gentle spirit of a long-suffering monk who is filled with tender love for others. Such tender love, he insists, is the only door to right thinking about the world. Thus, for him, there is no such thing as an irascible despiser of others who can be absorbed in serene contemplation of the cosmos. Some such contemplator may perhaps be found, but we can be sure that the contemplation is false, a lying and deceiving knowledge.

True knowledge about the creation will grasp the inner sense of the discourse about it, which distinguishes, in mysterious terms, between corporeals and incorporeals and providence and judgment. This is discourse that maps the paths of an ever more profound contemplation, in which the mind of the one at prayer is revealed as an incorporeal instrument created in the divine image and perfectly suited to receive the final blessedness for which it was originally created, namely, the knowledge of the Father through the Son in the Holy Spirit. God is Light (1 John 1:5), and the godly Light shines in its image!

> *The condition of the mind is the intelligible "height"*
> *Which resembles the color of heaven.*
> *Onto it the light of the Holy Trinity comes*
> *At the time of prayer.*
> —Evagrius Ponticus, *Skemmata* 4

All of the above suggests how to read Evagrius and how to approach the studies in this book. Evagrius's words are *discourse* about the monastic *life*. His words must be pondered slowly and at length, but above all they must be put into practice. The studies in this book are designed as exercises in pondering the discourse. They show the traditional ways by which the discourse provokes an interior movement in the fallen mind and guides it through the tortuous journey of recovering original blessings. The studies interpret the discourse always in the light of its aim—concrete practice.

Methodologically I comment on particular texts of Evagrius by reference to other of his texts and to other parts of the tradition of which he is so eminent a representative. This method is cumulative in its effect, and it mirrors the original process of the digesting of Evagrius's words by his first disciples. As they pondered what he said, more and more connections with other comments were made. The accumulation of insight begins to form a picture of the whole.

Along the way, I indicate only briefly the contemporary relevance of what Evagrius says for our own spiritual growth. This is not because there is not much that is relevant; it is a part of the method. Evagrius's relevance is that he allows a secure way out of merely contemporary points of view. For the relevance of this to fall into relief, it is enough to hear him well. This requires building bridges backward to a time different from our own and concentrating our efforts on that other time. In the conclusion, I will step back from this effort to hear him well and attempt to open a discussion of what this "hearing something new in something old" can contribute to our own spiritual growth.

As mentioned, the studies collected here bring together my research during a ten-year period. Each chapter has been published elsewhere, either as chapters in books featuring different authors or as contributions to scholarly journals. They have been slightly reworked here to form a coherent flow. Each chapter can stand on its own and could be consulted individually by a reader interested in the particular subject treated. But the collection has been arranged to function as a journey from start to finish. Let me indicate the sense of that arrangement for the reader who chooses to follow the whole unfolding.

The chapter on "spiritual progress" is an overview of all the works of Evagrius, and puts them in a proper order for reading that follows spiritual progress; in "one sitting" it surveys the whole of the Evagrian corpus and suggests how and where to take account of each particular work. The next, much shorter chapter on "spousal images" treats the whole scheme of Evagrian anthropology—that is, the relation of body, soul, and mind—but it does so under just one theme, albeit an attractive one: spousal images. "Penthos and Tears" considers attitudes with which Evagrius says we must begin our spiritual journey. Without understanding their role, we cannot advance further. "Love of Money" fits into this collection as a particular example of the way our master guide treats one of the eight principal evil thoughts that afflict the mind that would fix itself on contemplation and knowledge of the Trinity. By treating one of the eight, I hope all eight are somehow represented in the logic of the book's unfolding. "Apatheia" and "purity of heart" are terms (one from the philosophical tradition, the other biblical) indicating an intermediate goal in spiritual progress. The placement of the chapter here, in the middle of the collection, indicates this intermediate position. What precedes this chapter has to do with the first basic phase of the spiritual journey; what follows has to do with questions concerning those who have reached purity of heart. The chapter itself exposes some of Evagrius's most beautiful and useful teaching.

From this midpoint, the study turns to a question frequently considered by the monks of old: "abandonment by God." This is a risk that is run in the spiritual life only after reaching purity of heart, for then the monk is subtly tempted to become vainglorious and proud. Unless such pitfalls can be avoided, there will be no more spiritual progress; and indeed there will be an unraveling of the progress already made. This chapter is also the first to expand outward to see how Evagrius's teaching comes from and develops the tradition of other desert fathers. The chapter on the exegesis of Poemen expands even more outward from the "merely" Evagrian teaching and shows how the practice of the daily reading of the Word of God is the way in which all the wisdom of the desert was carried forward. Evagrius must be understood within this same stream. "The Fathers of Poemen" is a study that contests a contrast frequently drawn by contemporary scholars between Poemen, representing one type of Egyptian monasticism, and Evagrius, who is thought to represent another, less genuine type. This study unites many of the desert fathers around the teaching represented in an especially effective way in Evagrius. It argues that drawing such contrasts between Poemen and Evagrius causes us to miss the subtleties in both.

We are studying a monastic tradition from fourth- and fifth-century Egypt; and, as I said, my method is to treat it focusing on its original historical context. However, this tradition can become a useful treasure for any contemporary seeker of Christian wisdom. I myself am a monk, but I know that the usefulness of this or any other part of monastic tradition is not restricted to monks. I like to tell the people who visit my monastery that one of the things a monastery is good for is that it can put into particularly clear relief the ingredients that are necessary for anyone who is seriously seeking God. I invite my reader now to enter into this monasticism from the past. When the journey is over, I will indicate what I think are some of the ingredients that have fallen into clear relief and can be helpful to us in our search for God today.

1

Spiritual Progress in the Works of Evagrius Ponticus

In one of the chapters of the *Praktikos* Evagrius says, "The one making progress in *praktikē* reduces the passions, and the one making progress in contemplation reduces ignorance. There will one day be a complete destruction of the passions, but of ignorance there is one that has an end, but another of which there is no end, as they say" (87; p. 678).[1] This text is a clear expression—and characteristic—of the theme of spiritual progress as Evagrius conceives it.[2] Progress occurs in the two major phases into which he divides the monastic journey, a division for which he is so well known. There is progress in *praktikē,* which is shown in the reduction of the power of the passions. There is progress in knowledge, which is shown in the reduction of the power of ignorance. Furthermore, both types of progress are laid against the backdrop of a world beyond this present one, a world in which there is an end to the domination of the passions and an end, in some sense, to ignorance. But Evagrius suggests here the idea of infinite progress in knowledge, for the knower of God will never be able to grasp God entirely or adequately.[3]

The issue of spiritual progress as this brief text outlines it is evident in Evagrius in a variety of ways. In this fact Evagrius shows himself to be the heir of both monastic and philosophical traditions. I would like here to try to highlight the theme in Evagrius and see how it achieves a sharper focus

---

[1] The translations throughout are mine unless otherwise indicated. References to the text of the *Praktikos* are all to the edition of A. and C. Guillaumont, *Évagre le Pontique: Traité pratique ou le moine,* Sources Chrétiennes 170, 171 (Paris: Cerf, 1971). Vol. 170 is the introduction, and the critical edition of the Greek text is vol. 171. References to A. and C. Guillaumont, *Praktikos,* refer to this work.

[2] Spiritual progress is a typical theme in the monastic spirituality of the epoch. For a number of studies on various expressions of this, see *Spiritual Progress: Studies in the Spirituality of Late Antiquity and Early Monasticism,* ed. J. Driscoll and M. Sheridan; Studia Anselmiana 115 (Rome: Editrice Anselmiana, 1994).

[3] For this interpretation of the Evagrius text, see I. Hausherr, "Ignorance infinie," *Orientalia Christiana Periodica* 2 (1936): 351–62 and "Ignorance infinie ou science infinie?" *Orientalia Christiana Periodica* 25 (1959): 44–52.

11

in his work by referring to his principal writings in a sort of overview of the works. I will divide this overview into two major categories: first, progress as expressed in the relationship of separate Evagrian texts one to another and, second, progress as expressed within single works.

PROGRESS EXPRESSED IN THE RELATION OF EVAGRIAN TEXTS ONE TO ANOTHER

Some of Evagrius's works are intended by him to be understood in reference to each other, and this relationship expresses the order of spiritual progress. But whether Evagrius is explicit on this or not, it is possible to locate all the writings of Evagrius along some scale of spiritual progress. That is the project that I would like to undertake here. There is an ancient precedent for a project of this sort. Porphyry arranged the works of Plotinus according to an order of spiritual progress so that they would be read in a sequence that would promote spiritual progress in the reader.[4] The importance of this point in regard to reading Evagrius should not be underestimated. If he is read outside of a proper order, the door is opened wide for misunderstanding. And it is not simply a matter of a proper order for pursuing intellectual questions. The order of Evagrian texts represents a requirement about an order of actual progress in the life of virtue as a prerequisite for approaching texts that promote actual progress in the life of knowledge.

The Praktikos, *the* Gnostikos, *and the* Kephalaia Gnostica

This order of spiritual progress in works that relate to each other is seen most clearly in what Evagrius explicitly states to be a project in three parts, the *Praktikos,* the *Gnostikos,* and the *Kephalaia Gnostica.* He says in the letter that introduces these three, "I have divided the matter of *praktikē* compactly into a hundred chapters, and the matter of the life of knowledge into

---

[4] See P. Hadot, *Exercices spirituels et philosophie antique,* 2nd ed. (Paris, 1987), 45. Porphyry's arrangement, as explained by Hadot, was according to three stages: purification of the soul by detachment from the body, knowledge and passage beyond the sensible world, and conversion toward the mind and the One. Arrangement of philosophical teaching according to an order of spiritual progress was widespread throughout the various schools. For details, see P. Hadot, "Les divisions des parties de la philosophie dans l'Antiquité" in *Museum Helveticum* 36 (1979) 213–21. For this especially in Porphyry, see I. Hadot, *Le problème du Néoplatonisme Alexandrin* (Paris, 1978), 152–58.

fifty, plus six hundred" (*Praktikos,* prologue 9; p. 492). The hundred chapters of which he speaks are, of course, the hundred chapters of the *Praktikos;* the fifty, the transitional work the *Gnostikos;* the six hundred, the difficult and challenging meditations on the life of knowledge in the *Kephalaia Gnostica.* In this program of presentation we have the well-known Evagrian division of the monastic life into the two basic phases of *praktikē* and knowledge. The beginning phase of monastic life, *praktikē,* the active struggle for virtue, is begun with the *Praktikos,* but the aim of the *Praktikos* is to establish within the body, soul, and mind of the monk those conditions necessary for understanding the more lofty meditations of the *Kephalaia Gnostica.* The *Gnostikos* is a small transitional work between these two larger texts. No monk can begin his journey with the *Kephalaia Gnostica.* Indeed, history has shown that when the *Kephalaia Gnostica* is read outside of this context, it is subject to serious misunderstanding.[5] It is to avoid this kind of misunderstanding, which arises from failing to observe the order of spiritual progress, that Evagrius says immediately following the passage I just cited, "Some things we have veiled and made other things obscure, so that we might not give what is holy to dogs or cast pearls before swine (Matt 7:6). But it will all be clear to those who have begun to step in these same tracks" (ibid.; pp. 492–94). For our purposes we may understand "same tracks" as the proper order of spiritual progress.

Within each of these three related works there is likewise an order of progress appropriate to the subject matter of each. I will save the discussion of these orders for the second category of this study, when I will discuss order within the single works. For the present it is enough to note that these three works express in their relation to each other the whole sweep of the journey that the monk travels as he makes progress, from its beginning in *praktikē* to its goal of knowledge.[6]

Biblical Scholia

There is another genre within the Evagrian corpus that likewise expresses the order of spiritual progress; namely, the collections of biblical

---

[5] For the history of this text, understood and misunderstood through the centuries, see A. Guillaumont, ed., *Les 'Képhalaia Gnostica' d'Évagre le Pontique et l'histoire de l'origénisme chez les Syriens,* Patristica Sorbonensia 5 (Paris, 1962).

[6] To the notions expressed in the *Praktikos* the other Evagrian texts devoted primarily to *praktikē* can be subjoined. Thus, *On the Bases of the Monastic Life, On Evil Thoughts, On the Eight Spirits of Evil,* the *Antirrhetikos.* On the problem of classifying the works of Evagrius with cautions against too rigid a distinction between works devoted to *praktikē* and those devoted to knowledge, see Driscoll, ACW *Ad Monachos,* 29–31.

scholia. There are extant from the hand of Evagrius a large collection of scholia on the biblical book of Proverbs.[7] There is a smaller collection of scholia on Ecclesiastes, most of which have survived.[8] We know also that he perhaps composed scholia on the Song of Songs, though unfortunately no collection survives.[9]

In composing scholia on these biblical books Evagrius places himself in a tradition that goes back at least as far as Origen, who had already identified an order of spiritual progress in the progression from one of these biblical books to the other. Evagrius places himself directly in this Origenic tradition when he says in one of his scholia on Proverbs, "He who has enlarged his heart by purity will understand the reasons of God, reasons which concern *praktikē* and natural contemplation and theology. For all the material of the scripture is divided into three parts: ethics, natural contemplation, and theology. Proverbs corresponds to the first, Ecclesiastes to the second, and the Song of Songs to the third" (*In Prov.* 22:20).[10] In fact, for Evagrius a good spiritual father—someone accomplished in Christian gnosis—distinguishes himself as such, among other ways, by his ability to recognize to what particular stage of the spiritual journey a given verse of scripture is to be referred.[11] This applies throughout each verse of the scriptures, but here it is a case of knowing the stage of progress to which a particular book is in general to be applied.

In actual practice Evagrius will find in his meditations on verses from Proverbs material that refers to more than simply the life of *praktikē*. In other words, no more than Origen does Evagrius employ these distinctions rigidly. Yet the idealized scheme is evidence that Evagrius saw the scriptures themselves as the text on which a Christian philosophy would be based, that is to say, a Christian order of spiritual progress.[12] Origen himself had already made this claim for the scriptures, taking the progressive subject matter of Proverbs, Ecclesiastes, and the Song of Songs as evidence that Solomon, long before the Greeks, had set down the order of spiritual

---

[7] See P. Géhin, ed., *Évagre le Pontique, Scholies aux proverbes,* Sources Chrétiennes 340 (Paris, 1987).

[8] See P. Géhin, ed., *Évagre le Pontique, Scholies à L'Ecclésiaste,* Sources Chrétiennes 397 (Paris: Cerf, 1993).

[9] See A. and C. Guillaumont, *Praktikos* 1:36; see also P. Géhin, ed., *Scholies à l'Ecclésiaste.* Concerning the Canticle, Géhin writes, "c'est un livre qu'Évagre utilise peu et qu'il n'a certainement pas commenté" (*Scholies aux proverbes,* 20).

[10] G 247; p. 342.

[11] See *Gnostikos* 18, where Evagrius explains that it must be determined whether a verse is relevant to *praktikē,* natural contemplation, or theology and then where exactly within any of these three the verse refers. For example, if a verse applies to *praktikē,* does it refer to the irascible or to the concupiscible part of the soul, or perhaps to the rational part, and so on.

[12] Cf. P. Gehin's order in *Scholies aux proverbes,* 28–30, with references to these same divisions as conceived by Clement and Origen.

progress for the true philosophy: "Indeed he [Solomon] was not unaware that he was laying the foundations of the true philosophy and founding the order of its disciplines and principles" (*Commentary on the Song of Songs*, prologue).[13]

This scheme and the content of the biblical Proverbs themselves does give rise in Evagrius to a tendency to refer the verses of that biblical book to the first stage of monastic life, to *praktikē*. Nonetheless, whether in the genre of biblical scholia or some other style of text treating of *praktikē*, Evagrius very often refers the meditation to *praktikē's* goal in some aspect of knowledge. Thus, among the very first scholia on the opening verses of Proverbs, Evagrius explains the biblical verse "to know wisdom and instruction" (Prov 1:2) in this way: "It says he [Solomon] became king in Israel because he knew instruction and wisdom. And *wisdom* is knowledge of corporeals and incorporeals as well as the judgment and providence to be seen in them. *Instruction* is moderation of the passions which are seen in the passionate or irrational part of the soul" (*In Prov.* 1:2).[14] Evagrius has found at the very beginning of Proverbs two biblical words that refer to the two major stages of spiritual progress. Παιδεία refers to *praktikē;* σοφία refers to natural contemplation and prepares the mind for knowledge of the Holy Trinity. We shall not be surprised, then, to find in the proverbs that follow meditations on both these phases.

For similar reasons this classical scheme and the content of the biblical book of Ecclesiastes are suited to placing the knowledge of this visible, corporeal world in a position subordinate to the higher knowledge of an incorporeal world and this to the still higher knowledge of the Trinity. Thus, this biblical book's famous "vanity of vanities, all things are vanity" (1:2) is occasion for Evagrius to comment,

> To those who enter into the intelligible church and marvel at the contemplation of created things, the Logos says, "Do not think that this is the final end which is held in store for you by the gospel promises. All that is vanity of vanities before the knowledge of God himself. Just as after perfect health is restored, medicine is vain, so also vain are the reasons of aeons and worlds after the knowledge of the Holy Trinity." (*In Eccl.* 1:2)[15]

---

[13] Text in Die griechische christliche Schriftsteller der ersten drei Jahrhunderte (GCS), 33:76. Trans. Rowan A. Greer in *Origen: Translation and Introduction by Rowan A. Greer*, Classics of Western Spirituality (New York: Paulist, 1979), 232.

[14] G 3; p. 92; see also pp. 33–54 for a discussion of all the themes of Evagrian teaching that appear in the *Scholies aux proverbes*, especially 33–44, "Les Étapes du Progrès Spirituel."

[15] Géhin, ed., *Scholies à l'Ecclésiaste*, 58–60. Origen evaluates Ecclesiastes similarly: "And he [Solomon] included the second subject, which is called natural discipline, in Ecclesiastes, in which he discusses many natural things. And by distinguishing them as empty and vain

Unfortunately, Evagrius's scholia on the Song of Songs, if he ever actually wrote any, have been lost. We know only by reference to the tradition in which he stood that the scholia on these biblical verses would have been referred to the highest level of the knowledge of God.[16] We can only wonder to what heights the daring imagery of that biblical love poem might have inspired Evagrius. We get some glimpse in a composition like the following from his *Ad Virginem:*

> Virginal eyes will see the Lord.
> The ears of virgins will hear his words [cf. 1 John 1:1].
> The mouth of virgins will kiss their bridegroom [Cant 8:1].
> The sense of smell of virgins will run after the odor of his perfumes
>   [Cant 1:4].
> Virginal hands will handle the Lord [cf. 1 John 1:1].
> And purity of the flesh will be pleasing to him.
> The soul of the virgin will be crowned
>   and with her bridegroom she will live forever.
> A spiritual garment will be given her
>   and with the angels in heaven she will feast.
> Inextinguishable the lamp she will light
>   and the oil will not give out in her vessels [Matt 25:4].
> She will receive the riches of the aeons
>   and she will inherit the Kingdom of God [cf. Matt 25:1–13].[17]

The scholia on the classical trilogy of Proverbs, Ecclesiastes, and the Song of Songs bring to mind another set of biblical scholia composed by Evagrius: the *Scholia on the Psalms.* Evagrius situates recitation of the

---

from what is useful and necessary, he warns that vanity must be abandoned and what is useful and right must be pursued." And, "[a]fter Proverbs he [Solomon] comes to Ecclesiastes, which teaches, as we have said, that everything visible and corporeal is transitory and weak" (*Commentary on the Song of Songs,* prologue; GCS 33:76, 78; Eng. trans. Greer, *Origen,* 232, 234.

[16] Origen, *Commentary on the Song of Songs,* prologue: "Indeed, in the words of Song of Songs may be found that food of which the Apostle says, 'But solid food is for the perfect' and requires such people as listeners who 'have their faculties trained by practice to distinguish good from evil'" (GCS 33:62; Eng. trans. Greer, *Origen,* 218 cited here).

[17] See H. Gressmann, ed., "Nonnenspiegel und Mönchsspiegel des Euagrios Pontikos," *Texte und Untersuchungen* 39, no. 4 (1913): 151. This proverb shows much about the theme of spiritual progress, expressed first of all in the future tense of the verbs. As we shall see later in detail (see Chapter 2 below), the proverb is structured in an ascending order: (1) *Bodily* images reach their climax in "purity of the flesh." (2) Then there is the image of the virginal *soul* and its spiritual garment. (3) The image for the *mind* is an inextinguishable lamp and the riches of (a) the aeons and (b) the inheritance of the Kingdom of God, which is knowledge of the Holy Trinity. Cf. *Praktikos* 1–3. For how Evagrius would interpret Matt 25:1–13 in this context, see *Lt* 28:1; *In Prov.* 31:18; *G* 7; *V* 17, 43.

psalms within an order of spiritual progress, and it will be worth fixing its place before seeing the actual content of the scholia themselves. Some clue as to where psalmody fits an order of progress is given in various little chapters which indicate the role of psalmody in the monk's life. First of all, it has the role of calming the irascible part of the soul. In the *Praktikos* Evagrius says, "Psalmody and long-suffering and mercy put to rest an agitated irascibility and all of this at the appropriate times and in the appropriate measure" (15; p. 536). Or again, "In the one singing psalms irascibility is quiet" (*M* 98).[18] "Psalmody calms the passions and makes quiet the intemperance of the body" (*Prayer* 83).[19]

In these and similar statements Evagrius is referring the practice of psalmody to the life of *praktikē*, but psalmody also refers to the lower stages of knowledge. "Psalmody belongs to 'manifold wisdom' (Eph 3:10)" (*Prayer* 85).[20] With the Pauline expression "manifold wisdom," Evagrius consistently refers to the wisdom with which Christ creates the various worlds, and it is called manifold because of the diversity of the worlds (and all that is in them) to which fallen rational creatures—who differ among themselves according to the degree of their fall—have been assigned at the judgment (cf. *KG* I, 14; II, 1, 2, 21; III, 11, 57). Thus, the verses of the psalms have their calming effect on the irascible (a concern of *praktikē*) because they reach backward, as it were, into this part of the soul from the contemplation of Christ's manifold wisdom (a concern of knowledge). Yet this contemplation, which is equivalent to what Evagrius elsewhere calls contemplation of corporeals and incorporeals (see *Praktikos* 89), and contemplation of providence and judgment (see *M* 131–33) is not contemplation's highest goal. The highest goal is knowledge of the Trinity, which in this context Evagrius distinguishes from psalmody with the term *prayer*. Thus, in the passages already cited Evagrius says first, "Psalmody calms the passions and makes quiet the intemperance of the body," and then immediately adds by way of contrast, "Prayer makes the mind perform its own proper activity" (*Prayer* 83).[21] This proper activity is knowledge of the Holy Trinity.[22] Or again, first saying, "Psalmody

---

[18] See Gressmann, "Nonnenspiegel," 161.

[19] PG 79:1185B.

[20] PG 79:1185C. Here I am following a correction of the PG text in the edition by S. Tugwell, ed., *Evagrius Ponticus: Practikos and On Prayer* (published privately by the Faculty of Theology, Oxford, 1987).

[21] PG 79:1185B.

[22] Just to take examples from the *Kephalaia Gnostica* that specifically mention the mind and the Trinity, see *KG* I, 74; III, 6, 12, 13, 15, 30, 33, 69, 71; V, 52. For studies that examine this, citing many texts from other Evagrian writings, see I. Hausherr, *Les leçons d'un contemplatif: Le Traité de l'Oraison d'Évagre le Pontique* (Paris, 1960), 16–18, 93–96, 117–19, 147–49. G. Bunge, "Der Zustand des Intellektes," in *Das Geistgebet: Studien zum Traktat "De Oratione" des Evagrios Pontikos* (Cologne, 1987), 74–87; idem, *Evagrios Pontikos: Briefe*

belongs to 'manifold wisdom,'" he adds "but prayer is the prelude to immaterial and unmanifold knowledge" (*Prayer* 85).[23] Evagrius has chosen all his words carefully. Manifold wisdom refers to a material, diversified world. Prayer refers to an immaterial simplicity, God himself, in whose image the mind is made.[24] Thus, "Prayer is the activity which befits the dignity of the mind" (*Prayer* 84).[25] This distinction between psalmody and prayer explains Evagrius's otherwise enigmatic statement, "It is a great thing to pray without distraction, but it is greater to sing psalms without distraction" (*Praktikos* 69; p. 654).[26] Psalmody, being manifold, is distracting; therefore, to manage to pray psalms and avoid distraction is something of a feat.

This theory about the role of psalmody affects the sort of scholia that Evagrius composes on the various verses of the psalms, yet it is applied no more rigidly than the theory that locates Proverbs, Ecclesiastes, and the Song of Songs in an order of spiritual progress. Thus, psalm verses, according to Evagrius's commentaries, refer to the whole range of the spiritual journey from its beginnings in faith to its goal in knowledge of the Trinity.[27] Yet it is no accident that much of Evagrius's christology is found in his *Scholia on the Psalms*. It is because they refer to his manifold wisdom.[28]

Thus, Psalms in general and Evagrius's scholia on them in particular have a specific location in a scheme of spiritual progress. They refer to the initial stages of contemplative knowledge of the manifold wisdom with which Christ created the worlds, and they reach back from there to calm the irascible. They look forward to the higher contemplation of prayerful knowledge of the Holy Trinity. Both psalmody and prayer are gifts from God; and if one has not yet received them, Evagrius holds out hope for

---

aus der Wüste, Eingeleitet, übersetzt und kommentiert von Gabriel Bunge (Trier, 1986), 88ff., 137.

[23] PG 79:1185B. In this translation, I employ the clumsy word "unmanifold" in order to emphasize the contrast Evagrius wishes to emphasize. The Greek is τῆς ἀύλον καὶ ἀποικίλον γνώσεως.

[24] For more on the mind as the immaterial image of the immaterial God, see Bunge, "Der Zustand des Intellektes," 62–73; and Driscoll, ACW *Ad Monachos*, 344–48. See also the discussion below, p. 31 on the end of the *Gnostikos*.

[25] PG 79:1185B.

[26] For more extensive comments on the distinction between psalmody and prayer, see Hausherr, *Les leçons*, 115–20. See also A. and C. Guillaumont, *Praktikos*, 2:655; and Bunge, "Psalmodie und Gebet," in *Das Geistgebet*, 13–28.

[27] See, e.g., *In Ps* 24:20; 129:4–5; 137:7.

[28] See F. Refoulé, "La Christologie d'Évagre et l'Origénisme," *Orientalia Christiana Periodica* 27 (1961): 221–66. For the best study on Evagrius's christology, with many citations from the *Scholia on Psalms*, see G. Bunge, "La γνῶσις χριστοῦ di Evagrio Pontico" in *L'Epistula Fidei di Evagrio Pontico: Temi, Contesti, Sviluppi, Atti dell III Convegno del Gruppo Italiano di Ricerca su "Origene e la Tradizione Alessandrina,"* ed. Paolo Bettiolo (Rome, 2000), 153–81.

spiritual progress: "If you have not yet received the gift of prayer or psalmody, persevere and you will receive" (*Prayer* 87).[29]

The Chapters on Prayer *and the* Letter to Melania

Two other works of Evagrius need comment in a discussion that locates his writings in relation to each other: the *Chapters on Prayer* and the *Letter to Melania*. The *Chapters on Prayer* treat the highest stages of Evagrius's spiritual doctrine. Here he speaks of prayer in its most lofty sense of the mind's activity of focusing on knowledge of the Holy Trinity in whose image it was made.[30] It is important to recognize this as the fundamental subject matter of this treatise; otherwise, as happened in history and still happens among modern interpreters, one may take the *Kephalaia Gnostica* as containing Evagrius's loftiest teachings. The *Kephalaia Gnostica* are rather more concerned with the contemplation of Christ's manifold wisdom, and they consequently are a complex and detailed work, just as difficult to avoid distraction with as is psalmody itself. But the *Chapters on Prayer* drive to knowledge that lies beyond this. The work is probably addressed to Evagrius's friend Rufinus,[31] whom he considered to be ready for its contents. In any case, Evagrius makes clear in the dedicatory prologue that the life of *praktikē* is a necessary prelude to what this treatise contains, and he considers his reader already accomplished in *praktikē*. Leah is the biblical image for *praktikē* and Rachel a symbol for prayer. Evagrius says to his addressee, "Having served well for Rachel and received Leah, now you seek your beloved Rachel since the seven years have been fulfilled" (*Prayer*, prologue).[32]

To be sure, the chapters do not treat exclusively of prayer in its highest sense, but it is toward this prayer that all the meditations are designed to lead. This is the spiritual progress that the text promotes, and it does so through all the stages of monastic life as Evagrius consistently treats these. In his complex explanation of the significance of the number of 153 chapters, he concludes by calling it a triangular number, and he invites the reader to consider it "signifying knowledge of the Holy Trinity," a number reached by adding together "a lot of numbers," themselves producing a triangular number, "which you may consider to mean *praktikē*, natural

---

[29] PG 79:1185C. For a recent study on the whole of the *Scholia on Psalms*, see L. Dysinger, *The Relationship Between Psalmody and Prayer in the Writings of Evagrius Ponticus* (diss., Oxford, 1999); idem, "The Significance of Psalmody in the Mystical Theology of Evagrius of Pontus," *Studia Patristica* 30 (Louvain, 1997), 176–82.

[30] E.g., *Prayer* 1–3, 84, 86, 118–20. In this same vein, see *Praktikos* 3.

[31] See G. Bunge, *Briefe aus der Wüste*, 181 and 204 n. 61.

[32] PG 79:1165A.

contemplation, and theology" (*Prayer,* prologue).[33] Theology, a term Evagrius reserves for the highest form of prayer,[34] is reached only by making a
proper progress toward it. For as Evagrius warns in this treatise, "Just as it
does no good for someone with eye disease to stare directly at the sun at
high noon, so it would do absolutely no good for the impassioned and
impure mind to imitate the awesome and supernatural prayer 'in spirit and
in truth' (John 4:24)" (*Prayer* 146).[35] In other words, only with proper
progress toward prayer in spirit and in truth can it ever be reached.

Gabriel Bunge has questioned whether or not the *Letter to Melania* is
addressed to Melania. He believes that it was written to Rufinus.[36] In any
case, whether to Melania or to Rufinus, it is clearly a letter that is addressed
to someone who Evagrius thinks is spiritually prepared for its lofty contents. Reacting to the letter, we could perhaps borrow the exclamation of
the Lord's disciple from the Last Discourse of John's Gospel: "Here at last
you are speaking plainly" (John 16:29). This is not to say that its content
is in any way easy, but it is no longer veiled in the enigmatic proverbs in
scriptural language that only the initiated fully grasp after struggling with
such language in meditation. The reason that he is speaking plainly is that
the letter's addressee is capable of following a frank and open discussion of
the deepest dimensions of the Christian and monastic journey. Evagrius no
longer feels it necessary, as he said in his introduction to the *Praktikos,* the
Gnostikos, and the *Kephalaia Gnostica,* "to veil and obscure some things so
that we might not give what is holy to dogs or cast pearls before swine"
(Matt 7:6) (*Praktikos,* prologue 9; pp. 492–94).

It is important to be judicious in assessing the scope of such a remark.
This is not gnosticism's clandestine reserve of some truths for those few
with the spiritual substance that enables them to grasp secret knowledge.
It is rather Evagrius's respecting once again an order of spiritual progress.[37]
He knows that there is no insight into Christian truth without a whole way
of life behind it. Christian truth is not some deposit of secret knowledge
unveiled before a chosen few. Nonetheless, the deepest grasp of its mysteries is available only to those who have spent long years making progress

---

[33] PG 79:1167A. Cf. *Praktikos* 1, where the same division introduces the threefold work
of the *Praktikos,* the *Gnostikos,* and the *Kephalaia Gnostica.* See also *Gn* 49, discussed below
on p. 30.

[34] Cf. *Praktikos,* prologue 8; *Praktikos* 1, 84; *Prayer* 61; *M* 120, *In Prov.* 1:1; 22:20. For
this term in Evagrius's writings, see Driscoll, ACW *Ad Monachos,* 337–40.

[35] PG 79:1197D. For the consistent pneumatological and christological content assigned
to the expression "spirit and truth" in Evagrius, see G. Bunge, "The 'Spiritual Prayer': On the
Trinitarian Mysticism of Evagrius of Pontus," *Monastic Studies* 17 (1987): 196–98.

[36] See Bunge, *Briefe aus der Wüste,* 193–200.

[37] For the history of Matt 7:6 interpreted in this way, see A. and C. Guillaumont, eds., *Le
Gnostique ou a celui qui est devenu digne de la science,* Sources Chrétiennes 356 (Paris: Cerf,
1989), 38 n. 37.

along the road toward the passionlessness that makes love possible.[38] The *Letter to Melania* is addressed to someone who has made that journey. But not only that. It is likewise addressed to someone who has progressed through the various levels of knowledge that lead to knowledge of the Holy Trinity. To read the letter and assess its contents outside of this context, outside this order of spiritual progress, is once again to risk serious misunderstanding. Evagrius presumes that before one gets to the letter, the reader will have exercised oneself in distinguishing true knowledge from false knowledge and will be completely committed to the faith of the Catholic Church.[39] The talk of mystics very often must walk the tightrope of language that *could be* susceptible of heterodox interpretation. Evagrius risks walking that tightrope in this letter because he is confident that the reader is able to distinguish between true and false knowledge.

I have been suggesting here that the works of Evagrius must be read in a proper order, an order that represents a scheme of spiritual progress. This is Evagrius's own concern, and that it is his intention is reflected in the tone of the separate writings and the level at which he pitches each, a level in every case appropriate to some particular point along a progressive path of advancement toward the goal of knowledge of the Holy Trinity.[40]

We can turn now to a sampling of how a particular point of progress affects the way in which Evagrius structures individual texts and individual chapters within those texts.

PROGRESS EXPRESSED
IN INDIVIDUAL EVAGRIAN TEXTS

In this section we examine how the theme of spiritual progress appears in separate works of Evagrius. The potential for the study of this theme in Evagrius is very rich. Here I can indicate only some of the possible directions of study and suggest an approach to the texts which I think can help to uncover the theme.

It is important to recall at the outset that with Evagrius we are dealing with a particular genre of spiritual literature. These are texts written in the

---

[38] See *Praktikos*, prologue 8; *Praktikos* 81; *M* 67.

[39] See *M* 124–26. This chain is commented on in Driscoll, ACW *Ad Monachos*, 139–47.

[40] Evagrius himself is following a tradition in this position found among the philosophers and in Clement and Origen. The question is nicely summarized by A. and C. Guillaumont, in *Le Gnostique*, 37–40. It is true, of course, that once a work is written, it becomes "fair game" for any reader at all who wishes to approach it. My point here—and I think that of the ancients—is approaching the text with spiritual profit. Anyone at all may read the *Kephalaia Gnostica*, but not every reader will be prepared to profit from it.

short, cryptic style of the Bible's wisdom literature, texts designed to promote not only prolonged meditation but likewise the actual practice in life of the subject matter of the given proverb. These are words from a desert master given to disciples ready to expend the effort in mind and action that will lead to the word's deepest meaning.[41]

From a different perspective, these are likewise a style of literature marked by the broader philosophical traditions that shaped Evagrius, traditions in which written texts were to be conceived as "spiritual exercises," that is, as words requiring the inner and outer conversions that would promote the practitioner's progress along the path toward wisdom.[42] The importance of keeping this perspective in mind when reading Evagrius cannot be too strongly emphasized.

In what follows I would like to examine the theme of spiritual progress in the trilogy of the *Praktikos,* the *Gnostikos,* and the *Kephalaia Gnostica.* This will enable us to see the shape of spiritual progress as Evagrius conceives it across the whole spectrum of the monastic life, from its beginning in *praktikē,* through the various levels of knowledge, to its goal in knowledge of the Holy Trinity. In each of these three works I will examine the way in which the structure of the work as well as specific texts indicate that progress in the spiritual life is at issue. Then I will turn to a single text whose structure indicates the whole range of spiritual progress from beginning to end; namely, *Ad Monachos.* This text is a veritable road map guiding the way toward ever greater spiritual progress. I will present it as a summary of the more extensively conceived trilogy as well as a key for guiding a reader through all the works of Evagrius in such a way as to keep their many elements in proper balance.

The Praktikos

The *Praktikos* is Evagrius's most carefully constructed work devoted to *praktikē.* The work itself is structured according to an order of spiritual progress. Its overall design means to promote progress through the eight principal temptations that afflict a monk and then to describe the signs of passionlessness (ἀπάθεια), which will be the indications that a monk has made sufficient progress to pass on to the beginning stages of knowledge.[43]

---

[41] For more on this as applied to Evagrius, see Driscoll, ACW *Ad Monachos,* 157–95.

[42] For the notion of spiritual exercise as characterizing ancient philosophy, see P. Hadot, *Exercices spirituels.* For this as applied to Evagrius, see Driscoll, ACW *Ad Monachos,* 196–214.

[43] The structure of the *Praktikos* is studied at length by A. and C. Guillaumont, *Praktikos,* 1:113–25.

OVERALL STRUCTURE

After introductory proverbs that situate the upcoming meditations on *praktikē* within the broader context of knowledge as the monk's goal, Evagrius exposes the eight principal evil thoughts with descriptions of each designed to help the monk recognize how these thoughts will move in him (*Praktikos* 6–14). The order of these thoughts represents an order of progress either for good or for ill. For example, when one gives way to gluttony (γαστριμαργία), sexual temptations (πορνεία) are not far behind; and these in turn will expand into a general seeking after creature comforts represented by love of money (φιλαργυρία). Failure to achieve one's desires in any of these areas can lead in turn to anger (ὀργή) and sadness (λύπη) and then to the most oppressive temptation of all, listlessness (ἀκηδία). On the other hand, even when a monk has made progress against these evil thoughts, he is warned by Evagrius that he is then particularly susceptible to other kinds of temptations, particularly to vainglory (κενοδοξία) and pride (ὑπερηφανία).

Next Evagrius presents advice and solutions to each of the eight, again following the thoughts in their logical order. His advice is structured according to the three parts of the soul (*Praktikos* 15), locating the problem as being in the rational, the irascible, or the concupiscible parts and speaking of the virtues that must be in those parts instead (15–33). This advice is followed by six chapters that speak about the passions (34–39), that is, a general meditation on what moves evil thoughts in the irascible and concupiscible parts, together called the passionate part of the soul (38, 49, 78, 84). He observes that it is possible to make progress over the passions of the body to such an extent that one is eventually no longer troubled by them. However, the struggles of the soul, that is, those concerning relations with other people (35) will continue until death (36). After this a sort of demonology is presented with advice for the monk on how to conduct oneself in their presence, how to recognize and guard against their wily devices by observation, asceticism, and prayer (40–53).

In his study of the structure of this text A. Guillaumont sees the material I have discussed thus far as constituting a first part of the text. The second part, which extends from chapter 54 to 90, is devoted to the question of passionlessness, at which state the monk progressively arrives by his victory over the demons or passions.[44] There are a number of signs by which the condition of passionlessness can be detected: in the dreams the monk has (54–56), when the mind sees its own light at the time of prayer and is calm in the face of distractions (63–70), when each of the three parts of the soul acts according to nature (71–90). In other words, these are all indica-

---

[44] A. and C. Guillaumont, *Praktikos*, 1:118.

tions that some spiritual progress has been made. Indeed, there are degrees and nuances to the progress such that Evagrius distinguishes between a perfect and an imperfect passionlessness.[45] The text reaches a conclusion of the development with chapter 90, which prepares the way for the meditations on knowledge that follow in the next two works of the trilogy.[46] But to this there are appended ten others chapter that are apophthegmata of various fathers in the spirit of all that has preceded (91–100).

INDIVIDUAL CHAPTERS

The structure of this text clearly represents an order of spiritual progress. Any part of it could be studied more deeply and contribute thereby to the theme under examination here. I would like to offer just one example of how this might be done. I focus on chapters 63–70 of the *Praktikos*, a section of the work in which Evagrius treats of the superior forms of passionlessness. Of particular interest is how each of these chapters speaks of different signs by which progress toward the goal of *praktikē* can be detected.[47]

This unit of chapters begins with 63, which speaks of the mind beginning to pray undistractedly. This is a great sign of progress. The *Chapters on Prayer* speak of this as the ultimate goal of the life of the monk: "Undistracted prayer is the highest activity of the mind" (*Prayer* 18).[48] But Evagrius is not simply stating goals. Here he is concerned to share the observation—which is good advice—that the monk's struggle changes when he begins to pray undistractedly. The struggle grows more intense in a particular part of the soul; namely, in the irascible. The monk has made progress to the point that the passions of the body have been cut off (cf. *Praktikos* 36); but precisely because the demons feel threatened by this progress, they step up the battle in a more vulnerable part of the soul, the irascible. They work there because, according to one text, the irascible part of the soul is joined in the heart especially closely to the intelligible part, which is now turning itself toward this undistracted prayer (cf. *KG* VI, 84). The demons know that an agitated irascible can blind the mind (*KG* V, 27).

---

[45] Cf. *Praktikos* 60 and the comments of A. and C. Guillaumont, *Praktikos,* 1:108–10.

[46] *Praktikos* 90 reads, "The fruit of sowing: tears; that of the virtues: knowledge. And as tears accompany the sowing, so does joy accompany the reaping." The sowing is *praktikē;* the reaping is knowledge. For *Praktikos* 90, see A. and C. Guillaumont, *Praktikos,* 2:690.

[47] The subdivisions of the text that are printed in the critical edition of the Guillaumonts *Praktikos,* vol. 2, could well go back to Evagrius himself (see Guillaumont, *Praktikos,* 1:117 and 386–87). The chapters I am treating would thus be considered a unit by Evagrius himself.

[48] For this text, see Guillaumont, *Praktikos,* 2:646–47.

The grammatical structure of the sentence is worth observing in the context of a study of spiritual progress. The sentence is structured ὅταν... τότε, i.e., *when* a certain sign of progress appears, *then* a different kind of attack from the demons begins. These are precisely the kinds of signs that a monk and his spiritual father will need to pay attention to as they discern spiritual progress and adjust practices in the monastic life accordingly. In fact, in most of the chapters being studied here the grammatical structure is important for catching the nuances of what Evagrius is presenting. The ὅταν...τότε structure is not used again, but there is something similar in the way participles are related to main verbs. I will draw attention to this in some of what follows.

No. 64 speaks of "a sure sign" or we might say a "proof" of passionlessness: ἀπαθείας τεκμήριον. Such a τεκμήριον would be *when* (a participial construction) the mind begins to see its own native light and *when* (again, a participle) it remains quiet before visions in sleep and *when* (again, a participle) it can look at things without getting ruffled. There are three signs given here. The first, seeing the mind's own light, is a sign of the monk involved in the life of knowledge; for when the mind sees its own light, it is at its highest pitch, the purpose for which it was created.[49] The next two signs relate to a phrase in the previous chapter that spoke of the battle against the irascible taking place both by day and by night. At night the demons will present horrible visions to the monk in sleep, but no. 64 claims that it would be a sign of progress to remain calm before these. The battle by day against the monk would be based on whatever and whomever he might see being able somehow to agitate him. But no. 64 shows that a sign of progress would be to be able to look at anything or anyone at all with serenity.

No. 65 continues in the direction of this third sign of passionlessness. It says that the mind is strong *when* (again, a participial construction) it does not form images of anything in this world at the hour of prayer. Once more, we are speaking here of a sign of major progress, indeed, the goal of monastic life as Evagrius conceives it: imageless prayer.[50]

In no. 66 the grammatical structure of the sentence is a particularly clear expression of the intricacies of the spiritual life and the progress made within it. The core of the sentence is "a mind hardly senses any more the irrational part of the soul."[51] This is again a τεκμήριον of progress. But this

---

[49] Cf. *Skemmata* 2: "If someone would like to see the condition of the mind, let him be free of all representations and then he will see it as the color of sapphire or the sky. But to do this without passionlessness is impossible" (J. Muyldermans, *Evagriana* [Paris, 1931], 38). See also *Skemmata* 20.

[50] Cf. *Prayer* 114–20; *Skemmata* 20.

[51] The irrational part of the soul is what Evagrius usually calls the passionate part, but it means the same. See A. and C. Guillaumont, *Praktikos*, 2:651.

condition is modified by several participial phrases before the core sentence and by a genitive absolute afterwards. Thus, such a mind hardly senses the irrational part of the soul because "with God it has accomplished the life of *praktikē*" and also because it "has drawn near to knowledge." The genitive absolute casts its force over the whole sentence and explains how it is that the mind is now in such a condition: "knowledge catches the mind up on high and withdraws it from all perceptible things."

No. 67 renders no. 64 more precise, stating that passionlessness is not simply a soul that does not suffer any passion from things presently before it but likewise must include remaining undisturbed by any memories that come before the mind. Elsewhere in the *Praktikos* Evagrius explains that anything that is welcomed within with passion will later be remembered with passion (cf. 34). So, progress in passionlessness will need to include purifying the memories. This is especially true of the irascible part of the soul, where the monk has a tendency to remember injuries. But if injuries are remembered, it is as if there is no space left in the mind to focus on prayer. Thus, the memory must be carefully guarded if the monk is to pray as he ought.[52]

No. 68 is a chapter that is phrased in an intentionally provocative and paradoxical way. Clearly progress is at issue here, for Evagrius speaks of "the perfect one" and places the expression in apposition with "the passionless one," implying perfect passionlessness. What are the signs of this having solidly reached the goal of *praktikē*? He says, "The perfect does not practice temperance, and the passionless does not practice perseverance." To understand this paradox the chapter must be read together with no. 70, which speaks also of this same "perfect one" and describes him as "one in whom the virtues are established and who is wholly blended with them." This is strong language: *established, blended,* indeed *wholly blended.* This is describing not what might be a passing disposition of goodness but what is called "an excellent condition," an expression implying a stable and durable state.[53] In this condition one no longer is actively having to struggle with temperance, because "temperance belongs to the person who is troubled." Nor, strictly speaking, is perseverance necessary as an active struggle because "perseverance belongs to someone being troubled by the passions." Evagrius continues this paradoxical, very precisely reasoned, and even audacious manner of speaking in no. 70 when he says that the one wholly blended with the virtues "no longer remembers the law or the commandments or punishment, but he says those things and does whatever his

---

[52] *Prayer* 45, 47; *M* 13, with further comments in Driscoll, ACW *Ad Monachos,* 230–37.

[53] On this expression and its implications, see A. and C. Guillaumont, *Praktikos,* 2:603, 656–57.

excellent condition suggests." This is high progress indeed. This is perfect passionlessness.[54]

The Gnostikos

The *Gnostikos* is a short transitional work between the *Praktikos* and the *Kephalaia Gnostica*. Strictly speaking, its fifty chapters are not spiritual exercises in the same sense that the chapters of the other two works are.[55] This text is addressed to the monk who has reached passionlessness and is ready to move to meditations on knowledge. It is designed to keep such a monk always alert to continuing his vigilance in *praktikē* even as he advances to the specific exercises on knowledge that are contained in the *Kephalaia Gnostica*. The *Praktikos*, it could be said, contains the *content* of Evagrius's teaching on that subject; and the *Kephalaia Gnostica* contain the *content* of his teaching on various levels of knowledge. The *Gnostikos*, rather than presenting a content, is full of advice and warnings about proper entrance into knowledge and movement within it, advice that always keeps one eye vigilantly focused on guarding the progress attained thus far in the work of *praktikē*. All this being said, it is nonetheless true that this little work shows us much about how the theme of spiritual progress is a fundamental issue in effecting the transition from *praktikē* to knowledge.

The *Gnostikos* as a whole assumes that the monk who has reached some degree of passionlessness must now become a teacher to others. Indeed, it is in this work that Evagrius expresses himself most explicitly on the role of the spiritual father.[56] *Discerning* progress in another is a principal role of the father/teacher, whom Evagrius refers to as "the gnostic."[57] The first three chapters of the text mark the importance of this discernment:

---

[54] *Praktikos* 69, which is sandwiched between these last chapters discussed, has been treated above in another context. See above, p. 18. In the present context it can be noted that the chapter speaks of praying psalms undistractedly as a great sign of progress, a sign also of perfect passionlessness. To manage to pray the psalms in this way is to pray them like the angels, that is, not to be marked in the intellect by anything from the senses. Cf. *In Ps* 137:1. In the many λόγοι of the psalms, the monk sees through to (θεωρεῖν) the one Logos. Cf. *In Ps* 29:8.

[55] A. and C. Guillaumont make an observation in this vein (*Le Gnostique*, 26 with n. 11).

[56] On this, see especially G. Bunge, *Geistliche Vaterschaft: Christliche Gnosis bei Evagrios Pontikos* (Regensburg, 1988). As Bunge's work shows, there is much to be gleaned from Evagrius's other writings about his notion of the spiritual father, but then it is often by implication. In the *Gnostikos* Evagrius is explicit.

[57] On translating the term ὁ γνοστικός as "gnostic" and how this is to be distinguished from a member of heterodox gnostic sects, see A. and C. Guillaumont, *Le Gnostique*, 24 n. 2.

> Those accomplished in *praktikē* understand the reasons of *praktikē*, but gnostics will see the things of knowledge. (*Gnostikos* 1) The one accomplished in *praktikē* is the one who only has acquired passionlessness of the passionate part of the soul. (*Gnostikos* 2) The gnostic is the one who plays the role of salt for the impure and of light for the pure (*Gnostikos* 3).[58]

These three chapters form a smooth and direct transition from chapter 90 of the *Praktikos,* the last chapter of that work before the appended apophthegmata.[59] The thoughts expressed in these chapters are a bridge across a crucial passage in the journey of spiritual progress. Attention is focused first forward, toward knowledge (*Gn* 1). Then passionlessness is expressed as only a partial accomplishment in the path of spiritual progress (2). One can never rest at that point. Finally, the gnostic must look in two directions to be of service to others: he must be salt to the impure, that is, to those still involved in *praktikē;* he must be light to the pure, that is, to those who have entered knowledge (3).[60]

The spiritual father (the gnostic, the teacher) must exercise a detailed discernment of spiritual progress not only in those he teaches but also in himself. For himself he must be careful to be authentic in his teaching, never proffering lofty teaching only with a view toward impressing others (*Gn* 24). Furthermore, he is never to talk about God with sophisticated definitions but rather always to guard the mystery (27). It is important that he be approachable, not of too somber a countenance. Sour faces belong to those who do not truly desire the salvation of others (22).

But the father must be equally discerning of the point of progress that his disciples have reached. He is even to feign ignorance if questioned on some matter for which the disciple is not yet sufficiently spiritually prepared (*Gn* 23). Knowledge is not reached through theological disputes, and it is the duty of a father to turn the attention of those who do so back to the beginnings of knowledge, which lie in the conversion of life signified by *praktikē*. He must certainly not speak of the things of knowledge with the young, that is, with those who are still battling their passions; for this will only bring about their greater fall (25). It is enough for him to speak about those things necessary for salvation, which include all the teaching of *praktikē* but only partially the content of the realm of knowledge. More complex questions which can only scandalize are to be avoided (12, 13).

It is especially important that a father not teach beyond the capacity of his disciples and that if he should err in his content, it is better that he do

---

[58] Ibid., 88–91.

[59] See above n. 46.

[60] Cf. Matt 5:13–14: "You are the *salt* of the earth. You are the *light* of the world."

so in the direction of speaking too simply. Wait until the hearers urge, "Friend, go up higher (cf. Luke 14:10)," Evagrius advises (*Gn* 29). Monks around a father should be encouraged by him to talk about matters of *praktikē* but not about knowledge unless the father discerns someone capable of properly giving himself over to such (35). Some matters should simply not be brought up with either young monks or people who are not monks, for example, the highest reasons for the judgment, because this is a dimension of knowledge too easily misunderstood (36, 13). Some things are shared only with priests and then, at that, only with the better among them (14).

In a different vein, the father must be aware of the various reasons that cause a monk to experience a sense of being abandoned by God (a theme that will be discussed in more detail in a later chapter). This occurs once monks have reached a certain point of progress; and though it can seem a negative sign, its purpose is ultimately to safeguard humility as the monk makes progress. A father who understands this can be most useful for a monk who experiences a sense of abandonment (*Gn* 28). A father should be a good observer of all sorts of human characteristics and customs and walks of life; in a word, the differences among people. Observing these differences, he will be able to discern differences in levels of progress and will have something useful to say to everyone (15).

Thus the *Gnostikos* contributes to our understanding of the theme of spiritual progress in Evagrius by making discernment of progress a major characteristic of the gnostic, progress first of all in oneself and then progress in others. The capacity to teach properly and the proper content of teaching is largely dependent on a correct discernment of the point of progress in both teacher and disciple.

The *Gnostikos* also contributes to an understanding of spiritual progress from a different perspective. It speaks of certain virtues needed by the gnostic to maintain himself at his own level of progress. Evagrius uses the expression "knowledge safeguarded" and says that such knowledge itself both "teaches how it may be safeguarded and how one may make progress in it (*Gnostikos* 9)."[61] Most important among the virtues for the gnostic is gentleness, freedom from anger (*Gn* 4, 5, 31, 32). This actually is a constant stress throughout Evagrius's teaching.[62] But emphasizing this, Evagrius is also quick to add that all the virtues remain important since they

---

[61] A. and C. Guillaumont, *Le Gnostique*, 100. The Greek reads, ὅπως ἄν διαφυλαχθῇ καὶ ἐπὶ μείζονα προέλθοι.

[62] On this, see G. Bunge, *Vino dei draghi e pane degli angeli, l'insegnamento di Evagrio Pontico sull'ira e la mitezza* (Magnano, 1999).The way in which Evagrius considers gentleness and freedom from anger as permanently relevant to spiritual progress is expressed perhaps most clearly in the way in which proverbs on this issue are evenly placed throughout his work *Ad Monachos*. For a study of this, see J. Driscoll, "Gentleness in the *Ad Monachos* of Evagrius Ponticus," *Studia Monastica* 32 (1990): 295–321.

are all intertwined with each other, and the mind can be pulled away from knowledge at whatever point virtue is weakest (6). The practice of all the virtues (where gentleness is the most important) will express itself in concrete actions, most especially in the giving of alms. And if the monk has no alms to give, then he will set to work to earn some money so that he may (7). All these virtues must come to the fore especially in the act of teaching, which must be done without anger or sadness or care for the body (10), that is to say, with the fruits of *praktikē* well established. Before reaching the point of progress that Evagrius calls "being perfect," the monk should avoid frequent contact with many people; for, not yet having reached a good point in his progress, his mind will simply be filled with all kinds of imagination (11).

The *Gnostikos* bears the signs of careful structuring especially at its beginning and at its end. The beginning, as we have seen, carefully builds a bridge between *praktikē* and knowledge (*Gn* 1–3) and then launches the meditation by specifically drawing attention to the importance of absence of anger (4, 5). Then the other themes we have discussed here are intertwined throughout the text that follows, some pointing the attention to the condition of the teacher himself, others pointing the attention to the condition of the disciples. Then at the end of the work, similarly to the end of the *Praktikos,* a small collection of apophthegmata is appended (44–48) meaning to signal that the teaching here is in line with a tradition. The final two chapters conclude the work and open the door onto the *content* of knowledge, which will be dealt with in the third book of the trilogy, the *Kephalaia Gnostica.*

Again, let us observe the careful construction of the bridge to this next stage of spiritual progress. In the penultimate chapter Evagrius says, "The end of *praktikē* is to purify the mind and to render it passionless. The end of natural contemplation is to reveal the truth hidden in all created beings. But to distance the mind from material things and turn it toward its first cause, that is a gift of theology" (*Gn* 49).[63] Evagrius is ending the *Gnostikos* as he began the *Praktikos* with the mention of three stages of progress in the spiritual life: *praktikē,* natural contemplation, and theology (see *Praktikos* 1). In doing so he knits the two works tightly together by means of the literary device of inclusion, and he signals that in the *Kephalaia Gnostica* that follow the meditations will turn toward natural contemplation. But "the truth hidden in all created beings" is not a final point of progress. Thus does he point to the ultimate goal, represented with the term *theology,* as a turning of the mind toward God apart from all contact with material things.[64]

---

[63] A. and C. Guillaumont, *Le Gnostique,* 190–91.

[64] For this use of *theology,* see n. 34 above.

This ultimate goal is further emphasized by the final chapter of the *Gnostikos*. "Looking constantly toward the archetype, try to engrave its images [within], neglecting nothing of what would contribute to gaining that which is fallen" (*Gn* 50).[65] Here the mind of the gnostic is challenged always to look toward God himself, the archetype in whose image the mind is made. For though natural contemplation can reveal truth hidden in created and material things, this is only a pedagogical leading of the mind back to the Creator's most original intention for it. The mind is ultimately to be the immaterial image of the immaterial archetype, and as it makes progress on its way toward that, it is never to forget others, who are here described globally as "that which is fallen," that is, that mind which is fallen from its archetype.[66] Only in this carefully designated context can the reader properly now turn to the *Kephalaia Gnostica*. The reader is trained to recognize that its meditations are in large part devoted to natural contemplation but always in such a way as to point to what lies beyond and toward which one must always be making progress. Let us turn to that work now and try to uncover our theme there.

The Kephalaia Gnostica

The *Kephalaia Gnostica* are a lengthy and complex work, and the limits of this study do not permit more than several indications of how its chapters touch on our theme. However, limited as our observations may be, I think they can be instructive.

OVERALL STRUCTURE

As mentioned, the basic subject matter of the *Kephalaia Gnostica* concerns natural contemplation. This in indicated in the structure of the work itself: six "centuries" not of a hundred chapters but imperfectly of the number ninety; and six indicating the number of the days of the creation.[67] The 540 chapters that are generated according to this scheme range over a vast number of themes, all of which relate in some way to the knowledge being pursued at this point of spiritual progress. The vastness is both an image and an experience for the meditator of the "manifold wisdom" with

---

[65] A. and C. Guillaumont, *Le Gnostique*, 192–93.

[66] For this interpretation of "that which is fallen," see ibid., 193.

[67] Cf. the final exhortation after *KG* VI, 90: "Ponder our words, O brothers, and explain with zeal the symbols of the centuries according to the number of the six days of creation" (A. Guillaumont, ed., *Les six centuries des "Kephalaia Gnostica,"* Patrologia Orientalis 28, fasc. 1 [Paris: Firmin-Didot, 1958], 257).

which Christ created the worlds and of which we have already spoken above.

In this work, more than in all others, Evagrius refuses to shape his meditation in linear fashion. Guillaumont calls it polyphonic, noting how it is never just one thought developed at a time, but many together and complexly intertwined.[68] Nonetheless, he likewise notes that there is a dominant theme to each of the six centuries. These themes trace an order of spiritual progress. The first century is a first entry into the material of natural contemplation. Its meditations treat of cosmology and the present condition of created beings. The second and third centuries deal directly with making progress from this present condition; they speak of the contemplations whereby the mind may raise itself progressively to its primary condition. The fourth and fifth centuries focus on Christ and his role as Savior. The sixth century meditates on eschatology and the final restoration. Thus, from the first to the sixth century the meditating reader is offered the path of progress from the present condition to the future condition of knowledge that may be hoped for. This future condition, "final blessedness," is the subject matter proper to theology or essential knowledge. More than entering into this knowledge, about which it is not really possible to speak, the *Kephalaia Gnostica* point ahead to it, as a point toward which further progress must be made.[69]

INDIVIDUAL CHAPTERS

Among the 540 chapters in this work there are a number of series that could be examined according to our theme. I will briefly examine here a representative example, taken from the third century, that is, from the section of the work that speaks of the contemplations whereby the mind may progressively raise itself to its primary condition. There is a series on the various conditions of the mind proposed in chapters that occur in even numbers from *KG* III, 6, 8, 10, to 12. These are intertwined with another series, closely related to the theme yet different, concerning successive changes, running from *KG* III, 7, 9, 11, 13, 15, and carrying on in related themes to 17, 19, and 21, even as the first series can be read as continuing on to 14, 16, 18, 20, and 22 and indeed even farther.[70]

If we begin at *KG* III, 6, the meditation speaks of the "naked mind." This is the mind united to knowledge of the Holy Trinity and is the original condition for which it was created. It is the highest point of spiritual

---

[68] Guillaumont, *Les six centuries,* 36.

[69] For the expression "final blessedness" as referring to this stage, see *Praktikos,* prologue 8; *Ep Fid* 7, line 19; *In Eccl* 1:2. On the ineffability of the mystery at this point, see *Gnostikos* 41, *Inst ad mon.,* PG 79:1237C, D.

[70] For these series, see Guillaumont, *Les six centuries,* 101–7.

progress: "The naked mind is that which, through the contemplation which concerns it, is united to knowledge of the Trinity." No. 8 speaks of the mind in its "last clothing." The meditation is moving in a descending order. The last clothing of the mind is knowledge of "secondary beings," that is, beings in their fallen condition but including knowledge of their path of progress arranged for them by providence to the original condition. No. 10 continues the downward movement, speaking of the "imperfect mind." This is a mind in need of contemplation of corporeal nature, which in the Evagrian scheme is the starting point of progress in knowledge for those in a fallen condition. There are *logoi* hidden in the material creation, which when seen through (θεωρία in its literal etymological sense), lead eventually to knowledge of the immaterial Logos (see *Prayer* 52). No. 12 contrasts the "perfect mind" with the imperfect mind of no. 10. In so doing, Evagrius has created a couplet of no. 10 and no. 12, but he has also provided another name for "naked mind" of no. 6 and thus brought the meditation full circle. "The perfect mind is the one which easily receives essential knowledge." "Essential knowledge" is another expression for the "knowledge of the Holy Trinity" of no. 6.

We have here an order of spiritual progress that advances in circular fashion: the mind in its original condition, the mind in its last clothing before return to that condition, the mind imperfectly focused, the mind perfectly focused. And this meditation can be deepened by the other series with which it is intertwined. No. 7 speaks of changes for the nourishment of rational beings, all of them designed for eventually reaching what is called "the excellent change." Inside the meditation of the intertwined series this excellent change will be understood to be the change from the last *clothing* of the mind to the *naked* mind, from an *imperfect* to a *perfect* mind. No. 9, which is read next in this series, continues to speak of the changes and indicates that such changes are the deepest meaning of Christ's words, "Today and tomorrow I shall be casting out devils and working cures; on the third day I reach my goal" (Luke 13:32). We are clearly in a framework of spiritual progress in what is being proposed here, and Evagrius finds dominical warrant for his understanding.[71] The "excellent change" of the previous proverb is what Christ accomplishes on the third day, having progressed through *praktikē*, "casting out devils," today and tomorrow.

No. 11 can be read in this same series. It contrasts a corporeal nature with an incorporeal nature. The corporeal nature can receive the "manifold wisdom" of Christ, for indeed corporeal nature itself is the product of his wisdom. But it cannot receive Christ himself. With the term *Christ* Evagrius is speaking strictly, meaning the one "anointed" with knowledge,

---

[71] See also *KG* I, 90; IV, 26, where Evagrius constructs other meditations, seeing spiritual progress as the meaning of the Lord's words in this biblical text.

incorporeal in his original condition.[72] Christ is united in perfect knowledge to God, and an incorporeal nature is required to receive not his manifold wisdom but the wisdom of his Unity, and indeed, the Unity itself. This would be the excellent change (no. 7) accomplished on the third day (no. 9).

This interpretation is specified and deepened in no. 13. The wisdom of the Unity is indeed united to the nature that is "below it," that is, to corporeal nature. This is the manifold wisdom with which Christ created the worlds. It is a wisdom that comes "from the Unity" (that is, from God), and so this wisdom can be seen in what Wisdom has made, but the Unity itself cannot be seen in any of the natures to which it has been joined. The mind must be incorporeal to see the Holy Trinity, and such a mind can see the Trinity in incorporeal beings created in the Trinity's image.

By now the two series are very tightly intertwined. The series of even-numbered chapters on the conditions of the mind bends into a series on the soul, which, united as it is to a body, is likewise a condition of the mind. No. 14 contrasts a deficient soul with the perfect soul in no. 16. It is interesting to look at no. 15 from the other series as it stands sandwiched between these two. It speaks of the perfection of the mind, stressing again immaterial knowledge as being ultimately only knowledge of the Trinity itself. No. 17, the next in the odd-numbered series, continues to point to the progress that must be made toward "immaterial contemplation," and different angles on the mystery are proposed in no. 19 and no. 21. Meanwhile, the soul, introduced as the theme of meditation in no. 14 and no. 16, progresses through necessary purifications in no. 18, passing from "bodies to bodies" in no. 20. No. 22 comes at the issue from a different angle: the first movement of the mind away from the Unity. It is this movement that results in the mind finding itself in a soul joined to a body.

These are meditations of a difficult sort. It would be this kind of material that the *Gnostikos* was warning not to present to people who have not yet reached a point of spiritual progress appropriate to it. Without that, these chapters are easily subject to misunderstanding. But when these words are taught by a master who himself knows whereof he speaks (cf. *Gn* 27) and are received by disciples who have given evidence of their progress by justifiably urging, "Go up higher" (cf. *Gn* 29), then the chapters are instruments of progress through the manifold paths that constitute natural contemplation. They bring the prayerful reader to the borders no longer of knowledge of the created order and God's providence but rather to knowledge of God himself as non-numeric Trinity.[73] This is the essential

---

[72] Evagrius always means to imply this with his use of the term "Christ." See Bunge, *Geistliche Vaterschaft*, 34.

[73] Cf. *Ep Fid* 2, lines 17–21; 3, lines 1–54.

knowledge toward which the monk is always progressing; it is final blessedness; it is theology.

To return to the theme treated in the first part of this study concerning a proper order for reading the works of Evagrius, based on the order of spiritual progress, it is perhaps worth saying again that it is at this point, at the end of the *Kephalaia Gnostica* that I would locate the reading of the *Chapters on Prayer* and the *Letter to Melania*. Especially the *Chapters on Prayer* are designed now to train the monk for knowledge of a deeper level than what is covered in the *Kephalaia Gnostica*. They are always pointing toward the immaterial, naked, silent, imageless, light-filled knowledge of God.[74]

Ad Monachos

I would like to turn now briefly to a single work of Evagrius in which there is mapped out this entire journey which the *Praktikos*, the *Gnostikos*, the *Kephalaia Gnostica*, and the *Chapters on Prayer* detail. That is the text *Ad Monachos* (*M*). In this work we see in a glance, as it were, a journey of spiritual progress that begins with faith, the first virtue of *praktikē*, and concludes with the mind presented before the Holy Trinity. I have studied this work in detail elsewhere.[75] Here, in summary fashion, I would like to present the structure of that work as a scheme of spiritual progress. In that way I will bring these present reflections to an end. The structure can first be viewed schematically.

M 3 to *M* 62. The Key Structure: Faith → Love → Knowledge
M 3 to *M* 62. Proverbs interlacing love and temperance, the irascible and concupiscible parts of the soul. Proverbs following in part the order of the eight principal thoughts.

M 63 to *M* 72. The Center of the Text: The Relation between *Praktikē* and Knowledge
M 66 to *M* 68. The center of the center: passionlessness and knowledge
M 67. The center of the center of the center: passionlessness → love → knowledge.

---

[74] Unfortunately it is not possible here to study and comment on some of the series within the *Chapters on Prayer* where this kind of spiritual progress is being expressed. But see, e.g., 58–62 or, expanding the development, 52–64, or 117–23.

[75] See J. Driscoll, ACW *Ad Monachos*.

M 73 to M 106. Proverbs Grouped around a Spiritual Father
  M 74 to M 87. Fourteen proverbs on relations within the brotherhood
  M 88 to M 92. Five proverbs on a spiritual father
  M 93 to M 106. Fourteen proverbs training the soul for knowledge

M 107. The Turning Point of the Text: A Pure Mind in a Gentle Soul

M 107 to M 136. Proverbs Devoted Exclusively to Knowledge
  M 107 to M 110. The hierarchy of levels of knowledge
  M 118 to M 120. The christological anchor: Christ's relation to each
  phase of the spiritual journey
  M 123 to M 131. An intricate chain on the roles of wisdom and
  prudence in discerning the difference between true and false knowledge.

**M 136. The Culmination of the Monk's Journey: The Mind Presented
before the Holy Trinity**

After introductory proverbs, M 3 is a proverb with terminology that provides the structure of the entire text. The text begins with *faith*, the first of
the virtues as conceived by Evagrius. It drives toward *love*, the culmination
of the virtuous life. And love has as its purpose the *knowledge* of God, the
highest goal for the monk in Evagrian spirituality. The proverbs from this
beginning until the middle of the text are exercises in the various virtues to
be established in the irascible and concupiscible parts of the soul. The exercises follow in part the order of the eight principal thoughts, for which Evagrius is so well known in monastic literature. M 63 to M 72 are ten
proverbs that stand at the middle of the text, and the theme they treat
stands at the middle of the monk's spiritual journey: the relationship
between *praktikē* (the active struggle for virtue) and knowledge. This center has a center of three proverbs on the relationship of passionlessness to
knowledge. The key to understanding this is in the center proverb of this
center (M 67): *passionlessness* leads to *love* which leads to *knowledge*. There
is a new beginning in the text at M 73, and a coherent arrangement obtains
until M 106. Two sets of fourteen proverbs stand on both sides of a center of five whose theme is the spiritual father.
  I have called M 107 the turning point of the text. Gentleness is one of
the major ways in which Evagrius describes the goal of *praktikē*. A gentle
soul creates a mind pure enough for knowledge. This pure mind is the
text's turning point, and all the proverbs that follow are now concerned
exclusively with knowledge. In this section Evagrius defines the hierarchy
in levels of knowledge that he consistently expresses throughout his other
works. He develops an important chain on Christ's role in the monk's pro-

gressive mounting upward toward knowledge of God the Father. An intricate chain on the difference between true and false knowledge dominates this section and prepares the reader for the text's climax, which is the same as the climax for the whole spiritual life as conceived by Evagrius; namely, the mind presented before the Holy Trinity.

I think perhaps it is not necessary to summarize the foregoing discussion, for *Ad Monachos* does so. Spiritual progress begins, as does *Ad Monachos*, with faith, the first of the virtues. *Ad Monachos* finishes with the mind presented before the Holy Trinity. There is, in a certain sense, an end to the ignorance of the one who makes progress in contemplation; and there will one day be an end to the domination by the passions. But to progress in knowledge of the Holy Trinity, there will be no end.[76]

---

[76] Cf. *Praktikos* 87, as discussed on the first page of this chapter.

2

SPOUSAL IMAGES

E ven though no collection of scholia by Evagrius on the Song of Songs survives, we are not entirely in the dark about how he would understand that book's amorous images between bridegroom and bride and how he might apply them to the spiritual life. On a number of occasions Evagrius takes the image of bride from various places in the scriptures and uses it to understand the progress of the soul that seeks God. It is not an image that is confined to his teaching directed toward women, even if the image appears more frequently in such literature.[1] But the spousal images can move in both directions. Thus, for example, in the prologue to his *Chapters on Prayer,* most likely addressed to his friend Rufinus, he says, comparing his addressee to Jacob,

> For Rachel you have served well. You have received Leah, but now you want your beloved [Rachel] too. (*Prayer,* prologue)[2]

Here Leah is an image of the life of *praktikē,* the necessary prelude to the life of contemplation, represented by Rachel and the subject matter of the text that is to follow.

There is one text in which Evagrius is clearly inspired by images from the Song of Songs. It is, in effect, a scholion on some of its verses, knitted together with references to other scriptural images. This text gives us some clue of how Evagrius would have understood that biblical book within the traditional dynamic of Proverbs relating to *praktikē,* Ecclesiastes relating to natural contemplation, and the Song of Songs relating to theology.[3] The present study proposes to examine that text and to use it as an occasion to read also other texts where Evagrius uses similar images.

---

[1] S. Elm has studied this point in "Evagrius Ponticus' *Sententiae ad Virginem,*" *Dumbarton Oaks Papers* 45 (1991): 97–120. Elm sees the image as reserved to Evagrius's instruction to female monastics.

[2] PG 79:1165A.

[3] Evagrius reserves the term *theology* for the highest form of knowledge, that of the Holy Trinity. For a brief summary and reference to the relevant texts, see Driscoll, ACW *Ad Monachos,* 337–41.

Ad Virginem 55
Virginal eyes will see the Lord.
The ears of virgins will hear his words (cf. 1 John 1:1).
The mouth of virgins will kiss their bridegroom (Cant 8:1).
The sense of smell of virgins will run after the odor of his
    perfumes (Cant 1:4).
Virginal hands will handle the Lord (cf. 1 John 1:1).
And purity of the flesh will be pleasing to him.

The soul of the virgin will be crowned
    and with her bridegroom she will live forever.
A spiritual garment will be given her
    and with the angels in heaven she will feast.

Inextinguishable the lamp she will light,
    and the oil will not give out in her vessels (Matt 25:4).
She will receive the riches of the aeons
    and she will inherit the Kingdom of God (cf. Matt 25:1–13).[4]

It will be useful to enter immediately into commentary on this text, noting for the moment only briefly the context in which it is found. It is virtually the end of the collection of biblical-style proverbs composed by Evagrius in the work usually identified with the name *Ad Virginem,* a work frequently associated with *Ad Monachos,* like it in many respects.[5] The proverbs of *Ad Virginem* are addressed to a female monastic and range over many issues of the spiritual life, most of them associated with *praktikē.* No. 55 is clearly meant to function as a summary of the whole text.

As we examine it, it is first of all useful to observe that the text is structured in an ascending order of spiritual progress, moving from body to soul to mind. We will look at each of these in turn.

THE BODY

Evagrius speaks of the virgin's body and the purity that must be established therein by mentioning the five senses: sight, hearing, taste, smell, and touch. His formulation interweaves language from the Song of Songs

---

[4] H. Gressmann, ed., "Nonnenspiegel und Mönchsspiegel des Evagrios Pontikos," *Texte und Untersuchungen* 39, no. 4 (1913): 151.

[5] Gressmann published his critical edition of the two works together and connects them in his introductory remarks. For my understanding of the relation between the two texts, see Driscoll, ACW *Ad Monachos,* 28–29.

together with allusions to the opening verses of chapter 1 of the First Letter of John, and his combination appears seamless. This already is significant. It means to be an interpretation of the spousal images of the Canticle
in a christological key. John's "What was in the beginning, what we have
heard, what we have seen with our eyes...what our hands have touched,"
becomes virginal eyes that will see the Lord, ears that hear his words, hands
that handle him. But for the remaining senses, which John does not mention, Evagrius turns to the text of the Canticle: a mouth that kisses the
bridegroom (Cant 1:2; 8:1), a sense of smell that runs after the odor of his
perfumes (Cant 1:4).[6]

Evagrius's formulation imitates in its own way the rhetorical insistence
of the Johannine text, both of them expressing very concretely the reality
and the significance of the Lord's incarnation. True, we are dealing with
real bodies in the flesh: the Lord's and the virgin's. But also in both cases
the body points somehow beyond itself. In the case of the Lord, his body
is that of "the Word of Life...that was from the beginning" (1 John 1:1).
In the case of the virgin, it is "the purity of her flesh that will be pleasing"
to the Lord and so enable her soul and mind to be united with him.

Evagrius's use of the five senses is expressive of his basic understanding
of the body as an instrument for the soul's and mind's progress toward the
ultimate goal of knowledge of God (cf. *Praktikos* 49, 53, 82). The immediate goal for the body is to establish "purity of the flesh," as the last line
of this first part of the text expresses it. But this purity points beyond itself
to union with the Lord. This "beyond" is expressed, and indeed emphasized, in the future tense of all the verbs, one after the other. The future
seeing of the Lord, hearing his words, kissing his mouth, and so on are not
to be understood in a fundamentally carnal way, as the virtually unanimous
tradition of Christian interpretation of the Canticle affirms. These expressions all have a spiritual reference, corresponding sense by sense to the
nous, our chief instrument for the knowledge of God. In a key text Evagrius explains how:

> The mind also possesses five spiritual senses with which it grasps
> matters proper to itself. Thus, sight shows it intelligible objects
> nakedly. Hearing receives the reasons which concern these. The
> sense of smell enjoys their fragrance, uncontaminated by any
> falsehood, and the mouth receives their taste. Through touch it
> is confirmed in the accurate demonstration of the things per-
> ceived. (*KG* II, 35)[7]

---

[6] A comparison with the Greek text of Scripture shows that the vocabulary of Evagrius,
word by word, is clearly based on John's text and that of the Canticle in the LXX.

[7] A. Guillaumont, *Les six centuries des "Kephalaia Gnostica,"* Patrologia Orientalia 28, fasc.
1 (Paris: Firmin-Didot, 1958), 75. However, for this particular text there exists a Greek frag-

This text, perhaps at first sight a bit technical and dull, actually contains a rich and suggestive teaching. The five senses of the body have their counterpart in the *nous*. From the senses of the body we learn how those noetic senses are to be used, and we gain a language for speaking about realities otherwise inaccessible to us. The bodily senses provide metaphors for the more spiritual realities that are in fact experienced invisibly and ultimately even, in Evagrian language, immaterially.[8] Thus, noetic sight sees the intelligibility of objects, that is, their reason (λόγος) for existence in the scheme of God's providence and judgment. Hearing hears these reasons, what we might call silent words (λόγοι) that deliver understanding to the *nous*. Both smell and taste are concerned with a capacity to detect and savor the truth, while touch noetically "grasps" that truth with accuracy. The text from *Ad Virginem* presumes this teaching on the senses and develops it more personally for the one to whom the text is addressed. She is a virgin dedicated to the life of *praktikē*, that is, to the purification of her bodily senses; and what she shall ultimately see, hear, taste, smell, and touch is not a spiritual something but a Someone; namely, the Lord, her bridegroom.

This interpretation of these texts is both confirmed and neatly summarized in three chapters from the *Chapters on Prayer*. Evagrius says,

> We seek after virtues for the sake of the reasons (λόγοι) of created beings, and we seek these for the sake of the Logos who gives them their being. And the Logos is accustomed to manifest himself in the state of prayer. (*Prayer* 52)[9]

This Logos is the virgin's bridegroom, whom she "hears, touches, kisses, etc." in prayer, a term Evagrius reserves for the goal of the whole spiritual journey.[10] The next chapter continues this meditation:

> The state of prayer is the condition of passionlessness, which by a supreme love snatches up on high the mind in love with wisdom, the spiritual mind. (*Prayer* 53)[11]

Here passionlessness (ἀπάθεια), the immediate goal of *praktikē*, is the condition that allows one to advance to prayer. It corresponds to the

---

ment, on which my translation is based. See J. Muyldermans, *Evagriana: Extrait de la revue Le Muséon*, v. 42, augmenté de Nouveaux fragments grecs inédits (Paris, 1931), 58–59.

[8] For the immaterial nature of the nous, see *Praktikos* 3 with comments by A. and C. Guillaumont, *Praktikos*, 2:501–2; and Driscoll, ACW *Ad Monachos*, 344–48.

[9] PG 79:1177C.

[10] The *Chapters on Prayer* develop such an understanding, although in the prologue Evagrius acknowledges that there are actually two types of prayer, one that pertains to *praktikē*, the other to contemplation. See PG 79:1165C. Yet in the greater number of cases, "prayer" refers to this latter.

[11] PG 79:1177C.

"purity of the flesh" in the *Ad Virginem* text. In the same mood as that of the *Ad Virginem* text, this chapter speaks of love snatching the mind on high. It corresponds to "the Kingdom of God," which the virgin will inherit.[12] Later in the same work Evagrius offers a formulation that exactly follows the relationship between body, soul, and mind that we find in the text of *Ad Virginem*.

> Let the virtues which have to do with the body accord to those of the soul and let those of the soul accord to those of the spirit. And let these accord to immaterial and substantial knowledge. (*Prayer* 132)[13]

THE SOUL

Returning to the *Ad Virginem* text we can follow this same trajectory of spiritual movement. Evagrius is explicit in expressing the progress: "The *soul* of the virgin will be crowned." He immediately joins this to the principal image with which he is already working: "with her bridegroom she will live forever." We can perhaps best comment on this with a line from one of Evagrius's letters, which makes it clear that the purity of the virgin's flesh is not simply a matter of bodily temperance but ultimately of love. A virgin without love "is like that foolish virgin who was excluded from the bridal chamber because she was without oil, and her lamp went out" (*Lt* 28:1).[14] Indeed, everywhere in Evagrius's teaching love is the ultimate goal of the life of *praktikē*, and the only way that leads to knowledge of God (*M* 3, 67; *Praktikos* 81, 84; etc.). Thus, temperance, yes; but love is the ultimate crown of the virgin. "With her bridegroom she will live forever"— that is, "through love the mind sees Original Love, God. Through our love we see the love of God for us" (*Lt* 56:3).[15]

As Evagrius speaks here of the soul's being established in its progress, in addition to the images of crown and bridegroom, he also speaks of being clothed with a spiritual garment and feasting with the angels in heaven. The purity of the virgin's fleshly senses results precisely in a *spiritual* garment. It introduces her into a heavenly feast—we may presume wedding feast—with angels. Throughout the *Scholia on Proverbs*, angels frequently

---

[12] This interpretation of "Kingdom of God" will be established below.

[13] PG 79:1196A. See also *KG* III, 48, 61.

[14] W. Frankenberg, ed., *Evagrius Ponticus,* Abhandlungen der königlichen Gesellschaft der Wissenschaften zu Göttingen, Phil-hist. Klasse n.F. 13.2 (Berlin, 1912), 586.

[15] Ibid., 606

appear as the friends of those who make progress in the spiritual life. Characteristic is Evagrius's explanation of the biblical verse "Wealth acquires many friends" (Prov 19:4). Explaining each word in the text, he says,

> Wealth of knowledge and of wisdom acquires for us many angels..., for spiritual friendship is virtue and knowledge of God through which we join ourselves in friendship with the holy powers, if it is true that those who convert become cause for joy for the angels in heaven. (*In Prov* 19:4)[16]

Through her progress in virtue, the virgin has acquired friends—angels—who rejoice at her virtue and with whom she shares heaven's wedding feast of knowledge.

In the opening chapters of the *Praktikos*, Evagrius, always reading the scriptural text with extreme attention, distinguishes between the biblical expressions "Kingdom of heaven" and "Kingdom of God." He says,

> The kingdom of heaven is passionlessness of the soul, along with true knowledge of beings.

> The kingdom of God is knowledge of the Holy Trinity, coextensive with the substance of the mind and surpassing its incorruptibility. (*Praktikos* 2, 3)[17]

This distinction helps us to notice that Evagrius is using the same in constructing the ascending order of the proverb from *Ad Virginem*. First, we should observe that the proverb finishes with the expression "Kingdom of God," and we shall examine its significance below. But this allows us to give a precise sense to the word *heaven* in the part of the text we are presently examining. Heaven is "passionlessness of the soul" or, we may say, the purity of the virgin's flesh, completed with love. But passionlessness and love are the door to knowledge (*M* 66, 67, 68), which also has its ascending order: as the text in the *Praktikos* says, first knowledge of created beings, which will lead to knowledge of the Holy Trinity. In the present context we can understand "true knowledge of beings" to be accomplished by, among other things, penetrating the reasons (λόγοι) of the five senses.[18]

---

[16] G 189; p. 282. Cf. Luke 15:10. For the theme of friendship with the angels in these scholia, see P. Géhin, ed., *Évagre le Pontique, Scholies aux proverbes*, Sources Chrétiennes 340 (Paris: Cerf, 1987), 53–54.

[17] A. and C. Guillaumont, *Praktikos*, 2:498, 500. For detailed explanation of these texts see ibid., pp. 498–502 and Driscoll, ACW *Ad Monachos*, 344–48.

[18] In this regard it is useful to note again *Prayer* 132, cited above on p. 42.

THE MIND

The final part of the *Ad Virginem* proverb turns to the highest and most noble dimension of the virgin's being, the *nous* or mind. The specific word is not used, but anyone familiar with Evagrius's consistent and precise use of images cannot fail to recognize that we have here to do with the mind. For example, we may comment on "Inextinguishable the lamp she will light" by continuing the passage from the letter cited above. Evagrius has spoken of the foolish virgin who lacked oil for her lamp. And then he says, "I call 'lamp' the mind that was created to receive the blessed light but which because of its hardness fell from the knowledge of God" (*Lt* 28:1).[19] Thus, we see that this *Ad Virginem* proverb has described the entire path of return to the blessed light from which the mind of the virgin fell.

Since the lamp is by no means the only image that Evagrius uses to designate the mind, we can wonder what it is that may have induced him to do so in this particular proverb. Certainly he is thinking of the parable of the wise and foolish virgins, as the image of oil in the next line makes clear, as well as the other references to this same Gospel parable that we saw in the several other texts cited. This suits well the images of the virgin that he has developed in the first two parts of the proverb. But there is probably another Gospel text that is also moving around somehow in Evagrius's consciousness and that he would want a disciple trained by him to catch. Commenting on Proverbs 11:17, "A merciful man does good to his own soul, but the merciless destroys his own body," Evagrius says,

> Here with the word "body" he straightway is indicating the soul. Christ himself does this in the gospels where he says, "The lamp of the body is the eye," calling the mind "lamp," which is for receiving knowledge, and calling the irascible and concupiscible parts of the soul "body." (*In Prov* 11:17)[20]

An interesting exegesis is operating here. Evagrius takes the word *body*, found in the second line of the biblical proverb he is commenting on, to indicate *soul*, found in the first line. He justifies this interpretation by reference to Christ's having spoken in this same way. In the words of Christ to which Evagrius is referring—"the lamp of the body"—it is self-evident to him that "lamp" must refer to the mind. But since in the Evagrian anthropology the mind is related to the body only through the intermedi-

---

[19] Frankenberg, *Evagrius,* 586. Commenting on the word *lamp* in the book of Proverbs, Evagrius says, "The lamp is the pure mind filled with spiritual contemplation," *In Prov* 31:18 (G 375; p. 466).

[20] G 127; p. 224. Cf. Matt 6:22.

ary of the soul, the lamp that is the mind could only be a light for the soul
and not directly for the body. Thus does he conclude that by the word
"body" Christ meant "soul." The content of the proverb Evagrius is commenting on would also cause such an interpretation to make sense to him
because mercy is one of the primary virtues that establishes health in the
irascible part of the soul. Thus, being without mercy would destroy not the
body but the soul. In any case, it is clear that in the *Ad Virginem* text, the
image of the lamp refers to the virgin's mind; and it appropriately follows
what Evagrius says of the virgin's soul.

Concerning the virgin's lamp/mind, Evagrius says in the next line of the
proverb "the oil will not give out in her vessels." The formulation is taken
directly from the Gospel parable,[21] and Evagrius expects the reader to
notice this allusion and in meditation to fill out and apply its other details.
The oil must last as long as the bridegroom delays, and it is precisely this
that Evagrius is promising to the virgin whose body is pure and whose soul
has been crowned. *When* the bridegroom arrives, *then* she will go with him
into the wedding.

How does Evagrius expect the reader to understand the meaning of oil
in this text? Previous proverbs in *Ad Virginem* leave no doubt. It refers to
love, the concrete practice of charity. In no. 17, Evagrius says,

> Do not turn away the poor in their hour of tribulation, and oil
> will not be lacking in your lamp.

And again, at no. 43:

> The lamp of a virgin without mercy will be extinguished, and she
> will not see her bridegroom when he arrives. (*V* 17, 43)[22]

This is the characteristic link that Evagrius makes between love and
knowledge. It is a major and insistent theme in all of his writings.[23] He
often understands it in concrete and very practical ways. In the text of *Ad
Virginem* it has to do with care for the poor, but such advice is by no means
limited to this text.[24] In the *Gnostikos*, Evagrius describes the one who has
already entered the realms of knowledge as one who nonetheless concerns
himself always with giving alms, calling this "what the five virgins whose

---

[21] Compare Matt 25:4: ἔλαβον ἔλαιον ἐν τοῖς ἀγγείοις μετὰ τῶν λαμπάδων ἑαυτῶν with
the words of the Evagrian text: ἄσβεστον ἀνάψει λαμπάδα, καὶ ἔλαιον οὐ λείψει ἐν τοῖς
ἀγγείοις αὐτῆς.

[22] Gressmann, "Nonnenspiegel," 147, 149.

[23] Cf. J. Driscoll, "Gentleness in the *Ad Monachos* of Evagrius Ponticus," *Studia Monastica* 33 (1990): 295–321.

[24] For the same theme in *Ad Monachos*, see, nos. 25–30 with my comments in ACW *Ad
Monachos*, 81–82.

lamps went out did not have" (*Gn* 7).[25] In their notes on this text, A. and C. Guillaumont draw attention to one of the chapters of the *Kephalaia Gnostica:*

> The light which shines in the holy temples is a symbol of spiritual knowledge...which is fed by the oil of holy love. (*KG* IV, 25)[26]

In the last two lines of the *Ad Virginem* text we should recognize the designation of two levels of knowledge in an ascending order. "Riches of the aeons" refers to knowledge of the various worlds created as a result of God's providence and judgment.

> The Church of pure souls is true knowledge of aeons and worlds and of the judgment and providence which are in them. (*In Eccl* 1:1)[27]

Evagrius understands this knowledge to pertain to "the Kingdom of heaven," which is to be distinguished from "the Kingdom of God" in the last line. We already drew attention to the word *heaven,* used earlier in the proverb. We should hear it now between the lines or between the words "riches of the aeons." Elsewhere Evagrius is explicit. Commenting on the text in Ecclesiastes "He has placed the aeon in their heart," he says,

> That is, he has given the *reasons* for the aeon, for that is what the kingdom of heaven is, which is within us, according to the word of the Lord. (*In Eccl* 3:10–13)[28]

The exegetical logic employed here moves in several steps. Evagrius asks himself what the biblical verse could mean when it speaks of placing the aeon in the heart. He explains that it must be a condensed way of expressing "reasons for the aeon," since it is only that which could be in the heart and not an aeon itself. He feels secure in this interpretation because the Lord himself has said that the Kingdom of heaven is within us. And Kingdom of heaven for Evagrius includes precisely knowledge of the aeons.[29] Thus, the "riches" that the virgin will receive are this level of knowledge.

---

[25] A. and C. Guillaumont, eds., *Le Gnostique,* Sources Chrétiennes 356 (Paris: Cerf, 1989), 99.

[26] Guillaumont, *Les six centuries,* 145–47.

[27] P. Géhin, ed., *Évagre le Pontique, Scholies à L'Ecclésiaste,* Sources Chrétiennes 397 (Paris: Cerf, 1993), G 1, p. 58.

[28] G 15; p. 82. Emphasis mine. Cf. Luke 17:21.

[29] It is interesting to note that here and in the other four texts in which Evagrius makes reference to Luke 17:21, he substitutes "Kingdom of heaven" for Luke's "Kingdom of God,"

Such knowledge prepares her for the highest level of knowledge, the goal of her whole spiritual journey, here expressed as inheriting the Kingdom of God. The clearest confirmation we can have of this interpretation and of the precise content of this highest form of knowledge is in a text we have already seen:

> The kingdom of heaven is passionlessness of the soul, along with true knowledge of beings.
>
> The kingdom of God is knowledge of the Holy Trinity, coextensive with the substance of the mind and surpassing its incorruptibility. (*Praktikos* 2, 3)[30]

The goal to which the virgin is led is nothing less than knowledge of the Holy Trinity. But this is not a knowledge that can be had at arm's length, as if it were a mastering of a set of intellectual concepts. It is a knowledge "coextensive with the substance of the mind." We might say, working within the image of the present proverb, it is a knowledge that weds itself to the mind as to a bride, as to an instrument made pure again and ready to receive the penetration of her bridegroom, that is, this knowledge. Once received into the embrace of this knowledge, the virgin comes to understand that it "surpasses her mind's own incorruptibility," that is, although "true knowledge of beings" has shown her that her own mind has been created incorruptible and immaterial for knowledge of the immaterial God, once so knowing God, she realizes that God himself surpasses her utterly. She is with her bridegroom forever. This is her feast with angels, that is, other rational beings who enjoy the same knowledge. She is a lamp shining bright with this knowledge, a lamp never to be extinguished, for she has the oil that is love. Indeed, she can expect a spiritual posterity. Commenting on the biblical proverb, "If you keep these things, you will have posterity, and your hope shall not be removed," Evagrius explains

> He [Solomon, the author] considers right thoughts and spiritual contemplations the "posterity" of the mind. Wherefore, the soul that has no posterity is sterile, for it must be generated by the spiritual spouse. (*In Prov* 23:18)[31]

---

thereby rendering the verse serviceable to him according to the distinction between the two expressions which he wishes to maintain. On this, see Géhin, *Scholies à L'Ecclésiaste*, 85. See also: "The kingdom of heaven is the reasons of the aeons that were created and are to come" (*In Eccl* 3:15; G 19; p. 88). Cf. *In Eccl* 1:2; M 110, 116; *In Prov* 24:22.

[30] A. and C. Guillaumont, *Praktikos* 2:498, 500.

[31] G 256; pp. 350–52.

THE WIDER CONTEXT

I have focused this study on just one of the proverbs of Evagrius's *Ad Virginem* because I think it is of special interest and beauty. I have not entered into specific questions concerning the whole of *Ad Virginem*. This has been done elsewhere.[32] Nonetheless, it will be useful to note briefly this proverb's context within the whole and to draw some conclusions from all that we have seen.

The text we have examined, no. 55, is the middle of three proverbs that conclude the entire collection of fifty-six proverbs. In effect, no. 55 is the conclusion in terms of content, with no. 56 functioning as a sort of signing off. The proverb that precedes no. 55 is of interest because in it Evagrius warns against false teachers:

> I have seen men corrupting virgins in dogmas
>   and rendering vain their virginity.
> But you, daughter, listen to the dogmas of the Church of the
>   Lord,
>   and let nothing else persuade you.
> For the just shall inherit light,
>   but the impious shall dwell in darkness. (*V* 54)[33]

In the Latin and Syriac versions of *Ad Virginem* there follows a list of the dogmas that Evagrius considers important, virtually expressed in the form of a creed.[34] This proverb is similar to a series of proverbs in *Ad Monachos,* which are also concerned to warn against false teachers and to establish the relation between true dogma and the true knowledge that is the goal of the monastic quest (*M* 123–31). In these, too, there is the personal witness of Evagrius: "I have seen the fathers of these [false] dogmas" (*M* 126).[35]

---

[32] For the likely addressee of the text as a certain deaconess named Severa of the Mount of Olives community associated with Melania, see G. Bunge, "Origenismus-Gnostizismus: Zum geistesgeschichtlichen Standort des Evagrios Pontikos," *Vigiliae Christianae* 40 (1986): 24–54, here 35–39; and idem, *Evagrios Pontikos: Briefe aus der Wüste* (Trier, 1986), 180–81. For a study of much of the text's content, see S. Elm, "Evagrius Ponticus' *Sententiae ad Virginem,*" *Dumbarton Oaks Papers* 45 (1991): 97–120; and idem, "The *Sententiae ad Virginem* by Evagrius Ponticus and the Problem of Early Monastic Rules," *Augustinianum* 30 (1990): 393–404. For remarks on the relation of *Ad Virginem* to the rest of the Evagrian corpus, see ACW *Ad Monachos,* 28–29, 33–37.

[33] Gressmann, "Nonnenspiegel," 150–51.

[34] The Latin text is found in A. Wilmart, "Les versions latines des Sentences d'Évagre pour les vierges," *Revue Bénédictine* 28 (1911): 143–53, here, 150. For the likelihood of the Evagrian authorship of this part of the Latin and Syriac versions, see Bunge, "Origenismus-Gnostizismus," 32–33.

[35] Gressmann, "Nonnenspiegel," 164.

There is reference to the dogmas of the church: "Do not abandon the faith of your baptism" (*M* 124).[36] Such faith is necessary for the monk or virgin to discern between true and false knowledge. Whether or not the "creed" of the Latin and Syriac versions is authentic, by following the exhortation in reference to the dogmas of the church with no. 55, Evagrius is applying the content of that teaching to the virgin in a personal way. She will penetrate those dogmas for herself, seeing and touching her Lord as a spouse, being filled, as we have seen, with a knowledge of creation, which leads ultimately to knowledge of the Holy Trinity.

The final proverb of the collection simply ties a knot in all this:

> My words, O daughter, have been spoken for you,
>> let your heart keep my utterances.
> Remember Christ who guards you,
>> and do not forget the adorable Trinity. (*V* 56)[37]

The adorable Trinity is the Kingdom of God which the bride inherits.

What we have seen in our examination of this final proverb of *Ad Virginem* suggests modifying the sharp contrast that S. Elm draws between the mystical ascent as Evagrius conceives it for men and for women. On the basis of this same text, Elm draws such conclusions as, "in the case of women, the nature of this summit is entirely different, presented with entirely different *topoi,* and achieved by an entirely different method: mystical union with the divine is achieved not through *gnosis,* but through a heavenly wedding with Christ." Or, "A monk strives for an intellectual abstraction, namely, mystical knowledge. On the other hand, the fulfillment of a virgin's ascetic life is far more personal and concrete: it is union with the heavenly bridegroom, Christ. Consequently in the *Sententiae ad Virginem,* the λογιστικόν is not an issue." Again, "Γνωστική and its notions are of no concern to her. As a result of her capacity to achieve the highest aim of ascetic life, through a mystical wedding, she does not have to pursue the difficult path toward knowledge."[38]

For me these contrasts are drawn too sharply and result in too neat a division between the sexes. While taking into account the unique employment of images with which Evagrius constructs this particular text, Elm does not read them in the light of the other texts we have taken into consideration here, which is always necessary as a method for deriving all that Evagrius has tucked into his formulations. *Ad Virginem* was most likely addressed to a member of Melania's community on the Mount of Olives,

---

[36] Ibid., 163. For a commentary on the whole chain of ten proverbs in *Ad Monachos,* see ACW *Ad Monachos,* 139–47.

[37] Gressmann, "Nonnenspiegel," 151.

[38] Elm, "Evagrius Ponticus' *Sententiae ad Virginem,*" 112.

Melania whom Palladius called "the thrice blessed"[39] and whom he described as a "woman saturated with the Logos and in love with him, who turned the night into day" with her knowledge of authors like Origen, and who thereby freed herself from "false knowledge" to take wing as a spiritual bird flying upward to Christ.[40] The virgin addressed in this text, like the monks addressed in *Ad Monachos*, is to avoid false knowledge precisely to arrive at "true knowledge of beings," that is, the Kingdom of heaven, and thus to "inherit the Kingdom of God," that is, "knowledge of the Holy Trinity, coextensive with the substance of the mind and surpassing its incorruptibility" (*Praktikos* 2, 3). Thus, Γνωστική and its notions *are* of concern to her. The λογιστικόν *is* an issue for the virgin. It is "the lamp she will light," the lamp with which a Melania turned the night into day.

Evagrius has used spousal images rather naturally and appropriately in addressing himself to a virgin, but men and women alike in subsequent generations can profit from his formulation and be guided by its images. For both men and women the order and goal of the monastic journey remain fundamentally the same:

> Let the virtues which have to do with the body accord to those of the soul and let those of the soul accord to those of the spirit. And let these accord to immaterial and substantial knowledge. (*Prayer* 132)[41]

---

[39] Palladius's *Lausiac History* (*LH*) is thoroughly marked by Evagrian categories and language. See R. Draguet, "L'Histoire Lausiaque, une œuvre écrite dans l'esprit d'Évagre," *Revue d'Histoire Ecclésiastique* 41 (1946): 321–64; 42 (1947): 5–49. For Melania as "thrice blessed" (ἡ τρισμακκαρία Μελάνιον) see *LH* 5:2; 46:1. Μακάριος is a term that Evagrius generally reserves for the final goal of monastic prayer. For references, see Géhin, *Scholies à L'Ecclésiaste*, 157–58. Melania is also called "blessed" in *LH* 10:2; 18:28; 38:8, 9. She is "the holy and marvelous Melania" in *LH* 54:1 and ἡ ἄνθρωπος τοῦ Θεοῦ in *LH* 9.

[40] *LH* 55:3. G. J. M. Bartelink, *Palladio: La Storia Lausiafa* (Milan: Fondazione Lorenza Valla, 1974), 252. There is a double entrendre in what I have translated "woman saturated with the Logos... Αὔτη λογιωτάτη γενομένη ἤ καὶ φιλήσασα τὸν λόγον.... On its most immediate or literal level the text can be understood to mean that she was extremely intelligent or cultured and loved to read the scripture. This is how the Italian translator understands it: "Ella si rivelò donna di alta cultura e fu presa d'amore per le Scritture." (On the specific Christian sense of φιλολογεῖν as referring to dedication to the spiritual study of scripture, see K. Girardet, "Φιλόλογος und φιλολογεῖν" in *Kleronomia* 2 [1970]: 323–33.) But this translation, though literally correct, fails to express the overtones that Palladius's Evagrian theology would wish to imply. In any case, here we have a woman deeply immersed in knowledge as this is understood in Evagrian terms.

[41] PG 79:1196A.

3

PENTHOS AND TEARS

It is more than fifty years now since Irénée Hausherr published his important study *Penthos: La doctrine de componction dans l'Orient Chrétien.*[1] Since that time the book has served students of the Christian East well, and it is considered the standard general work on the subject. Hausherr's work is arranged according to various themes touching on *penthos:* a definition, its causes, means to it, obstacles to it, and so on. The book is a treasure chest of patristic texts bearing on the subject, spanning over a thousand years, bearing testimony to the importance of the theme and its persistent presence. Yet after more than half a century it is legitimate to ask, in no way intending to deny the service this book has provided, if it is not perhaps time to take up a fresh study of this theme. Many critical texts and fine monographs on the various authors that Hausherr cites have appeared in the last fifty years, and a methodology in patristic studies has been considerably refined in the last decades. A study as comprehensive as Hausherr's by the standards of our own time would require much groundwork and collaboration among various specialists and perhaps an approach to the subject more systematic than his. Perhaps what is needed today if we would envision a fresh study of this most important theme is first a series of individual studies on the various masters whom Hausherr so widely cites.[2] With a more systematic understanding of the teaching of these different masters on *penthos,* someone might be able with greater security to attempt again Hausherr's more thematic and global approach, perhaps giving the study a stronger chronological organization, an organization that also recognizes and articulates the different strands of a developing tradition.

In any case, in this present study I hope only to plant this suggestion and to offer a small sample of the sort of individual study that I think could usefully undergird a reexamination of the theme. I would like to examine

---

[1] I. Hausherr, *Penthos: La doctrine de componction dans l'Orient Chrétien* (Rome, 1944). English translation: *Penthos: The Doctrine of Compunction in the Christian East*, trans. A. Hufstader (Kalamazoo: Cistercian Publications, 1982).

[2] Recently a fine study has appeared: B. Müller, *Der Weg des Weinens: Die Tradition des "Penthos" in den Apophthegmata Patrum* (Göttingen, 2000).

penthos as it occurs in the writings of Evagrius and together with it the closely related subject of tears. When we look at the texts of Evagrius on *penthos* and tears, basically two points of general importance emerge: (1) They are something found especially in the beginning stages of the monastic life; but, as is typical for Evagrius, whatever concerns the beginning is also related by him to the end. In other words, *penthos* and tears have a scope; and that scope is pure prayer. (2) The second dimension that clearly emerges is that *penthos* and tears are closely related with the very important monastic problem of acedia or listlessness. We shall try to discover these two points as they are expressed in specific texts of Evagrius.

TEARS AT THE BEGINNING, BUT THE SCOPE IS PRAYER. THE CHAPTERS ON PRAYER 5–8

Four brief chapters, nos. 5–8, in Evagrius's *Chapters on Prayer* contain important information for us on how he understands our theme. These several chapters must be read in their context if they are to be fully appreciated. First of all, there is the context of the work itself. Among all the works of Evagrius, the *Chapters on Prayer* speak of the highest levels of prayer. It is a very advanced text, in my opinion perhaps his most advanced.[3] We are also virtually at the very beginning of this text. Numbers 1–4 speak in general terms. And when one knows the language of Evagrius and how he expects every word to be given its proper weight, then we are aware that in these first four chapters he has presented for our meditation the general structures of the spiritual journey within which the monk will move toward the goal of pure prayer. Numbers 1 and 2 speak of the preparation for pure prayer by the life of *praktikē*, the active struggle to establish virtue in the soul. Virtue in the soul establishes the mind (the νοῦς, Evagrius's consistent term for the instrument of prayer) in the stable condition required for prayer. Number 3 gives a definition of prayer, again using the term νοῦς: "Prayer is a conversation (ὁμιλία) of the mind with God...without any intermediary" (*Prayer* 3).[4] Number 4 moves within the same orbit of thought under the biblical image of Moses approaching the burning bush. His having to take off his shoes is an image for the monk of needing to rid himself of every passionate thought if he wants to "see him

---

[3] This opinion must be nuanced and carefully explained. See ACW *Ad Monachos*, 26–27, as well as chapter 1 above, "Spiritual Progress in the Works of Evagrius Ponticus." To say that it is his most advanced text is not to say that it is the most difficult. For this category the prize must surely go to the *Kephalaia Gnostica*.

[4] PG 79:1168D.

who is above all perception and all concepts and converse with him"
(*Prayer* 4).[5]

With no. 5 Evagrius addresses the first specific topic of his treatise, and
it is precisely tears and *penthos*.

> First of all pray to receive tears, so that by sorrowing (διά τοῦ πέν-
> θους) you may be able to calm the wildness that there is in your
> soul and obtain forgiveness from the Lord by confessing your
> offences to him. (*Prayer* 5).[6]

He could not have thrown the issue we are examining into greater relief.
He says, "First of all," in Greek, πρότερον, the very first word of the chapter which begins the meditation on specific themes. So tears are the beginning of prayer. That is to say, they are the beginning of what the monastic
life aims for; namely, that conversation of the mind with God. But tears are
a gift; they must be received. Indeed, one must pray for them. It should
also be noticed how closely tears are associated with *penthos* in this text.
They are the exterior evidence of the interior work of *penthos*. *Penthos* calms
or softens something wild within the soul. Such an image[7] gives some sense
of how *penthos* works interiorly. It must soften something hard, calm something that is wild. Something within must "first of all" change if the monk
is ultimately to arrive at pure prayer. So, the soul must be tamed for this. It
is one purpose that Evagrius attributes to tears and *penthos* in this chapter.
The other is forgiveness of sins. Confessing one's sins is among the first
steps of the monastic life and something that is to continue throughout.
Evagrius stands in the center of the whole tradition here. We see that it is
a confession that appropriately takes place with tears.

The next chapter reads

> Use tears to support every petition, because your Lord is greatly
> pleased to receive prayer made with tears. (*Prayer* 6).[8]

To understand this chapter it is useful to be aware that there are actually
two kinds of prayer in Evagrius. Speaking in a more general way, Evagrius
uses the word for the prayers that are uttered throughout the life of *praktikē*, swift expressions of needs and calls for help. Speaking more strictly, he
reserves the term for the goal of the entire monastic life. It is synonymous
for him with knowledge of the Holy Trinity.[9] In chapter 6 it is a question

---

[5] PG 79:1168D.

[6] PG 79:1168D.

[7] The Greek reads ἵνα δυνηθῇς διὰ τοῦ πένθους μαλάξαι τὴν ἐνυπάρχουσαν τῇ ψυχῇ σου
ἀγριότητα...

[8] PG 79:1169A.

[9] Οὐκοῦν καὶ προσευχῆς διττὸς ὁ τρόπος. Ὁ μέν τις πρακτικός, ὁ δὲ θεωρητικός (*Prayer*,

of the more general kind of prayer. Hausherr, in a different comment on this chapter, suggests that one can turn to chapter 38 to discover the sort of things for which the monk ought to pray:

> Pray first to be cleansed from passions, then to be delivered from ignorance and unawareness, and thirdly to be delivered from all temptation and abandonment. (*Prayer* 38).[10]

In praying to be cleansed from passions, one is praying to reach the goal of *praktikē*. In praying to be delivered from ignorance, one prays for the goal of gnosis or knowledge. The prayer to be delivered from temptation and abandonment is so that one will not be tempted to pride after having reached the goals of *praktikē* and knowledge.[11] For all these petitions Evagrius suggests tears. The language of this short chapter places us in the atmosphere of earnest pleading before a Sovereign (the Greek translated "Lord" here is ὁ δεσπότης). Tears are meant to be pleasing to him. They express one's earnest need and dependence on God for that which is petitioned. Or they express perhaps a certain fear that what is prayed for might not be received. Not to be delivered from passion and from ignorance or to be abandoned—the very thought is cause for tears.

With chapter 7 the reader experiences something that is typical in the written works of Evagrius. First, one is made to meditate in one direction; then the exercise shifts and something quite different is considered, or the same matter is considered from a different angle. After having praised the importance of tears, Evagrius now warns that they could be a cause of vainglory or pride.

> Even if you shed rivers of tears in your prayer, that is no reason for feeling conceited, as if you were superior to the populace. It is because your prayer has received help that you are able to confess your sins readily and to placate the Lord by weeping. So do not turn the antidote to passions into another passion, otherwise

---

prologue; PG 79:1165C). See also *Prayer* 98, "In the time of trials like these, make use of a short, intense prayer" (PG 79:1189A). For a useful study on continuous prayer as part of *praktikē* in Evagrius and in the whole desert tradition, see G. Bunge, "Betet ohne Unterlass," in *Das Geistgebet: Studien zum Traktat "De Oratione" des Evagrios Pontikos* (Cologne, 1987), 29–43. For prayer as knowledge of the Holy Trinity, see *Prayer* 58–61 with my commentary in ACW *Ad Monachos*, 338–40.

[10] PG 79:1176A. Cf. I. Hausherr, *Les leçons d'un contemplatif: Le Traité de l'Oraison d'Évagre le Pontique* (Paris, 1960), 20–21.

[11] For Evagrius's consistent understanding of the temptation to pride and his locating the question of abandonment precisely here, see Hausherr, *Les leçons d'un contemplatif*, 55. See also ACW *Ad Monachos*, 279–84, as well as chapter 6 below, "Evagrius and Paphnutius on the Causes for Abandonment by God."

you will only anger all the more him who gave you this grace. (*Prayer* 7)[12]

According to the teaching of Evagrius, vainglory and pride always assail the monk after he has in fact made some real progress in the spiritual life. To "shed rivers of tears" would be a sign of such real progress. Yet it is precisely here that Evagrius finds it necessary to remind the monk that if he has tears it is because he has been given them as a gift, as a grace. Remembering this is precisely the solution to vainglory and pride.

In this shift of direction in the meditation, Evagrius has nonetheless carefully kept in his formulation strong links with the two preceding chapters. The expression "it is because your prayer has received help" is counterpoised with "pray to receive tears" in chapter 5. And again we see two purposes for tears expressed in this chapter. The first, the ability "to confess one's sins readily" virtually repeats the expression from chapter 5, "obtain forgiveness from the Lord by confessing your offences to him." The second purpose of tears expressed here, "to placate the Lord by weeping," corresponds to "your Lord is greatly pleased...with tears" in chapter 6. In both chapters the word translated "Lord" is ὁ δεσπότης.

The final sentence summarizes the previous in a memorable and clever way. Tears are supposed to be the antidote to passions: they calm something wild in us; they lend earnestness to our prayers to be cleansed from the passions; and with them we confess our sins. Yet if they become cause for vainglory and pride, they simply have given rise to yet other passions. "So do not turn the antidote to passions into another passion." This would anger "the one who gave this grace" rather than please or placate him.[13]

If chapter 7 is an intricate and somewhat extended meditation, as far as such things go in Evagrius, chapter 8, the final chapter in this particular series, is striking and to the point.

> Many people who weep for their sins, while forgetting the purpose of their weeping, have gone out of their minds and turned astray. (*Prayer* 8)[14]

The danger of actually going out of one's mind can be a surprising warning to receive at this point, and Evagrius probably wants to create in his reader precisely this shock. Yet it is not unusual for him to speak of going crazy particularly in relation to pride. For him, pride is a form of madness

---

[12] PG 79:1169A.

[13] For this same idea represented elsewhere in the desert tradition, see in *The Apophthegmata Patrum*, Systematic Collection, chapter 3 on Compunction, no. 22 in the Greek version (Sources Chrétiennes 387, p. 162).

[14] PG 79:1169A.

because it carries one so far from the truth of one's utter dependence on God. If a monk lives the lie of thinking he has some reason for conceit because he "sheds rivers of tears," eventually he will be abandoned by God, an abandonment that is experienced as "utter insanity and madness, and visions of mobs of demons in the air" (*Praktikos* 14; p. 534).[15]

Two other ideas about tears are found again in this brief chapter. First, weeping is specified as being "for sins." Second, the notion of a "purpose" or goal (ὁ σκοπός) for weeping is mentioned. The immediate context has described this purpose from many angles: to calm the wildness, to obtain forgiveness, to please and placate the Lord. Why cry, says Evagrius, if not for these? Otherwise one is crying for show or for no good reason; and this, of course, is madness. But the expression "purpose for weeping" should also be understood in the broader context of this whole treatise and indeed in the broader context of the goal of the whole monastic life. There everything is done "showing to God our purpose (ὁ σκοπός) that whatever we do, we do for the sake of knowledge of him" (*Praktikos* 32; p. 574).[16] Thus, to come to knowledge of God is ultimately the purpose for weeping. To forget this is quite literally, as Evagrius says here, to turn astray (ἐκτρέπω), no longer following the only path that leads to true knowledge; namely, *praktikē's* path, which "first of all" (the πρότερον of chapter 5) begins with tears.

Before leaving this brief series of chapters, it is instructive to see how Evagrius continues the text after this initial meditation on tears and *penthos*. Chapters 9 through 12 can be considered another series concerned with the difficulties of prayer and the need to stand firm. "Work hard," he says; "do not relax"; "ward off"; "struggle." It is a meditation that counsels the monk to expect difficulties and the ruses of the demons. Then with chapter 13, there begins a long meditation on the importance of gentleness and love and their relation to prayer. These are virtues without which it is impossible ever to arrive at pure prayer. In Evagrius's understanding, they are the virtues par excellence.[17] So, we have seen *penthos* and tears in their broader context within the whole. The text has opened with a beautiful and dense meditation, biblically inspired, on pure prayer (chapters 1–4). The first specific issue that the text faces is precisely tears and *penthos* (chapters 5–8). Exhortations to stand firm (chapters 9–12) are followed by meditations that exercise the virtues of gentleness and love (chapters 13ff.).

---

[15] For a discussion of madness in relation to pride, considering a number of Evagrian texts, see ACW *Ad Monachos*, 281–82, as well as chapter 6 below, "Evagrius and Paphnutius on the Causes for Abandonment by God."

[16] ...τὸν σκοπὸν ἡμῶν δεικνύντες Θεῷ ὅτι πάντα πράττομεν τῆς αὐτοῦ γνώσεως ἕνεκεν.

[17] Cf. J. Driscoll, "Gentleness in the *Ad Monachos* of Evagrius Ponticus," *Studia Monastica* 32 (1990): 295–321.

Tears Related to Acedia
or Listlessness

If the texts from the *Chapters on Prayer* help us to see the fundamental role of tears in the monastic life,[18] there are other texts in which tears are related to acedia—which I prefer to translate as *listlessness*. Listlessness is a problem that afflicts the monk not at the beginning of the monastic life but long after he is involved in spiritual progress.

Chapter 27 in the *Praktikos* is part of a series of three chapters in that work that offer various remedies for listlessness. They are, first, tears; second, remaining in one's cell; third, remembering death. They are, of course, interrelated; but here I want to focus on what Evagrius says in chapter 27. The chapter offers a clear example of his famous method of antirrhetikos, that is, using words of scripture in the combat against a particular demon.[19]

> When we are oppressed by the demon of listlessness, we should divide our soul in two with tears, making one part console the other, (τὴν ψυχὴν μετὰ δακρύων μερίσαντες τὴν μὲν παρακαλοῦσαν τὴν δὲ παρακαλουμένην ποιήσωμεν) sowing good hopes in ourselves and singing David's words, "Why are you depressed, my soul, why do you disturb me? Hope in God, because I will praise him, the Saviour of my person, my God." (Ps 41:6) (*Praktikos* 27; p. 562)[20]

Against the demon of listlessness, Evagrius suggests using the verse of Psalm 41:6.[21] The image of dividing the soul in two is perhaps unusual, but it should be noticed that the idea is taken from the psalm itself. The psalmist is, so to speak, talking to himself, saying "Why are you depressed, my soul." That is, in this context, why are you letting the demon of listlessness overtake you? So, I use one part of myself to talk to another part of myself. The part I talk to is the part destined to be consoled; the part talking is the one consoling. For the purposes of the present investigation, it is worth noting that this division of the soul takes place "with tears." We

---

[18] "Fundamental role" is here intended in its strong sense, that is, the beginning of the journey toward pure prayer, the πρότερον of chapter 5.

[19] Evagrius has an entire work, the *Antirrhetikos*, devoted to this method, organized in eight chapters according to the eight principal evil thoughts or demons. Chapter 6 is concerned with listlessness.

[20] The English is slightly altered from S. Tugwell.

[21] In the *Antirrhetikos* at VI, 20, this same psalm verse is offered as a remedy. The thought expressed in Rom 15:4 is also perhaps guiding Evagrius here.

can perhaps better understand how Evagrius conceives this as happening by taking into account that the language of "consoling" in Greek here is the same language as in the beatitude on *penthos.* "Blessed are they who mourn (οἱ πενθοῦντες), for they shall be consoled (παρακληθήσονται)" (Matt 5:4). What the meditating monk (Evagrius or his reader) would notice is that the beatitude promises that the one who weeps—me!—is the same one who will be consoled: me again! The psalm verse fits this structure like a glove. "With tears" I speak to my soul and thereby "sow good hopes" for my future consolation. My present listlessness is thus broken, for this Word of God is a counter-word (an *antirrhetikos*) to the word or suggestion of the demon. My listlessness is broken because the psalm speaks of a future in which "I will praise God" again. My listlessness is broken because I have used tears, and the Lord's word has promised that those who weep shall be consoled.

It is tears that break the grip of the demon of listlessness. When a monk is in the grip of this demon, he thinks that no effort in the monastic life, no practice, is worthwhile.[22] Yet tears, in fact, are what "support every petition" for the things that need be asked for in prayer, as we saw in the *Chapters on Prayer,* chapter 38: to be cleansed from passion, delivered from ignorance, saved from temptation. If one prays for these things with tears, the demon of listlessness cannot remain near. In fact, the battle with this demon is a battle between tears or no tears. *Ad Monachos* 56 shows the demon winning: "The spirit of listlessness drives away tears." *Ad Virginem* 39 shows the reverse and the strength of the practice of tears: "Heavy is sadness; intolerable, listlessness; but tears before God are stronger than both" (*M* 56).[23]

A passage from *On Evil Thoughts,* chapter 18, can help to explain why a verse from the Psalms might be used against this demon.

> If a certain listlessness comes over us on account of our labors, let us run up a little onto the rock of knowledge (cf. Ps 60:3) and busy ourselves with the psalter, on which we pluck the chords of knowledge through the virtues. Let us pasture our sheep again beneath Mount Sinai so that the God of our fathers might call also to us from the bush and grace also us with the meanings (τοὺς λόγους) of signs and wonders (cf. Ps 104:27). (*On Evil Thoughts* 17)[24]

---

[22] For Evagrius's classical description of the effects of this demon, see *Praktikos* 12.

[23] H. Gressmann, ed., "Nonnenspiegel und Mönchsspiegel des Euagrios Pontikos," *Texte und Untersuchungen* 39, no. 4 (1913): 157; *V* 39, ibid., 149.

[24] P. Géhin, ed., *Évagre le Pontique, Sur les pensées,* Sources Chrétiennes 438 (Paris: Cerf, 1998), 212–14.

The use of the Psalter is a practical step that the monk under attack by this demon can take. In this and in other passages Evagrius understands the Psalter itself symbolically; it is more than a collection of prayers and sacred words, though it is also certainly that. However, the deepest sense of the Psalter is as something in which knowledge itself becomes the song through the vibration of the virtues. That is to say, the Psalter is somehow the expression and reality in the Sacred Scriptures of the whole range of the monastic journey, from its beginning in the practice of the virtues to its goal in the knowledge of God. But there is more. The Psalter is not just something outside the monk; it is somehow his deepest being, his νοῦς. In a scholion on the psalm verse "Praise the Lord on the harp, on the ten-stringed psalter sing psalms to him," Evagrius explains, "The harp is a soul accomplished in *praktikē* moved by the commandments of God. The psalter is a pure mind, moved by spiritual knowledge (ψαλτήριον δὲ νοῦς καθαρὸς ὑπὸ πνευματικῆς κινούμενος γνώσεως)" (*In Ps* 32:2).[25] Thus, the Psalter on which the chords of knowledge are plucked through the virtues is the very mind of the monk. By its various verses the monk is helped in his practice of virtue, in his battle with the demons, in his movements within the realm of knowledge. According to the passage from *On Evil Thoughts,* the thoughts of the mind—its sheep—are pastured once again beneath Mount Sinai, biblical symbol for the law or *praktikē,*[26] instead of being prey to the *logismoi* of the demons. Then God can call to this monk from the burning bush, biblical image of knowledge, and show him the *logoi,* the deepest inner sense, of signs and wonders. All this hope is offered to the listless monk if he will but mount the rock of knowledge and play the Psalter there.[27]

The Psalter in its many and varied dimensions is suited in a general way for aiding the monk in the practice of virtue and in various levels of knowledge.[28] Evagrius's scholia on the Psalms amply demonstrate this. But we

---

[25] PG 12:1304C.

[26] Moses, the biblical figure around whom Evagrius's thought is constructed here, is a symbol of natural contemplation (cf. *KG* II, 64) and, as we have already seen in *Prayer* 4, also for pure prayer. This is because he was "the most gentle of men" (Num 12:3), the virtue par excellence of the life of *praktikē*. For this use of Moses elsewhere, see *Praktikos* 38 and *Lt* 27, 36, 41, 56.

[27] It is not difficult for any reader in a tradition like Evagrius's to understand the rock as an image of Christ, based on a similar exegetical procedure in 1 Cor 10:4, where Paul gave an interpretation that was to become authorative in the many occurrences of the word *rock* in scripture: "For they drank of that spiritual Rock that followed them: and the Rock was Christ." For a discussion of other texts in which Evagrius understands the word *rock* in this way, see ACW *Ad Monachos,* 287.

[28] Cf. *Prayer* 85: "Psalmody belongs to 'manifold wisdom' (Eph 3:10)" (PG 79:1185C). Here I am following a correction of the PG text in the edition by S. Tugwell.

also have from Evagrius some specific applications of the Psalms to the problem of listlessness. In addition to the texts we have already examined, we find in the *Antirrhetikos,* that collection of biblical verses to use in battle against the eight evil thoughts, some eighteen passages from the Psalms in the chapter on listlessness. Some of these are directly relevant to the present investigation, for they show again that the battle with this demon is in part a battle about tears. In the *Antirrhetikos* Evagrius often focuses the scriptural passage he offers to be used against a particular demon by describing some specific dimension of that demon's attack to which the verse can be applied. Thus, for example, he says,

> For the soul that, on account of the evil thought of listlessness, does not want to pour out tears during the night; but tears are a great medicine against the visions of the night that come from listlessness; this medicine was wisely applied by the prophet David to such passions when he said, "I am wearied with my groanings; I shall wash my bed every night; I shall water my couch with my tears" (Ps 6:7). (*Ant* VI, 10)[29]

This is the struggle already observed as so succinctly expressed in *Ad Monachos* 56: "The spirit of listlessness drives away tears." Another remedy is offered for this same problem several chapters later. "For the soul that thinks that tears are of no value in the battle against listlessness and has forgotten what David did and said: 'My tears have become my bread day and night' (Ps 41:4)" (*Ant* VI, 19).[30] In this same chapter of the *Antirrhetikos* Evagrius also suggests the Psalm verse found in *Praktikos* 27—Psalm 41:6.[31] There it is a question of arousing hope and consolation in the listless monk. The Psalm teaches one part of the soul to say to the other, "Hope in God." This division of the soul into two parts takes place "with tears." Tears, and *penthos* in general, are ultimately about hope and maintaining hope especially against the demon of listlessness.[32] Despite all the difficulties of *praktikē* and its seeming to last forever without bearing fruit,[33] if the monk accompanies his monastic asceticism with tears and an attitude of *penthos,* there are good grounds for the hope of reaching knowledge.[34]

---

[29] W. Frankenberg, ed., *Evagrius Ponticus,* Abhandlungen der königlichen Gesellschaft der Wissenschaften zu Göttingen, Phil.-hist. Klasse n.F. 13.2 (Berlin, 1912), 522.

[30] Ibid., 524.

[31] See above, p. 57.

[32] A number of other chapters in the *Antirrhetikos*'s remedies against listlessness are focused directly on the issue of hope. See VI, 12, 14, 18, 22.

[33] See *Praktikos* 12 on listlessness: "[the demon] suggests to him that he still has a long time to live, conjuring up before his eyes a vision of how burdensome the ascetic life is" (A. and C. Guillaumont, *Praktikos,* 2:526; trans. Tugwell).

[34] On the relation of hope and knowledge, see especially *In Ps* 70:14. For a beautiful prayer

This practice and attitude as a regular part of monastic practice are expressed in another text from *Praktikos* 57, where tears are found together with compunction (ἡ κατάνυξις), a word to be very closely associated with *penthos*.[35] Chapter 57 is found in a part of the work (57–62) which identifies the state that is close to passionlessness or *apatheia*, the goal of *praktikē*.

> There are two peaceful states of the soul: one grows from natural seeds, the other results from the withdrawal of the demons. The first has as its consequence humility together with compunction, and tears and unbounded yearning for God and immeasurable zeal for work; the second has as its consequence vainglory together with pride, which capture the monk when the other demons go away. Anyone who perceives the beginnings of the first state of peace will be all the more acutely aware of the assaults of the demons. (*Praktikos* 57; p. 634)[36]

After the defeat of the demon of listlessness, "the soul is taken over by a peaceful condition and by unspeakable joy" (*Praktikos* 12; p. 526).[37] It is this condition about which Evagrius is speaking also in this chapter, but in addition he consistently teaches that after the defeat of this demon and as the monk draws near to the borders of passionlessness, two other demons of a different order are in a position to attack; namely, vainglory and pride. We have already seen this idea in the series of chapters examined from the *Chapters on Prayer* (see 7, 8). This chapter then is a warning for the monk who approaches the goal of *praktikē*. Evagrius distinguishes two kinds of peaceful state in the soul. Both are good, but the one that allows for the possible entry of vainglory and pride is the more risky. What can guard against such a risk? The other kind of peaceful state, the one that "grows from natural seeds." Evagrius borrows a Stoic idea here according to which natural seeds of the virtues are placed in us from birth, which, if cultivated, produce their proper fruit.[38] It is interesting in the context of the present investigation to find tears and compunction listed as some of what follows from these natural seeds of the virtues. They are found together with "humility…unbounded yearning for God and immeasurable zeal for work." All these work together to protect the peaceful state of the soul. In

---

to be said to Christ with tears and formulated with phrases from Psalm 30:3, see *On Evil Thoughts, Long Recension* 34 (PG 40:1241B-C).

[35] See Hausherr, *Penthos*, 14ff. for the evidence; in English, 7ff. In the Systematic Collection of the *Apophthegmata Patrum*, see the stories collected in chapter 3, entitled Περὶ κατανύξεως.

[36] Translation Tugwell, slightly altered.

[37] Translation Tugwell.

[38] See A. and C. Guillaumont, *Praktikos*, 2:635.

other words, basic virtues and practices from *praktikē* must continue to be lived even after the monk reaches the peaceful state and enters into knowledge.[39] Among these, we are not surprised to find tears, since they are the "first of all" (cf. *Prayer* 5) in the journey toward pure prayer; they are the "antidote to passions" (cf. *Prayer* 7) so long as one does not "forget their purpose" (cf. *Prayer* 8); they are stronger than sorrow and listlessness (cf. *V* 39). Nor are we surprised to find tears together here with compunction, an attitude closely associated with *penthos*. We saw that tears with *penthos* calm the wildness of the soul (cf. *Prayer* 5). Here tears and compunction protect a peaceful state of the soul. They form part of the whole πολιτεία[40] of a monk, together with zeal and yearning. Yet there is some sense in which actual tears keep emerging in these texts as a hinge around which other virtues and practices revolve. With language similar to chapter 57 of the *Praktikos*, Evagrius elsewhere says, "Zeal and yearning and mortification of the body cultivate tears, and tears cleanse the soul from sin just as a whetstone lifts rust from iron."[41] Monastic zeal and yearning and mortification—in a word, the whole ascetical life—mean to cultivate tears; for tears cleanse the soul from sin and so ready it for pure prayer, "the conversation of the mind with God" (cf. *Prayer* 3). This, for Evagrius, is the hidden meaning of the psalm verse "They that sow in tears shall reap in joy." His scholion is, "Those who undertake *praktikē* with hard work and tears are they who 'sow in tears, but those who share in knowledge without hard work are the ones who 'reap in joy'" (*In Ps* 125:5).

CONCLUSION

Two texts can serve as a conclusion to this investigation of tears and *penthos* in the writings of Evagrius. Each is characteristically short, but I think we are now in a position to see how much of his teaching Evagrius has compressed into these brief lines. When one knows the teaching of Evagrius on this topic as it has been outlined here—that is to say, when one is familiar with his themes and what he emphasizes; when one is a disciple of his—then a scholion like the following strikes as a marvelous and memorable summary of the details of that teaching. It is a comment on this verse from Ecclesiastes: "It is better to go to a house of mourning (εἰς οἶκον πένθους) than to go to a house of drink, since such is the end of every

---

[39] Cf. *M* 63: "Knowledge keeps guard over a monk's way of life (πολιτεία)" with my commentary in ACW *Ad Monachos*, 285–86.

[40] See previous note.

[41] *Institutio ad monachos*, in the supplement by J. Muyldermans, *Le Muséon* 51 (1938): 201 n. 7.

man (καθότι τοῦτο τὸ τέλος παντὸς ἀνθρώπου), and the living will give good to his heart" (Eccl 7:2). Evagrius comments:

The end of man is beatitude (Τέλος τοῦ ἀνθρόπου ἡ μακαριότης ἐστίν). And if the Lord in the gospels calls mourning blessed (Εἰ δὲ μακαρίζει τὸ πένθος…) in the place where he says "Blessed are those who mourn, for they shall be consoled," then rightly does Solomon say here that the end of man is mourning, because he fills with spiritual goods those who live in mourning. (*In Eccl* 7:2)[42]

Τέλος and μακαριότης are words that Evagrius consistently associates with the goal and purpose of monastic life.[43] Thus, he begins this scholion with what is a common piece of his vocabulary and a constant theme of his teaching: the end (τέλος) of man is beatitude (μακαριότης). Within the logic of how his commentary unfolds, the word *beatitude* helps him find his way to the Lord's words in the Gospels, words that, of course, are paradoxical: the mourning are blessed. Evagrius seizes this paradox and throws it into relief by relying on the inspired words of Solomon, whom he takes to be the author of Ecclesiastes and whose words already beautifully express the paradox. So Solomon says, "The end of man is *penthos*." Indeed, the Lord's words can be the only explanation of why Solomon would say, "It is good to go to a house of *penthos*."

Of course, the human author of Ecclesiastes, in saying "The end of every man is mourning," probably did not imagine his statement being interpreted in so positive a tone. But two clues in the text, which Evagrius's exegetical tradition would attribute to the intentions of the Holy Spirit,[44] guide Evagrius to this particular interpretation. First, he has found the word τέλος in the text, and his tradition tells him that this is a "code word" for the final goal of everything in Christian and monastic life. Second, he has found the word πένθος in the text. He knows this word to be in the Beatitudes as well—the Beatitudes which likewise describe the τέλος of life as μακαριότης. So Evagrius's logic here is tightly biblical, and it is based on a syllogism that the meditating monk must complete. Solomon can say, "The end of man is *penthos*" because the Lord has said, "Blessed are those in *penthos*, for they shall be consoled." This consolation, of course, and not *penthos* itself, is the final blessedness; but the paradoxical formulation of the scholion means precisely to lend hope to those who are in mourning,

---

[42] P. Géhin, ed., *Scholies à L'Ecclésiaste,* Sources Chrétiennes 397 (Paris: Cerf, 1993), 156.

[43] For references, see ibid., 157–58. For a discussion, see ACW *Ad Monachos,* 222–23, 245–46.

[44] On the importance of a sympathetic understanding of this tradition for a proper grasp of how Evagrius moves within a scriptural text, see ibid., 17–22.

which we have seen should be every monk. For to those in such mourning, future blessedness is promised.

In countless ways in his writings, Evagrius constantly moves his reading disciples back and forth between the two basic phases of monastic life, *praktikē* and knowledge. This present scholion does that in such a way as to show how tears and *penthos* move back and forth between these two dimensions of the monastic journey. They are a permanent part of *praktikē*, but they are precisely what gives the monk hope, for he is already blessed if he is now mourning. It is the sowing in tears and the reaping in joy.

This Psalm verse, a scholion on which we have already seen, is the inspiration for the chapter which concludes the main body of Evagrius's work the *Praktikos*.[45] He says:

> The fruit of sowing is sheaves, and the fruit of the virtues is knowledge. And as tears accompany sowing, so joy accompanies reaping. (*Praktikos* 90; p. 690)

These brief lines mean to summarize the eighty-nine chapters that have preceded it in the *Praktikos,* all of the chapters being in various ways instructions on the life of *praktikē*. But these lines mean also to point ahead to what follows, for the *Praktikos* is the first part of a three-part work; and now the monk's meditations will be turned toward the joy of knowledge as expressed in the *Gnostikos* and the *Kephalaia Gnostica*. For the purposes of this present investigation it is instructive that Evagrius, even being ever so brief, places tears in this important transitional position. *Penthos* and tears are ultimately about hope, the hope that present labor, present sorrow, present listlessness have a future consolation in store. In this monastic tradition actual tears are meant to flow. We must try to understand why precisely tears and why precisely the mourning that is *penthos* are what offer this hope. They do so because actual tears soften something wild within. They undergird the monk's every petition both for progress in *praktikē* and for reaching the goal of knowledge, and so they please the Lord who is being petitioned. They break the grip on a heart made cold by listlessness and so plant seeds of hope. They wash, they really do effectively wash sins away. They accompany a great yearning for God—indeed, they express it—and they flow beside the zeal with which the monk undertakes his task.

In the writings of Evagrius we have a privileged glimpse of where precisely the widespread theme of *penthos* in ancient monasticism finds its place. The theme is not unique in Evagrius; he is one of its representatives. Each of the great masters of the past leaves us with a particular angle from which to view and profit from the wisdoms of the tradition. In the texts we have examined here, one can taste the style and unique incisive twists that

---

[45] For this as the conclusion, see A. and C. Guillaumont, *Praktikos,* 1:120–21.

so characterize the writings of Evagrius. Yet one is also struck by the fact that here again Evagrius shows himself heir of the tradition that precedes him and one who forms that which follows. This influence on subsequent monasticism is seen with special clarity—it would be one example among many possible—in the prologue of the *Rule of St. Benedict*. Although one could say it, one need not say that in this text Benedict sounds like Evagrius or is directly influenced by him. However, this much at least must be said: Evagrius and Benedict are talking about the same thing.

> The good of all concerned may prompt us to a little strictness in order to amend faults and to safeguard love. Do not be daunted immediately by fear and run away from the road that leads to salvation. It is bound to be narrow at the outset. But as we progress in this way of life and in faith, we shall run on the path of God's commandments, our hearts overflowing with the inexpressible delight of love. (*Rule of Benedict*, prologue, 47–49)[46]

Or again:

> We must know that God regards our purity of heart and tears of compunction, not our many words. (*Rule of Benedict* 20:3)

Or again:

> Every day with tears and sighs confess your past sins to God in prayer. (*Rule of Benedict* 4:57)

Finally, in the chapter that explains that the life of a monk ought to be a continuous Lent, St. Benedict says,

> This we can do in a fitting manner by refusing to indulge evil habits and by devoting ourselves to prayer with tears, to reading, to compunction of heart and self-denial. (*Rule of Benedict* 49:4)

---

[46] Trans. *RB 1980, The Rule of Benedict in Latin and English with Notes,* ed. T. Fry (Collegeville, 1980).

4

THE EVIL THOUGHT
"LOVE OF MONEY"

L ove of money (φιλαργυρία) is counted by Evagrius as one of the
eight principal evil thoughts with which the monk must do battle.
Developing his understanding with forceful images drawn from
scripture and of his own crafting, he teaches that desiring money wrongly
is the root of all evil, bringing others in its train. Voluntary poverty and
concrete acts of charity toward the poor are the antidotes to love of money.
But neither poverty nor even charity is a goal in itself for Evagrius. These
open the door to the only true wealth and our true goal: loving knowledge
of the Holy Trinity. What we do with money determines in a fundamental
way whether or not we will reach this goal for which we were created.

Evagrius was the first of the desert fathers to transmit in writing the
apophthegmata of other fathers. It is to him that we owe the account of
the memorable gesture and saying of the monk who sold his personal copy
of the Gospels and said, "I have sold the book which told me to sell all I
have and give to the poor" (Matt 19:21 par.) (*Praktikos* 97).[1] This little
story can serve to express right from the start of this brief study some of
the principal themes of Evagrius's understanding of the question of money,
as this was imparted to him by his own spiritual guides in the desert.

First of all, we see that what the monk did in selling his Gospel book was
inspired by the scriptures themselves. Indeed, the teaching of the desert
fathers on any practice of the monastic life always sought to let itself be
shaped under the inspiration of scripture. Second, the story shows us a
concrete action very important to desert monastic practice; namely, caring
for the poor. Third, we may note that the scope here is not merely some
exterior physical austerity or style of life, but rather love expressed in caring for others. Finally, we could comment on this story with a meditation
on the same Gospel verse that Evagrius uses elsewhere. He says, "Go, sell

---

[1] A. and C. Guillaumont, *Évagre le Pontique: Traité pratique ou le moine*, Sources Chrétiennes 170, 171 (Paris: Cerf, 1971), 704.

what you have and give to the poor; and taking up the cross, deny your-self, so that you will be able to pray without distraction" (*Prayer* 17).[2] This is typical of a style Evagrius uses to comment on a biblical text. He cites a well-known verse and then changes a part of it in order to make his point. The change, of course, is not a betrayal of the text's meaning but rather a penetration of it or an application of it to a particular point. With his gloss on this verse, Evagrius shows that poverty is not an end in itself but neces-sary to the supreme goal of the monastic life: undistracted prayer. For Eva-grius, undistracted prayer is equivalent to "you will have treasure in heaven" and "then come follow me" of the Lord's words as they are known more familiarly.

These points can form a sort of outline for the investigation that follows. Evagrius's understanding of this question fits into the larger context of his well-known discussion of the eight principal evil thoughts—*logismoi*—(also called passions and sometimes evil spirits or demons) with which the monk must do battle. Obviously, each of the eight would be worthy of study; this chapter offers one possible example of how to do so. We have spoken in the first chapter about a major theme that can act as an optic for tying together many of Evagrius's writings; namely, spiritual progress. In the second chapter we spoke about positive qualities and practices: *penthos* and tears. Now we can take one example of the direct battle in which the monk must be engaged against all eight evil thoughts. Each of the eight has its own characteristics and poses a special danger, but each one is also related to the others and so can be understood only in relation to them.

SCRIPTURAL INSPIRATION

Evagrius not infrequently cites 1 Timothy 6:10 as he meditates on this question: "Love of money (φιλαργυρία) is the root of all evil."[3] But he pre-sumes that the monk will know or discover the fuller context of this state-ment. Indeed, the scriptures at this point express very well what Evagrius's teaching and that of the whole desert tradition are; and it is clear that this teaching derives from this fundamental text. Thus, "Those who want to be rich are falling into temptation and into a trap..." (1 Tim 6:9) and "some people in their desire for it have strayed from the faith..." (v. 10) and "but you...pursue righteousness, devotion, faith, love, patience, and gentle-ness" (v. 11). Virtually every word and idea here is an important part of

---

[2] PG 79:1172A.

[3] φιλαργυρία is the technical name that Evagrius uses to describe this *logismos*.

Evagrius's teaching. The inspired text, then, will be a guide for him of how fundamental is the problem of love of money.[4]

Evagrius's work *On the Eight Spirits of Evil* is a collection of individual sayings, each designed for lengthy meditation, organized according to the order of the eight principal evil thoughts. In the first of two chapters devoted to love of money, Evagrius begins by citing 1 Timothy 6:10. He takes the image of the root seriously, and in his own meditation develops it. If it is a "root," Evagrius reasons, then whoever wants to get rid of all the passions should get rid of the root: "Whoever wants to get rid of the passions, let him pull out the root." Thus, what one does about money is identified as a fundamental question of the spiritual life. "If you prune the branches well and love of money remains, it will do you no good because, even though they have been trimmed, they will immediately bloom again" (*Eight Spirits* 7).[5]

Evagrius—typically—follows this scriptural image with images of his own, each meant to provide a different metaphor for understanding some dimension of the kind of problem the monk is dealing with. Thus, "the rich monk is an overloaded ship which the waves of a storm will immediately sink." Or "the monk who possesses nothing is like an eagle that flies high and descends for food only when need constrains it." The one with many possessions "is like a dog tied to a chain; when he is made to go somewhere, he drags the chain behind him." "The sea is never filled even though huge rivers flow into it, and the desire of the one who loves money is never filled by however many riches." The goal is not "to enslave the free mind to many masters" (νοῦν ἐλεύθερον δεσπόταις πολλοῖς). The monk without goods does not have to work to maintain them but "dedicates himself to prayer and reading" (*Eight Spirits* 7, 8).[6]

Scriptural images and Evagrius's own development of these is a basic dimension of whatever he teaches. The reader is expected to pause and meditate on the image, let it grow within, and thus function as either a forceful warning or a consoling encouragement. We should continue to be aware of it in what follows.

Evagrius also uses the scriptural text as a divinely given tool to throw in the face of particular manifestations of this evil thought. This is a method that he advances against all eight of the evil thoughts, most completely developed in his work *Antirrhetikos*. But the antirrhetic method also emerges in his scholia on the Psalms. For example, of Psalm 10:30 he says, "This verse is to be directed against the wealthy," and then cites it: "He lies in wait in secret like a lion in his den. He lies in ambush to seize the poor;

---

[4] For examples of 1 Timothy 6:9–11 in Evagrius, see *On Evil Thoughts* 1, 3, 21, 22; *Eight Spirits* 7; *Lt* 6, 52.

[5] PG 79:1152C.

[6] PG 79:1152–54.

to catch the poor, by drawing him to himself" (*In Ps* 10:30).[7] Psalm 61:11 "is to be said to those who are greedy"; namely, "If wealth should flow in, do not set your heart upon it" (*In Ps* 61:11).[8] Or "to the rich who have no children and still do not give any alms to the poor," one can say Psalm 38:7: "He stores up treasure, and does not know for whom he gathers it."[9] The method is simple, but when one trusts in the power of the divine word, it is full of effective force.

AN ANALYSIS OF THE WAY THE EVIL THOUGHT LOVE OF MONEY WORKS

One of the things for which Evagrius is especially appreciated is his sagacity in analyzing the actual way an evil thought insinuates itself into the mind of the person engaged in spiritual combat. His work *On Evil Thoughts* contains his most extensive development on this topic, and so it is significant that right at the very beginning of this work Evagrius offers what is for him a lengthy analysis of love of money in relation especially to two other evil thoughts: gluttony and vainglory. "To put it briefly, it is not possible for someone to fall toward a [particular] demon without having first been wounded by those in the front line of combat." It is not possible to agitate the irascible part of the soul if one is not fighting for food, riches, or glory.[10] Sadness and anger—other evil thoughts—arise from frustration at not obtaining one of these. Very effectively Evagrius notes that these are the three basic temptations posed to Christ: first food, then riches, then glory. This threesome becomes traditional in later Byzantine theology. In any case, this example of the Lord is fundamental: "he taught us also through these things [by refusing the temptations] that it is impossible to ward off the devil without despising these three thoughts" (*On Evil Thoughts* 1).[11]

One particular dimension of this temptation that Evagrius warns against is the thought that causes a monk to imagine a long old age in which he is likely to be afflicted with illnesses with no one to care for him. Thus, it

---

[7] PG 12:1196.

[8] J. B. Pitra, *Analecta sacra spicilegio Solesmensi parata,* vol. 3 (Paris, 1883), 70.

[9] Ibid., 30.

[10] The irascible part of the soul is one of its three parts, together with the concupiscible and the rational. Reestablishing health in all three parts is the goal of the monastic life. See *Praktikos* 89 for a classic expression of this doctrine, omnipresent in Evagrius.

[11] P. Géhin, ed., *Évagre le Pontique, Sur les pensées,* Sources Chrétiennes 438 (Paris: Cerf, 1998), 152. See comments by Géhin (pp. 149–53), citing many other Evagrian texts in this same vein. For these three *logismoi* as the temptation faced by Christ, see especially *Lt* 6 and 39.

would be only reasonable, the thought intimates, to hoard money for such a future (*Praktikos* 9; *Eulog* 11). But the only solution to counteract this kind of thinking is the firm statement: "It is impossible for love to exist together with someone who has riches. For love is a destroyer not only of riches but also of our transitory life itself" (*Praktikos* 18; p. 546). Here once again we see that the issue is not an arbitrary physical austerity but love itself. Love takes no account of this transitory life. For Evagrius, the Lord's words, "There is no greater love than this, to lay down one's life for one's friend" (John 15:13), can be fulfilled concretely by giving up the security that money provides in order to be free to love others.[12]

Evagrius's analysis, however, can run even deeper than this. In a different chapter of *On Evil Thoughts* he is careful to put the blame not on money itself but on the way we desire it or use it. Things are good in themselves, Evagrius wants to say. To explain how the problem emerges he engages in the following distinctions and lines of analysis. In the evil thought of love of money there can be distinguished the mind (νοῦς) itself, the thought (νόημα) of gold, gold itself, and the disordered passion for it. The first three are good in themselves, and so the sin must lie with the last, which is said to be engendered by free will, constraining the mind to make an evil use of what God has created (*On Evil Thoughts* 19).[13] So Evagrius can be precise: the avaricious monk is not the one who has money but the one who desires it wrongly. It is possible to have a great deal of money and not fall into this sin. Such, for example, could be the case with the procurator of the monastery. "A lover of money is not the one who has goods but the one who desires them. It is said, in fact, that the procurator is 'an intelligible purse' (βαλάντιον λογικόν)" (*Gn* 30).[14]

POVERTY AS A CONCRETE MONASTIC PRACTICE

We have seen that at issue here is something that determines whether or not the other demons that afflict a monk are allowed to enter or not. At issue is the root of all evil and success or failure with the greatest of all commandments: love. At issue is a right understanding of the good things of God's creation. Gold is beautiful. The mind that can think it is beautiful. The thought itself of gold is a process to be admired. But desiring gold

---

[12] This connection with the Johannine verse is made by A. and C. Guillaumont, with further commentary (*Praktikos,* 2:546–47).

[13] Evagrius likes this example and uses it also at *On Evil Thoughts* 4, 8, 24.

[14] A. and C. Guillaumont, eds., *Le Gnostique,* Sources Chrétiennes 356 (Paris: Cerf, 1989), 142.

wrongly is absolutely deadly. So what, concretely, can a Christian do to avoid wrong desire, to be free of self-seeking for the sake of love? Evagrius answers that voluntary poverty can help a great deal.[15] This is a feature of initial conversion to the monastic life. In the prologue of the *Praktikos* Evagrius speaks of the highly symbolic dimensions of the monastic habit, which shows, among other things that monks "love poverty and flee greediness."[16] This actually is a defining feature of the monastic way, but it always has a scope beyond itself.

> The one who possesses nothing knows the pleasure of living without care....You chase away the crowd of demons every time you refuse to give your heart over to material worries....You will carry the cross without distraction if you refuse the desire for possessions....Let the one who has chosen the ascetical practice of renunciation defend himself with the rampart of faith, fortify himself with charity, make himself firm with hope. (*Eulog* 11)[17]

The choice of voluntary poverty should be considered in the biblical category of "offering." In a scholion on a verse from Ecclesiastes, Evagrius distinguishes between types of offerings to God: offerings from the soul, from the body, and from outside the body. Of offerings that come from something exterior to the body, riches and possessions are mentioned. So the choice of poverty is meant to be a kind of offering, a sacrifice, a gift freely offered to God (*In Eccl* 5:3).[18]

THE GOAL: TRUE RICHES IN KNOWLEDGE OF GOD

We have seen, then, that voluntary poverty—the renunciation of material goods—is a defining feature of monastic life. But there is a risk in putting a spotlight on this question, as we are doing in this chapter. We may fail to see it in its fuller context. That would be especially misleading in Evagrius, where many elements and practices are held in delicate balance with each other. Poverty is not the ultimate goal of the monastic life, nor even its most essential defining characteristic. Evagrius is always consistent

---

[15] See *Ant* 5:15, 30; *Lt* 39:4; *M* 16.

[16] A. and C. Guillaumont, *Praktikos*, 2:490.

[17] PG 79:1108B.

[18] P. Géhin, ed., *Évagre le Pontique, Scholies à L'Ecclésiaste*, Sources Chrétiennes 397 (Paris: Cerf, 1993), 120–22.

on what this latter is, even if he has different expressions for it. The goal is always and only knowledge of the Holy Trinity. I have argued elsewhere that Evagrius's little work *Ad Monachos* can function as an interpretive key to all his other works because its intricate structure means to be a kind of model of all the various ingredients of the spiritual life. Proverbs on particular themes are arranged in a mathematical structure that reflects the same proportions and relationships that these themes hold in the actual spiritual life.[19] In *Ad Monachos* we see the issues of poverty and love of money treated in the same way they are presented in the rest of his thought, expressed in chains of proverbs that are a pithy summary of what he teaches also elsewhere.

The first three-quarters of the text offer primarily various meditations on the life of *praktikē*, the active struggle for virtue; the last quarter stresses contemplation and knowledge of the Trinity as the final goal of the monastic journey. Early in the first part of the text, Evagrius introduces two extended meditations on poverty and riches. Its early appearance indicates that it is part of the initial conversion of monastic life. But the chains of proverbs on this theme are strategically sandwiched between other chains stressing the importance of love and forgiveness of injuries. Love and hate are contrasted in the style of the biblical sapiential books in a general proverb about monastic life: "Anachoresis in love purifies the heart; anachoresis in hate agitates it" (*M* 8).[20] This prepares the reader for hearing the first proverb on poverty in the framework of this love and hate contrast: "Just as love rejoices in poverty, so hate is pleased by wealth" (*M* 16).[21] We have already noted this idea. Poverty is for the sake of love and not an end in itself. But in the very next proverb Evagrius points poverty even beyond the question of love to the final goal of the monastic life: "The rich man will not acquire knowledge…" In all his writings, from every angle of every practice and virtue, Evagrius tries to show what precise relationship practice and virtue have with the goal of knowledge. He will constantly remind the reader/disciple that virtue and practice are not ends in themselves, but necessary means toward knowledge. Riches, he here warns, will make knowledge impossible; and in the rest of the proverb just cited, he alludes to the Lord's own words as his authority for this absolute position: "and the camel will not enter through the eye of a needle" (Matt 19:23–26). In the following proverb he is still insisting on the same theme: "The one who loves money (Ὁ φιλῶν ἀργύριον, playing on the technical name for the evil

---

[19] See ACW *Ad Monachos.*
[20] H. Gressmann, ed., "Nonnenspiegel und Mönchsspiegel des Euagrios Pontikos," *Texte und Untersuchungen* 39, no. 4 (1913): 153.
[21] Ibid., 154.

thought: ἡ φιλαργυρία) will not see knowledge, and he who amasses it will become dark in himself" (*M* 17, 18).[22] One of Evagrius's preferred images for knowledge is a light that appears interiorly to or in the one praying.[23] Here the thought is just the opposite: riches will create a kind of interior darkness. As the monk continues to meditate on such proverbs, he begins to grasp ever more deeply the spiritual logic at work. Attempting to amass riches agitates the soul, inciting either anger or sadness and thus preventing love; love is the only door to knowledge; knowledge is an interior light, nothing less than the very light of the Holy Trinity within oneself.

At this point in the text Evagrius leaves the theme of poverty and riches to introduce another series of meditations, but it is not long before he returns to the earlier theme again and even more insistently than in the chain of three proverbs just examined. The next series is *Ad Monachos* 25–30. The striking thing about this chain of six proverbs is that each of the six mentions some dimension of the question of poverty and relates it directly with knowledge, usually expressed under some biblical image. But it is not only this relation to knowledge that is noteworthy. This chain's position in the text likewise relates poverty closely to the question of love. The first and last members of the series speak of a concrete charitable action or the failure thereof, thus indicating once again how closely questions about money are related to charity: "The monk who gives no alms will himself be in need, but the one who feeds the poor will inherit treasures" (*M* 25). Or, "He who is merciful to the poor destroys irascibility" (*M* 30). *Irascibility* (θυμός) is almost a code word signaling in this text and others that Evagrius is speaking very concretely about love,[24] and, indeed, the next meditation in the text to unfold after *M* 30 continues this very theme.

Between the proverbs that speak of these concrete actions of giving alms (*M* 25) and being merciful to the poor (*M* 30) Evagrius has placed four other proverbs that express in especially condensed form the themes we have already seen elsewhere. "Better poverty with knowledge than wealth with ignorance" (*M* 26). So knowledge is the real wealth: "An ornament for the head: a crown; an ornament for the heart: knowledge of God" (*M* 27). Or again—repetition causes the insight to sink in more deeply—"Procure knowledge and not silver, and wisdom rather than much wealth" (*M* 28).[25]

---

[22] Ibid., 154.

[23] For a discussion of this widespread image in Evagrius's writings, see G. Bunge, *Das Geistgebet: Studien zum Traktat "De Oratione" des Evagrios Pontikos* (Cologne, 1987), 62–87, where many texts of Evagrius on this question are discussed.

[24] Cf. *In Prov* 22:2 (G 234): "The rich man purifies his irascible part through almsgiving and thus acquires love. The poor man through his poverty learns to be humble" (P. Géhin, ed., *Scholies aux proverbes,* Sources Chrétiennes 340 [Paris: Cerf, 1987], 328).

[25] Gressmann, "Nonnenspiegel," 155.

CONCLUSION

To summarize: according to Evagrius, who let himself be firmly guided by the biblical text, love of money (φιλαργυρία) is the root of all evil. It agitates the irascible part of the soul and thus prevents love. Without this root pulled out, other passions will overtake the soul, making it increasingly difficult to establish love, which is the culmination of all the virtues. Without love, there is no passage to the knowledge of the Holy Trinity, the ultimate goal and final blessedness. This is the naked content of Evagrius's teaching. But, as we have seen, Evagrius does not deliver his content naked. He clothes it in striking images, for the most part drawn from the scriptures. Such images are not mere decoration but, under the practice of meditation, become part of the very content itself. Only the practice of such meditation can verify the forcefulness of this particular way of teaching. The rich man is like a camel attempting to go through the eye of a needle, an overloaded ship, a dog dragging a chain, a person filled with darkness.

Perhaps the most forceful image of all is the one we can use to close this chapter. It is an image that makes clear the personal dimensions of the question of love of money and its christological perspective. It is an image that gains greater force for being rooted in the actual events of salvation history. With it Evagrius shows that each one of us, in deciding what he will do about money and riches, is involved in that same salvation history and must decide for himself into which of several patterns he will fall. "Judas the traitor received an intelligible richness and spiritual goods, but he did not know how to use them, because for the sake of gain he betrayed the wisdom and the truth of God" (*In Eccl* 5:17–19).[26] Obviously Evagrius would expect each baptized Christian to see himself under this description of Judas before his fall. Each one has received intelligible richness and spiritual goods. This is nothing less than discipleship and friendship with Jesus. To seek material wealth instead of this—"Judas was a thief" (John 12:6)— is to betray Jesus and to exchange material wealth for knowledge, here expressed as "the wisdom and the truth of God." It is obvious where wisdom lies.

The time and context of Evagrius's teaching—the fourth century, the Egyptian desert—are very much different from our own. Yet his is a wisdom that still calls out to us in our own time. As monasticism can do in any age when it is healthy, it wants to be a clear sign for the whole church of some of the fundamental issues of the Christian life. The work of creating a radically clear image is perhaps the particular vocation of the monastic life, but monastic life means to show what each Christian must incorporate

---

[26]G 43; Géhin, *Scholies à l'Ecclésiaste*, 138.

into his or her own life. The monastic life of Evagrius's time reminds all Christians in our time that loving money wrongly may be considered the very root of all evil. From it stems a host of other problems. The important thing is to use material goods for the building up of love and never to let desire for these impede our love and concern for others. Then the mind is free, as it was created to be, for loving contemplation and knowledge of the Holy Trinity. This is the true wealth. Nothing is sweeter, nothing more valuable.

5

APATHEIA AND PURITY OF HEART

S eizing a particular word in the biblical text, as the genre of scholia requires, Evagrius comments on the word *gift* in the following text from the book of Proverbs: "He that has pity on the poor lends to the Lord; and he will recompense to him according to his gift" (Prov 19:17). Evagrius says, "Here he calls 'gift' purity of heart, for it is in proportion to our passionlessness [*apatheia*] that we are judged worthy of knowledge" (*In Prov* 19:17).[1] This text contains in a condensed form virtually all I would like to speak about in this chapter. Here we find the expression "purity of heart" in apposition with the technical term *apatheia;* and both are related to knowledge (*gnōsis*), Evagrius's term for the final goal of the monastic life.

It is commonly observed that Evagrius was especially influential in introducing this word of Stoic origins, *apatheia,* into the monastic vocabulary, or at any rate of firmly establishing it there.[2] Jerome was unmeasured in his criticism of Evagrius on this point.[3] It is often claimed that for this reason Cassian, who transposed much of Evagrius's teaching into a Latin key and did not hesitate to transliterate Greek terms, intentionally avoids the use of *apatheia* and regularly replaces it with the expression "purity of heart."[4]

---

[1] See P. Géhin, ed., *Évagre le Pontique, Scholies aux proverbes,* Sources Chrétiennes 340 (Paris: Cerf, 1987), 294.

[2] Evagrius takes this from Clement. See A. Guillaumont, "Le gnostique chez Clément d'Alexandrie et chez Évagre le Pontique," in *ΑΛΕΞΑΝΔΡΙΝΑ, mélanges offerts à Claude Mondésert* (Paris: Cerf, 1987), 195–201, here 198. A. and C. Guillaumont, *Praktikos,* 1:103. For Clement, see J. Raasch, "The Monastic Concept of Purity of Heart and Its Sources: III, Philo, Clement of Alexandria, and Origen," *Studia Monastica* 10 (1968): 13–24.

[3] Jerome, *Letters* 133; CSEL 56:246. Most scholars agree that Jerome has not correctly understood Evagrius on this point. Nonetheless, his letter was influential in promoting a misunderstanding among Latin readers.

[4] S. Marsili, *Giovanni Cassiano ed Evagrio Pontico: Dottrina sulla carità e contemplazione,* Studia Anselmiana 6 (Rome, 1936) 115 n. 1; *Praktikos* 103; A. and C. Guillaumont, *Praktikos,* 1:103 n. 6; C. Stewart, "From λογος to *verbum*: John Cassian's Use of Greek in the Development of a Latin Monastic Vocabulary," in *The Joy of Learning and the Love of God: Essays in Honor of Jean Leclercq* (Kalamazoo: Cistercian Publications, 1995), 20–21.

This "common knowledge" is correct in its main lines, but it requires some nuance. Mark Sheridan has shown that Cassian's use of *puritas cordis* and other such terms to express what Evagrius intends by *apatheia* is probably motivated not so much by a desire to avoid a term that Jerome—and also Augustine!—had not looked favorably upon as by the fact that he, Cassian, was very familiar with Latin philosophical vocabulary and that there were other terms available to express what the Greeks expressed with *apatheia*.[5] Sheridan's study is an important contribution to reading Cassian with a keener eye fixed to spot his own reliance on traditional Latin terminology and for coordinating this with the biblical expression *puritas cordis*. But it also suggests to me a line of investigation worth pursuing in this present chapter; namely, with what other vocabulary does Evagrius express what he also expresses in his use of the word *apatheia*? In fact, it is mistaken to think that Evagrius speaks of the particular phase of spiritual progress that *apatheia* is concerned with only by using this one particular Stoic term. One could get this impression if one were to know Evagrius on this issue only through the *Praktikos*, which is a work in which the main subject matter is precisely *apatheia*, where the term itself is used many times and where all of the chapters serve to fix with clarity what Evagrius means by it and what its role is in the context of the larger spiritual journey that the monk undertakes. But in other works of Evagrius there is an ample number of texts that show that he uses also other vocabulary, more biblical and including "purity of heart," to express *apatheia*. These are the texts I propose to examine here.

The examination can unfold in three steps. First, I will summarize Evagrius's teaching on *apatheia* as it is found in the *Praktikos*. His precise vocabulary in this work will provide us with a set of lenses for recognizing the same things expressed with other terminology. Second, I will examine texts from Evagrius's scholia on the biblical book of Proverbs. This will be an exercise in accumulating relevant texts, in the random order that they occur, following the same random order that the genre of scholia creates. A particular word or phrase of the biblical text is chosen and commented on. In a third step I will examine the use of both *apatheia* and other terminology for the same concept in Evagrius's *Ad Monachos*, a text in which he locates much of his spiritual vocabulary within a textual structure that shows clearly the relation of one term to another.

In 1970 Juana Raasch wrote, "Evagrius makes little use of the Scriptural term 'heart' but prefers to speak of *katharotes* as a quality of the *psyche* or

---

[5] M. Sheridan, "The Controversy over ἀπάθεια· Cassian's Sources and His Use of Them," *Studia Monastica* 39 (1997): 287–310. J. Raasch, "The Monastic Concept of Purity of Heart and Its Sources: V, Symeon-Macarius, the School of Evagrius Ponticus, and the Apophthegmata Patrum," *Studia Monastica* 12 (1970): 32.

the *nous.*"[6] When she wrote, primarily summarizing the studies of S. Marsili, as she says, who wrote in 1936, some of the important critical texts of Evagrius's work that have since been published were not available. And little attention had been given by scholars to Evagrius's letters or to his *Ad Monachos,* considered to be of minor importantance within the whole corpus. Nearly thirty years later we are in a much better position to understand Evagrius on this precise question. Thus, in all three steps of this investigation, we shall focus especially on the terms, *heart, purity of heart,* and *apatheia.* Although our main purpose will be to know Evagrius on the question, we will see, in relation to the earlier remark about Cassian's use of Evagrius, that Cassian not only had other Latin philosophical terminology available to him, but he also had in Evagrius himself an extensive use of "purity of heart" to signify *apatheia.*

APATHEIA IN THE *PRAKTIKOS*

There are major studies on Evagrius's understanding of *apatheia* in the *Praktikos.*[7] Thus, our purpose here will be only to summarize with a view to fixing precisely the meaning of the term. The Platonic threefold division of the soul is a major dimension of Evagrius's anthropology. These are the rational part (λογιστικόν), the irascible part (θυμικόν), and the concupiscible part (ἐπιθυμητικόν). The spiritual struggle of the monk is conceived as a battle for establishing virtue in these various parts. Different virtues are suitably established in a part of the soul to which they correspond, while various vices can also be identified as trouble in one or another part of the soul.[8]

For Evagrius there are two major divisions of the spiritual life: *praktikē,* where the concern is purifying the passionate part of the soul;[9] and knowledge, where the rational part of the soul devotes itself to contemplation and knowledge.[10] Thus, the monastic life as conceived by Evagrius is the

---

[6] Raasch, "Monastic Concept of Purity of Heart: V," 32.

[7] For thorough studies, see A. and C. Guillaumont, *Praktikos,* 1:98–112, together with individual comments on the various chapters in the whole of vol. 2. Also G. Bunge, *Evagrios Pontikos: Praktikos oder Der Mönch, Hundert Kapitel über das geistliche Leben* (Cologne: Luthe-Verlag, 1989).

[8] The classical expression of this in Evagrius is *Praktikos* 89, where the various parts of the soul are clearly identified along with the corresponding virtues. This clear statement can function for all other occurrences of the terms in the writings of Evagrius. See also *Praktikos* 15.

[9] Thus, *Praktikos* 78: "*Praktikē* is the spiritual method which purifies the passionate part of the soul" (A. and C. Guillaumont, *Praktikos,* 2:666).

[10] Cf. *Praktikos* 89. There are divisions within the realm of knowledge also.

entire struggle to rid oneself of *evils* (related to the passionate part) and *ignorance* (related to the rational part) and to establish in the soul *virtue* (related to the passionate part) and *knowledge* (related to the rational part). For Evagrius there can be no knowledge in the higher part of the soul without virtue first being established in the passionate part of the soul. The technical term for virtue established in the passionate part of the soul is *apatheia,* or passionlessness.[11] It is not a final goal, but an intermediary one.

The *Praktikos* is Evagrius's principal work devoted to this stage of the spiritual life. It can be seen there that *praktikē* basically consists in doing combat with evil thoughts. The text analyzes eight principal evil thoughts (also called demons) and offers sage advice for how to defeat them. The advice is structured according to the three parts of the soul (*Praktikos* 15), locating the problem as being in the rational, the irascible, or the concupiscible parts and speaking of the virtues that must be in those parts instead (15–33). This advice is followed by six chapters that speak about the passions (34–39), that is, a general meditation on what moves evil thoughts in the irascible and concupiscible parts, together called the passionate part of the soul (cf. 38, 49, 78, 84). Evagrius observes that it is possible to make progress over the passions of the body to such an extent that one is eventually no longer troubled by them. However, the struggles of the soul, that is, those concerning relations with other people (35) will continue until death (36). After this, a sort of demonology is presented with advice on how to conduct oneself in their presence, how to recognize and guard against their wily devices by observation, asceticism, and prayer (40–53).

In their study of the structure of this text, A. and C. Guillaumont see the material I have discussed thus far as constituting a first part of the text. The second part, which extends from chapter 54 to chapter 90, is devoted to the question of passionlessness, at which state the monk progressively arrives by his victory over the demons or passions.[12] There are a number of signs by which the condition of passionlessness can be detected: in the dreams the monk has (54–56), when the mind sees its own light at the time of prayer and is calm in the face of distractions (63–70), when each of the three parts of the soul acts according to nature (71–90). In other words, these are all indications that some spiritual progress has been made. Indeed, there are degrees and nuances to the progress such that Evagrius distinguishes between a perfect and an imperfect passionlessness.[13] The

---

[11] This literal English translation of the Greek term is useful once this clear meaning is established; namely, that it signifies no longer being troubled by the passionate part of the soul. Thus, in what follows where the English *passionlessness* or *passionless* are used, it will always be for the Greek ἀπάθεια or ἀπαθής.

[12] A. and C. Guillaumont, *Praktikos*, 1:118.

[13] Cf. *Praktikos* 60 and the comments of A. and C. Guillaumont, *Praktikos*, 1:108–10.

text reaches a conclusion of the development with chapter 90, a chapter that prepares the way for the meditations on knowledge that follow in the next two works of the trilogy, the *Gnostikos* and the *Kephalaia Gnostica*.

Perfect passionlessness means that health is established in the two passionate parts of the soul, the concupiscible and the irascible. Then these two parts work together to maintain the soul in this state and to leave it free for its higher part, the rational, to function for knowledge. The concupiscible part *desires* virtue and knowledge. The irascible part *fights* the evil thoughts that attack all three parts of the soul. In the passionless soul, thoughts from the passionate part no longer mount up to darken the mind (cf. *Praktikos* 74) and thereby is the rational part ready to pass into knowledge.

This summary can serve to provide us now with what I earlier called a set of lenses to discern other ways and other terms Evagrius uses to speak about this same reality.

THE SCHOLIA ON PROVERBS

When the language is taken from the philosophical tradition, it allows for a clear and precise articulation of the many various dimensions of the spiritual journey. In Evagrius and most others who function in similar theological traditions, this philosophical language does not contaminate the Christian content but makes it possible to think about it more profoundly. Thus, the distinction of the rational, irascible, and concupiscible parts of the soul, together with *apatheia* as a term describing health in the latter two parts, enables a clear understanding of particular issues that must be dealt with in order to reach the ultimate goal of contemplative knowledge of the Holy Trinity.

In what follows we shall see how Evagrius ponders these issues also under the influence of biblical language. His philosophical framework allows him to penetrate the biblical text more deeply. At the same time the biblical language is itself decisive, enabling him to make connections and shape insights that would not be possible to him if left to the philosophical tradition alone. Perhaps nowhere is this so clear as in what Evagrius says of the ubiquitous biblical word *heart*.[14] He does not use it as a simple bib-

---

[14] The word *heart* is rarely used in a metaphysical sense in classical Greek writing, as J. Raasch shows in "The Monastic Concept of Purity of Heart and Its Sources: I," *Studia Monastica* 8 (1966): 9–11. Evagrius's frequent use of this word is owing to his saturation in the biblical language. In general I find Raasch's studies to be too suspicious of what she calls "Hellenism," contrasting this with a pure Gospel tradition which the former gradually contaminates. For examples of this suspicion, see "The Monastic Concept of Purity of Heart and

lical code word for one or other part of the soul, as this is conceived by Greek philosophy. Instead, we find him using it across all three parts and beyond.[15] With this term he is able to show the dynamic and inextricable interconnections that exist among all the various dimensions of the inner life. We can see this now by what I called above an exercise in the accumulation of texts from his biblical scholia.

Scholia on Proverbs 19:17 (G 199; Géhin, p. 294). It will be useful to look again at the scholion with which this study opened. This short saying yields a rich meditation for the reader who is familiar with the discussion of *apatheia* from the *Praktikos*. Commenting on a verse from Proverbs, "He that has pity on the poor lends to the Lord; and he will recompense to him according to his gift," Evagrius says,

> Here he calls "gift" purity of heart, for it is in proportion to our passionlessness (ἀπάθεια) that we are judged worthy of knowledge.

The biblical verse is bound to inspire Evagrius, for it speaks of "having pity on the poor." For him this would fall into the category of *praktikē*, and in fact he considers such a practice to be of major importance in establishing virtue in the irascible part of the soul.[16] The Proverbs text goes on to say that God will recompense the one who helps the poor according to his gift. Evagrius often will take one particular monastic practice or one particular

Its Sources: II, Among the Second Century Apologists and Anti-Heretical Writers and in the Literature of the Third Century, Not Including the Alexandrians," *Studia Monastica* 8 (1966): 87–88; "The Monastic Concept of Purity of Heart and Its Sources: III, Philo, Clement of Alexandria, and Origen," *Studia Monastica* 10 (1968): 54–55; "The Monastic Concept of Purity of Heart and Its Sources: IV, Early Monasticism," *Studia Monastica* 11 (1969): 271, 293, 308; "The Monastic Concept of Purity of Heart and Its Sources: V, Symeon-Macarius, the School of Evagrius Ponticus and the Apophthegmata Patrum," *Studia Monastica* 12 (1970): 27.

[15] More often than not, *heart* indicates the soul, as Evagrius understands this; but it should not be thought that this is a hard and fast rule. It is in fact the duty of the gnostic—Evagrius's term for one who is passionless and enjoys contemplation—to teach others how particular texts in scripture are to be understood as referring to one or other part of the soul, or one or other stage of spiritual progress (see *Gn* 18, 19, 20). Thus, in one place Evagrius can say, "The Scripture applies many other names to the soul and its representations, of which it is only possible to list a few which apply to the soul: mind, soul, heart" (*In Prov* 25:26; G 317; Géhin, *Scholies aux proverbes,* 408). Evagrius goes on to list twenty-two other scriptural names. Yet elsewhere he can say, "It is in fact a habit of the divine Scripture to say 'heart' in place of 'mind'" (*In Ps* 15:9; PG 12:1216A).

[16] "The rich man purifies his irascible part through almsgiving" (*In Prov* 22:2 [G 234; Géhin, p. 328]). "The monk who gives no alms will himself be in need, but the one who feeds the poor will inherit treasures" (*M* 25). "He who is merciful to the poor destroys irascibility" (*M* 30). H. Gressmann, ed., "Nonnenspiegel und Mönchsspiegel des Euagrios Pontikos," *Texte und Untersuchungen* 39, no. 4 (1913): 155.

biblical word and let it stand for the whole. So he does here with the word "gift." If the scripture speaks of "recompense according to the gift," such recompense could only mean for Evagrius knowledge. And he makes that point explicit in this short explanation. But he also wants to explain "according to his gift," and thus does so within the logic of his understanding of passionlessness, since in a general way he knows that it is "in proportion to our passionlessness" that we come to knowledge.[17] Worthy of note for the scope of this present study, Evagrius rather spontaneously introduces the expression "purity of heart" as another way of saying passionlessness. The scholion thus lines up in very neat order the following: purity of heart, *apatheia*, and knowledge.

I have chosen to comment on this particular scholion first because I think it immediately pries loose that too narrow understanding of Evagrius as a monastic thinker who uses only philosophical categories and vocabulary to express himself on this question. In this case "purity of heart" stands directly for what also is expressed by the term *apatheia*. But if we examine other texts now, we will see that the word *heart* itself does not stand for just one or several parts of the soul that Evagrius's philosophical language allows him to distinguish. It moves across a wide spectrum.

Scholia on Proverbs 3:15 (G 30; Géhin, p. 124). "She [wisdom] is more valuable than precious stones; no evil thing shall resist her." It is the second half of this verse that Evagrius feels required to explain: "It is only in front of wisdom that the demons are powerless because they are not able to throw evil thoughts into the heart of one who has become wise. For the mind (νοῦς) that is touched by the contemplations of wisdom becomes unreceptive to impure thoughts."

Although the word *heart* is not in the biblical text being commented on here, it comes naturally to mind for Evagrius to express his thought. It is a commonplace in his teaching to speak of the battle against evil thoughts; and if in the *Praktikos* he speaks of such thoughts troubling one or other part of the soul, named according to the classical Platonic division, here he speaks more generally of thoughts in the heart. But also of considerable interest in this text is the fact that "heart" stands in virtual apposition to the word *mind* (νοῦς), Evagrius's technical term for our fundamental instrument of contemplation.[18] Purity is at issue here, expressed negatively.

---

[17] Recall the distinction between imperfect and perfect passionlessness that was noted in the *Praktikos*. The expression "judged worthy of knowledge" (καταξιούμεθα γνώσεως) in this scholion is similar to a second title to Evagrius's work the *Gnostikos*, found in some manuscripts. This work is concerned with those who have reached perfect passionlessness. See A. and C. Guillaumont, *Le Gnostique*, Sources Chrétiennes 356 (Paris: Cerf, 1989), 20.

[18] For what I hope is a useful summary of Evagrius's understanding of this term, see my ACW *Ad Monachos*, 5–9.

In one moment the talk is of evil thoughts in the heart; in the next of impure thoughts in the mind—two ways of saying the same thing.

Scholia on Proverbs 17:24 (G 168; Géhin, p. 264). "The countenance of a wise man is sensible; but the eyes of a fool go to the extremes of the earth." "The heart of 'a fool' is an 'extreme' evil."

The exegetical tradition within which Evagrius works, which derives, of course, its general lines from Origen, often has a tendency to move quickly from references to some dimension of the material world to an interior sense relevant to the human condition. That is the case here, where "earth" and indeed its "extremes" are rather naturally taken in this text as representing extreme evil, since it is a fool that is being spoken about here. For the purposes of this present study, we want to notice that Evagrius effects the passage to this interior sense by means of the word *heart*. The literal sense of the verse is something to the effect that the "material" eyes of a fool wander all over the place. For Evagrius, the spiritual sense refers to the heart. So, here *heart* becomes a general word for the interior, which can either be in evil, indeed in extreme evil, or—unsaid here but certainly implied—in wisdom or knowledge.

Scholia on Proverbs 19:7 (G 191; Géhin, p. 286). "A good thought (ἔννοια) will draw near to those that know it (τοῖς εἰδόσιν), and a prudent man will find it." "Here he has called the knowledge of God a 'thought' and 'those who know it' are the pure of heart."

In the biblical text Evagrius finds two words whose general sense fits well his understanding of the goal of monastic life, ἔννοια and εἰδόσιν. In this scholion he simply renders that explicit by using his preferred and more precise term, knowledge of God, τὴν τοῦ Θεοῦ γνῶσιν. Wanting to explain who it is that will know this, he adds that it will be the pure of heart, an expression that seems to come rather naturally at this point, as a means of expressing what he does so often; namely, the intimate relation between *praktikē* and knowledge. The pure of heart (= *praktikē*) will have the knowledge of God. Once again, then, we have the expression "pure of heart" put directly in relation with the whole goal of the monastic quest, knowledge of God.

Scholia on Proverbs 21:20 (G 228; Géhin, p. 324). "A desirable treasure will rest on the mouth of the wise; but foolish men will swallow it up." "The wisdom of the Lord 'will rest' (ἀναπαύσεται) in the heart of 'the wise,' but 'foolish men' (ἄφρονες) will destroy it."

The exegetical method used here is a quick and simple movement to the spiritual level of the text, repeating the scriptural verse and substituting for the literal sense of "treasure" the spiritual sense "wisdom," for the literal

sense of "mouth" the spiritual sense "heart." There is a logic to these sub-
stitutions. Evagrius could not have failed to be struck by two words in the
biblical text, ἀναπαύσεται and ἄφρονες, both of which have precise meanings in his theological vocabulary.

The word ἄφρονες is the opposite of φρόνιμος or φρόνησις (prudence), a
virtue that Evagrius so consistently associates with wisdom that when one
is mentioned, the other is implied, if not also explicitly mentioned. In the
Praktikos, where so much of the discussion is based on the three parts of
the soul, Evagrius locates, as has been said, various virtues in these different parts. Wisdom and prudence are placed together in the rational part of
the soul.

> The task of prudence is to command [the battle] against the
> opposing powers and to protect the virtues and to throw up a
> front against vices; also it regulates what is neutral according to
> the circumstances. [The task] of intelligence is to arrange har-
> moniously everything which contributes to our goal. [The task]
> of wisdom is to contemplate the reasons for the corporeals and
> the incorporeals. (*Praktikos* 89; pp. 682-84)

What is interesting in this conception is how virtues in the rational part
of the soul are looking in different directions, as it were. Wisdom contem-
plates and is directed toward knowledge, while prudence is directed toward
praktikē, commanding the battle against the demons. Intelligence manages
some harmony between the two. Another text from the *Praktikos* confirms
this interpretation, and in it the other word that concerns us, ἀνάπαυσις,
is also used.

> Rest (ἀνάπαυσις) is wisdom's, but work is yoked to prudence. For
> there is no procuring of wisdom without war, and there is no suc-
> cessful war without prudence. For prudence has been entrusted
> with opposing itself to the irascibility of the demons, forcing the
> powers of the soul to act according to nature and preparing the
> way for wisdom. (*Praktikos* 73; p. 660)

Within the logic of such vocabulary, one could almost say that Evagrius
could not have explained the expression "a desirable treasure will rest"
otherwise than by seeing it to mean "wisdom will rest." But what about
the substitution of the word *heart* for *mouth*? It could, of course, simply
be a word with which Evagrius expresses the interior meaning of the text.
Yet as we seek in this present study to understand the relation between Evagrius's use of *apatheia* and his use of the heart, another text sheds some
further light on the question. In *Ad Monachos* Evagrius says, "In the gen-

tle heart, wisdom will rest; a throne of passionlessness: a soul accomplished in *praktikē*" (*M* 31).[19]

The vocabulary of this proverb as well as the general idea expressed in it is based on the Lord's words, "Come to me, all who labor and are heavy laden, and I will give you rest (κἀγὼ ἀναπαύσω ὑμᾶς). Take my yoke upon you, and learn from me; for I am gentle and lowly in heart (πραΰς εἰμι καὶ ταπεινός), and you will find rest for your souls (καὶ εὑρήσετε ἀνάπαυσιν ταῖς ψυχαῖς ὑμῶν)" (Matt 11:28–29). It is not only the terms *gentle* and *rest* that Evagrius borrows from the Gospel passage; also the way he uses the terms *heart* and *soul* reflects their use in the Gospel. The gentle heart of the proverb stands in relation to the gentle heart of the Lord in the gospel passage. The monk will learn to have a gentle heart by learning from the Lord.[20] The Lord promises rest for *souls,* and the proverb from *Ad Monachos* connects soul with passionlessness. That in the proverb *wisdom* is said to rest in the gentle heart is a formulation based on another dimension of the Gospel passage; namely, "learn from me."

In all the passages examined here, a number of similar questions continue to turn up with different vocabulary: the relationship between *praktikē* and knowledge, the role of wisdom and prudence in relation to these, the heart and the soul as both the place for the battle that prudence undertakes and the place where wisdom will rest, passionlessness as the link between these two. Evagrius himself can be used to summarize all this:

> The soul which has rightly done *praktikē* with God and has loosed itself from the body reaches those places of knowledge where the wings of passionlessness bring it to rest and from where it receives those wings of the holy dove which it spreads out wide through the contemplation of all the aeons and then comes to rest in the knowledge of the adorable Trinity. (*On Evil Thoughts* 29; Géhin, p. 256)[21]

Scholia on Proverbs 22:20 (G 247; Géhin, p. 342). "And you inscribe them [the words of the wise] three times in yourself, in view of counsel and of knowledge, on the breadth of your heart."

---

[19] I comment on this proverb at length in ACW *Ad Monachos,* 249–59.

[20] Evagrius cites this Gospel text in a passage where he lists examples of gentleness. He mentions Moses, David, and "even the Savior himself [who] commanded us to be imitators of his gentleness, saying, 'Learn from me, for gentle am I and humble in heart and you will find rest for your souls'" (*On Evil Thoughts* 13; P. Géhin, ed., *Évagre le Pontique, Sur les pensées,* Sources Chrétiennes 438 [Paris: Cerf, 1998], 198).

[21] This same text is found in *KG* II, 6. The Greek for "rest" in this passage is based on καταπαύειν. The passage draws its use of the dove imagery from Ps 54:7. Cf. *In Ps* 54:7. A similar distinction in a rest associated with *praktikē* and another associated with knowledge is found at *KG* III, 68.

The one who has enlarged his heart by purity will understand the reasons of God, reasons which concern *praktikē*, and natural contemplation and theology. For all the material of the scripture is divided into three parts: ethics, natural contemplation, and theology. Proverbs corresponds to the first, Ecclesiastes to the second, and the Song of Songs to the third.

This is an important scholion for our present investigation because in it we find purity of heart associated not only with *praktikē* but also with two levels of knowledge that Evagrius regularly distinguishes: natural contemplation and theology.[22] The biblical trilogy of Solomon's books—Proverbs, Ecclesiastes, and the Song of Songs—is associated with these three dimensions of spiritual progress.[23] Thus, here "heart"—the enlarged heart, the pure heart—has for its object every dimension of the monastic life, from its beginnings in *praktikē* to its highest levels in knowledge of theology.

If this accumulation of various texts is acquainting us with a certain frequency of the concept "purity of heart," this is the first time we have encountered the idea of an enlarged heart. The immediate inspiration for Evagrius on this particular occasion comes from the biblical text itself. "Breadth of your heart" (ἐπὶ τὸ πλάτος τῆς καρδίας) becomes in his comment "the one who has enlarged his heart" (ὁ πλατύνας...τὴν καρδίαν αὐτοῦ). However, the image of an enlarged heart occurs frequently in Evagrius, as well as enlargement as a general concept, and is regularly used to refer to the realms of knowledge.[24]

Scholia on Proverbs 24:27 (G 291; Géhin, pp. 282, 284). "Prepare your works for your exodus, and equip yourself [to go] into the field."

> Our Lord in the Gospels called the world a "field" [Matt 13:38], and now Solomon calls the contemplation of the world a "field." But the "field" in the Gospels is that of man composed of body and soul, for it is of the senses; while the "field" spoken of here is of the mind alone, for it is intelligible and composed of the reasons of this world. This is the "field" into which the pure of heart enter.

Again the reader is struck in this scholion by the close association between purity of heart and the goal of knowledge. It is worth untangling

---

[22] By "natural contemplation" Evagrius means knowledge of the created world. By "theology" he means knowledge of the Holy Trinity. Cf. *Praktikos* 1–3.

[23] Much could be said on this point. See chapter 1 above.

[24] Cf. *In Prov* 1:20–21 (G 12); 18:16 (G 184); *In Ps* 4:2; 17:37; 80:11; 118:32, 96; *M* 135.

how Evagrius arrives at such a conclusion. He begins by employing an exegetical device common to the Alexandrian tradition; namely, interpreting a word in one part of the scripture with a clearer explanation of it from another part. In this case, he proceeds by citing the highest authority, the Lord himself, who explictly begins an explanation of one of his own parables by saying, "The field is the world." That will definitely establish, at least in general terms, how the word "field" in the Proverbs text is to be understood, but on observing the two texts closely Evagrius notices a difference. The world of the Gospel parable is clearly the world of this present life and the present human condition, where man is composed of body and soul; for in this world of the parable, weeds are sown by the Evil One and are allowed to grow along with the good wheat until harvest time.

Looking at the Proverbs text, Evagrius reasons that it cannot be the same world that is spoken of there. The language of "preparing works" makes him think in general terms of *praktikē*. The exodus spoken of makes him think of the passage from *praktikē* to knowledge. ("Here he calls the soul's exit from evil and ignorance an 'exodus'" [*In Prov* 1:20-21 (G 12)].[25]) In the proverb's second line, therefore, going into a field (i.e., a world) cannot be the world where the Evil One still sows weeds but must be the world that one enters in the exodus from evil and ignorance. That world is an intelligible one, which the "mind alone" can know. A mind still immersed in the struggles of body and soul cannot enter that intelligible world.[26] But a concise way of referring to the world where such struggles are past would be "pure of heart." It is not a world of the senses but "the contemplation (θεωρία) of the world."[27] Thus, the pure of heart will enter into the intelligible world and its reasons, which the mind alone can perceive.

Scholia on Proverbs 27:8 (G 332; Géhin, pp. 420-22). "As when a bird flies down from its own nest, so a man is brought into bondage whenever he estranges himself from his own place." "The 'place' of the heart is virtue and knowledge; and if a man 'estranges himself' from it, he falls into evil and ignorance and becomes a slave since 'Everyone who commits sin is a slave of sin.' (John 8:34)."

---

[25] Géhin, p. 102. For similar interpretations of "exodus" see also *In Prov* 8:3 (G 99); *KG* IV, 64; V, 6, 21, 30, 36, 68, 71, 88; VI, 47, 49, 64; *M* 21, 54. On these texts from *Ad Monachos*, see ACW *Ad Monachos,* 241, 267–69.

[26] It should be noticed that Evagrius is carefully using the language with which he describes the various conditions in which rational creatures find themselves after the fall: body, soul, mind. The mind alone is at the root of the original creation, and it will also describe the final condition.

[27] In the strong sense of θεωρία, "seeing through" the world of the senses. What is seen are the "reasons of the world," also spoken of in the scholion, of which the intelligible world is composed.

Evagrius moves immediately to a spiritual sense of the literal meaning of the text, expressing the interior sense of "place" as "heart." Here his application covers the whole range of the interior life, the two main realms of virtue and knowledge, whose opposites are evil and ignorance. Thus, "heart" here serves to express the proper place of the one who lives the monastic life. Going away from the heart—from virtue and knowledge—is to be a slave to sin.[28]

PURITY OF HEART IN THE *AD MONACHOS*

We have seen that the *Praktikos* offers a neat and orderly exposition of Evagrius's teaching on *apatheia*. In the biblical scholia the discussion on the same comes as it may, according to the order of the biblical text and the words found therein. This genre does not permit an orderly presentation of Evagrius's thought. Now, however, having trained our eye to spot the issue of *apatheia* as it is exposed in biblical language, particularly with the use of the word *heart*, it is possible to conclude this chapter by returning to the Evagrian text that does permit an orderly presentation; namely, the *Ad Monachos*.

I have spoken of this text elsewhere at length and have argued that its structure contains a secret that Evagrius expects the careful reader to uncover.[29] Its 137 proverbs unfold in an order of spiritual progress that begins with faith, the first virtue of *praktikē*, and concludes with the mind presented before the Holy Trinity, the goal of the entire monastic life. The particular place within this structure where a specific issue—a virtue, a vice, a level of knowledge—is treated is a key to how Evagrius conceives that issue in relation to the whole. The language of *Ad Monachos* is heavily biblical. This is clear, among other ways, in the abundant use of the word *heart* in the text. Thus, in this text the reader has, as it were, the best of both worlds: an orderly presentation similar to what is found in the *Praktikos*, and a heavily biblical language, similar to what is found in the scholia.

Evagrius uses the word *heart* evenly throughout the entire text. Therein it is closely associated with *apatheia*, but it has other functions and refer-

---

[28] This examination of proverbs has not been exhaustive on the proverbs from the *Scholia on Proverbs* that relate to this theme. Other relevant texts would be the following: *Scholia on Proverbs* 6:27–28 (G 82); *Scholia on Proverbs* 8:5 (G 100); 16:33 (G 152); 17:23 (G 166); 22:15 (G 244); 25:20: (G 312); 26:23 (G 328).

[29] J. Driscoll, "A Key for Reading the Ad Monachos of Evagrius Ponticus," *Augustinianum* 30 (1990): 361–92; idem, ACW *Ad Monachos;* idem, *The Mind's Long Journey to the Holy Trinity: The Ad Monachos of Evagrius Ponticus* (Collegeville, MN: Liturgical Press, 1993).

ences as well. A brief review of these uses, always following the order that is a key to understanding them, will serve to summarize in an orderly way all that we have seen so far.[30]

> Anachoresis in love purifies the heart;
> anachoresis in hate agitates it. (*M* 8)

This first appearance of the word *heart* in the text speaks of its purity. This saying is part of the first chain of proverbs with which Evagrius moves the reader from meditations on faith, the first of the virtues, to love, the goal of *praktikē*. Thus, love, here meaning practical charity toward others, is what purifies the heart.

> Where evil enters in, there also ignorance;
> but the hearts of holy ones will be filled with knowledge. (*M* 24)

Here, interestingly, "heart" is referred to the final goal of monastic life, knowledge. As we have already seen in some of the scholia, it is a term that can at one and the same time refer to the life of *praktikē* and the purification that must be worked there, and to the life of knowledge. The same is true in a proverb that follows closely after:

> An ornament for the head: a crown;
> an ornament for the heart: knowledge of God. (*M* 27)

Or again,

> In the gentle heart, wisdom will rest;
> a throne of passionlessness: a soul accomplished in *praktikē*.
> (*M* 31)

In this tightly constructed proverb the whole range of monastic life is exposed in its two basic phases. As noted above in the commentary on *Scholia on Proverbs* 21:20, "wisdom resting" is a standard way Evagrius expresses a dimension of the life of knowledge. Of course, no one enters that rest without the work of *praktikē*, expressed in three different phrases here, each of which summarizes the goal in a different way. Passionlessness is equivalent to the soul accomplished in *praktikē*. And a more biblical way for saying the same is "gentle heart." With this expression Evagrius often summarizes the goal of *praktikē*, a particular version of what he means by a pure heart.[31]

---

[30] I have already commented more amply in ACW *Ad Monachos* on all the texts that I will cite here.

[31] See J. Driscoll, "Gentleness in the *Ad Monachos* of Evagrius Ponticus," *Studia Monastica* 33 (1990): 295–321.

The heart is the place of struggle for the monk, as in the following:

> Like a strong south wind on the sea,
> so is irascibility in the heart of a man. (*M* 36)

> Better a fast with a pure heart
> than a feast in impurity of soul. (*M* 44)

This is a clear example of the parallel sense of "heart" and "soul," the question of purity being always at issue. And purity is always a struggle against evil thoughts, as the proverb that follows immediately in the text shows:

> He who completely destroys evil thoughts in his heart,
> he is like the one who dashes his children against the rock.
>   (*M* 45)

An angelic dream gladdens the heart, while a demonic one agitates it (*M* 52). The heart is made to glow after the struggle with listlessness, the most oppressive evil thought of them all (*M* 55). And again, evil thoughts should never be allowed to linger in the heart (*M* 58), even if it is temptations that test the heart of a monk (*M* 60). In a strategically located proverb that treats of pride, "the original evil," Evagrius warns, "Do not give your heart to pride" (*M* 62).

At the center of the text of *Ad Monachos* Evagrius has placed a chain of ten proverbs which in this placement functions as a hinge for the movement from *praktikē* to knowledge. Each of the ten proverbs treats this theme (*M* 63 to 72). At the center of this center are three proverbs that treat *apatheia* or passionlessness (*M* 66 to 68), thereby expressing its crucial role in the whole of spiritual progress. In the first of these three proverbs, the word *heart* appears once again:

> Without milk, a child is not nourished,
> and apart from passionlessness, a heart will not be raised up.
>   (*M* 66)

The word *heart* continues to be used in the text, but hereafter the references consistently refer the heart to knowledge. The monk who "keeps his heart" will be filled with knowledge (*M* 94). Humiliation of the irascible raises up the heart (*M* 100). "Without knowledge the heart will not be placed on high" (*M* 117).

In the final movement of the text, Evagrius constructs proverbs that move in a crescendo toward the final proverb, which speaks of the mind being presented before the Holy Trinity. Along this way, the heart and its purity remain at issue.

The wisdom of the Lord raises up the heart;
his prudence purifies it. (*M* 131)

Here once again are the twin virtues of wisdom and prudence, which operate in the rational part of the soul. In this proverb their object is the heart. The heart raised up by wisdom is the heart that enjoys contemplation of "the reasons for the corporeals and the incorporeals."[32] The prudence that purifies the heart is the work of *praktikē*, where we saw the task of prudence is "to command [the battle] against the opposing powers and to protect the virtues and to throw up a front against vices."[33]

Finally, in the proverb that immediately precedes the "mind presented before the Holy Trinity" (*M* 136) one reads

Contemplations of worlds enlarge the heart;
reasons of providence and judgment lift it up. (*M* 135)

Here one encounters again what was noted as a frequent image in Evagrius: the enlarged heart.[34] It is precisely contemplation that does so. Thus, the heart is not just something purified in *praktikē* but is in some sense the very instrument of contemplation, enlarged, lifted up by knowledge of different kinds.

CONCLUSION

Examination of the scholia on Ecclesiastes and on the Psalms would continue to build the case that is unfolding before us, as would many passages from Evagrius's letters.[35] The case briefly stated is this: Evagrius makes frequent use of the expression "purity of heart"; by it he expresses in biblical language what he also expressed with precision in a term borrowed from the philosophical tradition through Clement, that is, *apatheia* (passionlessness). Purity of heart and passionlessness are different ways of saying the same thing. It is not the final goal of the monastic journey but the necessary intermediate threshold that must be passed on the way to contemplation and knowledge of the Holy Trinity.

Our examination has also shown that "purity" is one issue for Evagrius and the "heart" another. If the term *apatheia* has the advantage of

---

[32] As according to *Praktikos* 89, cited above in the comment on *Scholia on Proverbs* 21:20.

[33] Also according to *Praktikos* 89, cited above in the comment on *Scholia on Proverbs* 21:20.

[34] In the commentary on *Scholia on Proverbs* 22:20. See n. 24 for other references.

[35] See, e.g., *In Eccl* 5, 39, 44, 48, 63, 64, 68, 72; *Lt* 12:2; 14; 17:3; 25:6; 27:1; 39:5; 54:2; 56:2; 58:3.

expressing that dimension of things which concerns the concupiscible and irascible parts of the soul no longer being disturbed by the passions, the term *heart* allows Evagrius to speak more fluidly across various dimensions of the inner life. With it he sometimes refers to these parts of the soul, at other times to all three parts, then to one part only, but also to the mind, or the mind as it is united with the soul. Heart is certainly the object of purification in the work of *praktikē*, but it is also the instrument used for contemplation.

In explaining that it is ultimately the instrument for contemplation or knowledge that must be purified, Evagrius moves very naturally from what may first seem a more philosophical term, *mind* (νοῦς) to what may seem the more biblical term, *heart*. But this natural movement only shows that the sharp distinction between philosophical and biblical is not made by Evagrius. It tends to be more our problem than that of these ancients.

> To be sure, it is not the mind itself which sees God, but rather the pure mind. "Blessed are the pure of heart, for they shall see God" (Matt 5:8). Note that he does not praise purity as blessed but rather the one seeing [i.e., contemplating]. Purity is passionlessness of the reasonable soul, but seeing [contemplating] God is true knowledge of the one essence of the adorable Trinity, which those will see who have perfected their conduct here and through the commandments purified their souls. (*Lt* 56:2)[36]

Evagrius is extremely consistent in his talk about the inner life. His vocabulary is both philosophical and biblical, but he coordinates these two sources to speak just one language, which may be described as Christian and monastic. One of the most characteristic dimensions of his thought is the division of the monastic journey into the two stages of *praktikē* and knowledge. Yet just as characteristic is his never losing an opportunity to unite these two, teaching in one moment that the purity of *praktikē* is not an end in itself, and in the other that the knowledge which is the goal is not possible apart from purity. The biblical text itself instructs him always to keep in balance these two dimensions.

> I have faith in God that you will reap thirty and sixty and a hundredfold the fruit thanks to the purity of your lives. "For blessed are the pure of heart; they shall see God." (*Epistula Fidei* 36)

---

[36] W. Frankenberg, ed., *Evagrius Ponticus,* Abhandlungen der königlichen Gesellschaft der Wissenschaften zu Göttingen, Phil.-hist. Klasse n.F. 13.2 (Berlin, 1912), 604.

In the pure heart another heaven is imprinted, of which the vision is light and the place spiritual. (*Lt* 39:5)[37]

The state of prayer is the condition of passionlessness, which by a supreme love snatches up on high the mind in love with wisdom, the spiritual mind. (*Prayer* 53)[38]

---

[37] Ibid., 592.
[38] PG 79:1177C.

6
EVAGRIUS AND PAPHNUTIUS ON THE CAUSES FOR ABANDONMENT BY GOD

I n the three chapters that follow now I would like slowly to open up the concentrated focus on Evagrius that has prevailed so far in these studies to the wider monastic world of which he was a part. One way of doing this is to trace the influence of a particular father on a major theme in Evagrius's teaching. That is what is undertaken here in this chapter. The father in question is the great Paphnutius, and the theme is abandonment by God. This particular theme can follow usefully on the examination just completed of purity of heart; for, as we shall see, the fate that awaits monks who fail to reach purity of heart or remain fixed in it is a salutary abandonment by God. What exactly does Evagrius mean by this rather shocking expression, "abandonment by God"?

In chapter 47 of the *Lausiac History* (*LH*), Palladius describes a visit made by himself and "blessed Evagrius and blessed Albanus" to the monks Cronius and Paphnutius. Their visit, undertaken within the traditional practice of going to consult the fathers, had a specific purpose. They wanted to ask them about "the causes why some of the brothers can deviate or vacillate or fall from a proper way of life" (47:3, lines 23–25).[1] In fact, the visit and the question were prompted by recent events within the desert communities that were disturbing to the three questioners. A great ascetic had suddenly died at his work. Another was digging a well and in the process was somehow buried alive. A third had died of thirst crossing the desert. Then, as now, people who wish to make progress in the spiritual life

---

[1] τὰς αἰτίας τῶν παραπιπτόντων ἢ καὶ ἐκπιπτόντων ἀδελφῶν ἢ σφαλλομένων ἐν τῷ καθήκοντι βίῳ. The Greek text used here is in G. J. M. Bartelink, *Palladio, La Storia Lausiaca* (Milan: Fondazione Lorenza Valla, 1974), which is basically the text prepared by C. Butler, *The Lausiac History of Palladius*, 2 vols. (Cambridge, 1898, 1904), with emendations, many later suggested by Butler himself. This edition has the advantage of numbered paragraphs and lines, making the text easier to cite. The introduction by C. Mohrmann is helpful for understanding the textual complexities. But essential for this is G. Bunge in *Quatre ermites égyptiens, d'après les fragments coptes de l'Histoire Lausiaque,* trans. A. de Vogüé (Bellefontaine, 1994), 17–80.

wonder about such things and what purposes God may have in allowing them. But what really troubled the three questioners was the moral fall of some very accomplished monks of the desert. Their names are given us: Stephen, Eucarpios, Heron of Alexandria, Valens of Palestine, and Ptolemy the Egyptian of Scete. Palladius makes it clear that the questions of the three visitors are provoked by the finishes that these "bad monks" had made. "Therefore we asked, 'What was the cause by which men who live in the desert could be fooled in their thinking and end up in such a state of intemperance?'" (*LH* 47:5, lines 35–37).[2]

Paphnutius offers them an answer.[3] It is a theologically sophisticated answer, and we shall examine its content here shortly. But the tendencies of Palladius's work[4] combined with the fact that Evagrius is explicitly mentioned here as one of the party of visitors has raised the question whether there is any historical reliability to Palladius's assigning this teaching to Paphnutius. In fact, as we shall see, what Paphnutius says here appears amply developed in the writings of Evagrius. Thus the question: Has Palladius simply put the teaching of his old master Evagrius in the mouth of a venerated father, or is this Palladius's best effort at remembering his visit and the teaching that he and his companions received from Paphnutius?[5] Cassian also, in his third conference, reports an encounter with Paphnutius, during the course of which he teaches in a way quite similar to what is reported here by Palladius; but this is perhaps best explained as a dependence by Cassian on Palladius's text.[6]

A. and C. Guillaumont argue that this textual relationship between the two weakens the probability of the authenticity of Paphnutius's reported discourse, not to mention that we may have to do here with two different figures named Paphnutius. For the Guillaumonts this, combined with the similarities between Evagrius's teaching and that reported of Paphnutius, leads them to conclude, "Il est fort possible que celui-ci [Pallade] ait fait exposer par Paphnuce, qu'il dit 'très gnostique,'—et de façon incomplète, piusque deux causes de déréliction sont seulement retenues—la doctrine de son maître Évagre."[7]

The incompleteness of Paphnutius's teaching in comparison to that of Evagrius—as we shall see, Evagrius gives five reasons for a monk's being abandoned by God, while Paphnutius gives two—actually can argue more

---

[2] The translations of the text are mine.

[3] He is called by Palladius Παφνούτιος ὁ γνωστικώτατος (*LH* 47:5, l 38).

[4] Palladius's work is considered to be thoroughly marked by Evagrian categories. See below n. 8.

[5] Facing this question, even if it cannot be finally resolved, helps in reading the Evagrian material with a sharper eye.

[6] Thus, Butler, *Lausiac History of Palladius*, 2:224–25; cf. Cassian, *Conference* 3, 20.

[7] A. and C. Guillaumont, *Le Gnostique*, Sources Chrétienne 356 (Paris: Cerf, 1989), 142. For the whole argument, see pp. 141–42.

strongly, I think, in favor of the authenticity of what Palladius reports here. If we may presume that Palladius knew Evagrius's teaching on the question, what reason would he have for abbreviating it as he "puts it into the mouth of Paphnutius"? Not only concerning the main question but also in regard to other parts of Paphnutius's discourse, there are links with other Evagrian themes, but here again only in what, by comparison, would have to be called abbreviated form. For what purpose? That Palladius is intentionally obfuscating to set his reader off the Evagrian scent is not likely, especially in a chapter that explicitly mentions Evagrius's involvement in the visit. Perhaps a simpler and more likely explanation is that Palladius has reported, as best as he can remember, the teaching that he, together with Evagrius and Albanus, received from Paphnutius; and that Evagrius was launched in a certain direction by this teaching, which he later developed himself.

I do not propose to be able to settle this problem in the present study, nor is it my direct purpose here. I hope rather to study the teaching on abandonment as reported in chapter 47 of the *Lausiac History* together with the teaching of Evagrius on the same. Such an exercise is worth doing in its own right, apart from determining whether or not the teaching is that of a historical Paphnutius. Yet this much we may at least learn in the process; namely, that Evagrius's teaching is surely not entirely his own invention; that, like most of his other teaching, the teaching on abandonment is rooted in a tradition that precedes him; that concrete circumstances and problems gave rise to the teaching in the first place and made it relevant for Evagrius's own life; and that, as he did with other parts of the tradition, Evagrius, of course, has put his own mark on it, made it clearer, made a neater presentation of it, and deepened it through his particular experience.

Ever since R. Draguet's studies on the *Lausiac History,* a phrase from his title has become shorthand among scholars for referring to the strong Evagrian stamp that Palladius's work displays: "une œuvre écrite dans l'esprit d'Évagre."[8] But it is perhaps necessary to nuance the significance of this most certainly correct description. It is too simplistic to think that this means that Palladius has merely recast his stories from the desert and the teachings of the fathers reported there and made them his ploy for promoting the teachings of Evagrius, which are otherwise *sui generis* and thus not representative of the genuine spirit of Egyptian monasticism. Evagrius is not only a very capable and creative spiritual master who certainly gives his own particular stamp to what he teaches, but he is first a spokesman for

---

[8] R. Draguet has convincingly demonstrated that the *Lausiac History* is very much shaped and marked by the theological and spiritual framework of Evagrius. This position has been generally accepted since his article, "L'Histoire Lausiaque, une œuvre écrite dans l'esprit d'Évagre," *Revue d'Histoire Ecclésiastique* 41 (1946): 321–64; 42 (1947): 5–49.

a tradition that precedes him. Being among the first to write about it from within and to reflect on it theologically, he has, of course, contributed much to its shaping. But what he teaches has its roots in fathers who precede him and in the wisdom accumulated through experiences that are broader than his own. Thus, "a work in the spirit of Evagrius" needs to mean that we have to do here not just with the spirit of one peculiar innovator but rather with the tradition that he represents. Palladius takes advantage of the focus, order, and spiritual logic with which Evagrius speaks the wisdom of desert monasticism.[9]

Applying this to the question at hand, there is no reason to exclude a priori that Evagrius's teaching on abandonment has its roots in fathers he may have asked about it, in the tradition that he came to the desert to learn. Be that as it may, certainly Evagrius offers a profound and clear · teaching on the theme. By studying it in the context of his reported visit to Paphnutius, whether this is Paphnutius's authentic teaching or not, we can gain some feel for the context in which Evagrius proffered his own teaching, generally so leanly expressed. This context will help us to see that Evagrius's teaching, in short scholia and brief chapters, has its roots in very concrete experiences—his own and that of the monks with whom he shared a way of life.

I propose to conduct this study in four parts. In the first part I will examine the five fallen monks who are mentioned in chapter 47 of the *Lausiac History* and whose fall occasioned the question put to Paphnutius. In fact, elsewhere in the *Lausiac History* there are chapters on three of these monks which describe their falls. The two others are spoken of also in Syriac fragments that likely are the work of Palladius. We will see that Evagrius had

---

[9] Denying Evagrius a place closer to the mainstream of the currents of Egyptian monasticism began with the first Origenist crisis at the end of the fourth century, continued with the denunciations of Jerome, and was confirmed in the second Origenist crisis in the sixth century, with the specific condemnation of Evagrius, together with Origen and Didymus, in the Second Council of Constantinople in 553. This damaged image is accepted by many modern scholars who continue to be influenced by the ancient texts that draw a strong contrast between intellectually active monks (usually lumped together as "Origenists") and the simpler, less-educated, and (so the texts presume) holier and more humble monks. That this contrast between two types of monks is a too-heavy-handed interpretation of the actual situation in fourth-century Egyptian monasticism is amply illustrated in the work of G. Bunge, especially his "Évagre le Pontique et les deux Macaire," *Irénikon* 56 (1983): 215–27; 323–60. See also S. Rubenson, *The Letters of St. Anthony: Origenist Theology, Monastic Tradition and the Making of a Saint* (Lund, 1990); and M. Sheridan, "Il mondo spirituale e intellettuale del primo monachesimo egiziano," in *L'Egitto cristiano: aspetti e problemi in età tardo-antico*, ed. A. Camplani (Rome, 1997), 177–216. For a view also suggesting a more careful interpretation of the implications of Draguet's studies, see C. Mohrmann's introduction in *Palladio, La Storia Lausiaca*, xxii–xxiii. On the second Origenist crisis, see D. Hombergen, *The Second Origenist Controversy: A New Perspective on Cyril of Scythopolis' Monastic Biographies as Historical Sources for Sixth-Century Origenism* (Rome, 2001).

personal knowledge and involvement with the monks in question. In the
second part of this study, Paphnutius's answer to his questioners can be
exposed and examined in its own right. In a third part, I will offer a reaction to this teaching from the standpoint of the teachings of Evagrius in
general. Finally, in a fourth part, with a broader context hopefully thus
established, the texts of Evagrius's own teaching on abandonment can be
examined.

THE FALLEN MONKS

Valens

Earlier in his account, Palladius has a series of three chapters in which he
tells the story of three of the five monks mentioned in chapter 47, monks
whose falls occasioned the question about abandonment put to Paphnutius. In the way the accounts unfold, the framework of Evagrian thought
that is typical of Palladius sometimes comes to the fore. The first of those
mentioned is Valens. "He was Palestinian by birth but a Corinthian in his
character" (*LH* 25:1, lines 1–2). The reference is to St. Paul, who attributed to the Corinthians the passion of being puffed up (τὸ πάθος τῆς φυσι-
ώσεως) (1 Cor 4:18ff.). What is central to Evagrius's teaching on
abandonment is thus immediately introduced. Virtually all of it centers on
pride and how it may be avoided and overcome. This Valens had lived
many years "with us," says Palladius, and reached "such a level of pride that
the demons were able to fool him" (*LH* 25:1, lines 4–5).

What the demons did was this: Valens was weaving in the dark and lost
his needle. A demon produced a light that enabled him to find it, and
Valens mistakenly presumed that it was his own holiness that produced the
miraculous convenience. He became so puffed up by this that he came to
the point even of despising "participation in the mysteries" (τῆς κοινωνίας
τῶν μυστηρίων αὐτὸν καταφρονῆσαι) as something that he did not need
(*LH* 25:2, lines 11–13).[10] Later, as another example of pride, when Macarius their priest, whom Evagrius always considered one of his special masters,[11] had sent to him a portion of sweets that guests had brought, he
grabbed the messenger and said, "Go and tell Macarius: 'I'm not your infe-
rior that you need to send me an offering.'" Macarius thus understood that
he was deceived by the demon and went to admonish him the next day,
but, alas, to no avail (*LH* 25:3, lines 18–23).

---

[10] The reference here is to the celebration of the Eucharist.
[11] See Bunge, "Évagre le Pontique et les deux Macaire," 215–27, 323–60.

This defiance was enough to make it clear to the demon that the monk was now completely in his grasp. So he arranged a vision of himself as the Savior and appeared to him ἐν φαντασία in the midst of thousands of angels. One of these says to the deluded monk, "Christ is pleased with your observance and the boldness with which you speak and so has come to see you." He is then instructed to bow the knee to him and adore him when he sees him in the distance, which he promptly does. It is clear that the demons are making sport with him, but he is still unaware of it. The next day he rushes off to the church, where he announces to the assembled community, "I have no need of communion, for I have seen Christ today." This was too much for the fathers, who adopted strong measures indeed. They bound him in chains for a year, and this together with their prayers brought about his cure. Palladius finishes his account by explaining that the reason he is telling this and the following stories is because "often even virtue becomes the occasion for a fall."[12] Then he quotes Ecclesiastes: "I have seen a just man perish in his justice, and this too is vanity" (Eccl 7:15).[13]

The reader is struck in this account by several clear connections with themes in Evagrius, and once again the old question will pose itself: Has Palladius fabricated a story for illustrating Evagrian themes, or has Evagrius's own teaching been shaped by his personal awareness of events like the one recounted here? For me it is this latter that is the more natural explanation, though it is probably not possible to arrive at a definitive conclusion. In any case, what are the connections with Evagrius?

In the *Chapters on Prayer* Evagrius speaks from many different angles of a monk's experience with pure prayer, the goal of monastic life as he and his tradition conceive it. In some of the chapters he speaks of its positive characteristics; in others, of possible dangers. Chapters 73 and 74 are formulations at which Evagrius could have arrived by his own reflection and reflection with other fathers on the kind of delusion the monk Valens underwent. It is enough to cite Evagrius's own words for the connection to appear evident. The several explicit mentions of vainglory should be noted. This is a passion associated with monks who have made real progress on some levels. It should also be noted that Evagrius makes reference to the ideas of some other unnamed father on the matter.

> 73. Once the mind is praying purely and without interference from the passions, the demons no longer assault it from the left, but from the right. They propose some divine radiance to it or some shape taken from the things the senses feel at home with,

---

[12] For all the above, see *LH* 25:4–6.

[13] Evagrius has a scholion on this text, which will be examined below.

so that the mind will think that it has perfectly attained to its goal in the matter of prayer. An experienced ascetic said that this comes about because of the passion of vainglory and because the demon which fastens on to the place around the brain sets up a vibration in the veins.

74. I think that the demon touches this place and manipulates the light that surrounds the mind as he pleases, and this is how the passion of vainglory is stirred to produce a line of thought which shapes the mind so that it will lightheadedly try to locate the divine, substantial knowledge. Someone like this is not troubled by carnal, unclean passions, and is apparently standing before God in purity, so he reckons that there is no opposing force still at work in him and this makes him suppose that the apparition he sees is divine, though in fact in comes to him from the extreme cunning of the demon manipulating, by means of the brain, the light which is attached to the mind and so shaping the mind, as we have said. (*Prayer* 73, 74; PG 79:1181D–1183A)[14]

We may regard this as a well-considered analysis of the delusions experienced by a monk like Valens, whose story offers us a concrete *Sitz im Leben* for the concern with imageless prayer that runs throughout the *Chapters on Prayer*. Such concern should be understood not as some foreign esoteric Neoplatonism imported by Evagrius into more purely conceived Christian traditions, but as his and his tradition's extreme prudence before monks whose pride in their ascetic accomplishments brings them to imagine that they are having visions of Christ, not to mention that they no longer feel the need for sharing the eucharistic mysteries.

As we shall see below, when we examine Evagrius's own texts on abandonment, he frequently speaks of the demons making sport with the vainglorious and proud monk, even as Palladius reports here. Yet there is divine providence involved in God's allowing this to happen; for, as in the present case, it eventually results in the monk's cure.[15]

Heron

The story of Heron has a less happy outcome—or at least a more ambiguous one. He lived close to Palladius, was his "neighbor," and is

---

[14] Trans. Tugwell, pp. 39–40.

[15] G. Bunge notes that even the method of binding a monk in chains is known to Evagrius as a part of this theme, to which his *Lt* 52:4 makes allusion. See G. Bunge, *Briefe aus der Wüste* (Trier, 1986), 369–70.

reported to have spoken offensively to "the blessed Evagrius." Yet Palladius gives him his due. He describes him as a refined young man, gifted with intelligence and a pure life (*LH* 26:1). But this becomes precisely the problem. In the monastic understanding, pride is based on some real gifts and ascetic accomplishments. Something in Evagrius's own success as an esteemed father must have bothered Heron, for one day he said to him, "Those who obey your teachings are deceived, for there is no need to listen to other masters than Christ himself" (*LH* 26:1, lines 5–8).

In this confidence of a direct link to Christ, Heron shows himself similar to Valens, as he does also in another attitude. "He no longer wanted to approach the mysteries" (*LH* 26:2, lines 11–12). So he also was put in chains. Yet as the story unfolds, Palladius still feels constrained to give him further his due. "He was extremely frugal in his way of living" (*LH* 26:2, lines 12–13), eating and drinking very little. He could recite many Psalms by heart, knew by memory the Letter to the Hebrews, the prophet Isaiah, and parts of Jeremiah, Luke's Gospel, and the Proverbs (*LH* 26:3). Yet his pride made him restless in his cell, which he eventually left to head off for Alexandria, his city of birth. There he frequented the theater, the hippodrome, and taverns, where he eventually fell to the standard series of the passions: gluttony, wine loving, and desire for women. Having taken up with an actress, he suddenly found himself seriously diseased to the point that his testicles fell off. This returned him to divine thoughts. He confessed to the fathers but was unable to take up his old asceticism, for he died several days later.

This startling story was upsetting for Evagrius, Palladius, and Albanus. How was it, they wondered, that a monk so accomplished could fall so hard? Why did God permit it? And what is the meaning of his disease and his death? These were their questions purportedly put to Paphnutius. Evagrius himself will later teach that the accomplished monk who thinks himself self-sufficient will suddenly find himself immersed in the most squalid of carnal desires.[16] Shameful though it be, there is a providence involved. We shall see how in the teachings of Paphnutius and Evagrius.

Ptolemy

The story of Ptolemy unfolds more simply, but the same basic themes are present. He was a great monk, or at least a great ascetic, living for more than fifteen years in a place seemingly impossible to inhabit. But "because

---

[16] *Praktikos* 13, especially "sometimes it also hands over to the demon of fornication the one who, just a little before, was being tied up and forced to be a holy priest." See also *Praktikos* 14. A. and C. Guillaumont, eds., *Praktikos*, 2 vols., Sources Chrétiennes 170, 171 (Paris: Cerf, 1971), 2:528–35.

he became a stranger to the teaching and the company of holy men, as well as communion in the mysteries," he came to the point of affirming that these things have no value (*LH* 27:2, lines 10–13). He too leaves the desert and falls prey to gluttony and wine loving, his basic problem being summarized as "never speaking with anyone" (μηδενὶ μηδὲν ὁμιλοῦντα, *LH* 27:2, line 15), that is, being self-sufficient, never asking the advice of the fathers. As of this telling, Ptolemy is still not cured. The account finishes with words from the Book of Proverbs: "Those who have no head (κυβέρνησις) fall like leaves" (Prov 11:14), a text on which Evagrius comments by simply citing two New Testament verses: "Tossed about by every wind of teaching and shipwrecking in the faith."[17] This sad story puts a certain force behind Evagrius's frequent pleas that the monk not merely devote himself to bodily asceticism,[18] or likewise his insistence on the importance of consulting the fathers.[19]

Stephen

The monks Stephen and Eucarpios, mentioned in chapter 47 of the *Lausiac History,* are not spoken of in any of the received versions of the text. However, in his critical edition of the Syriac materials of the *Lausiac History,* R. Draguet has published in an appendix two fragments that tell the stories of two fallen monks, Stephen and Eucarpios. The stories, though slightly more lengthy than the three chapters thus far examined, certainly appear to be from the hand of Palladius; and they read in the same tenor as the rest of the *Lausiac History.* In both stories the author has firsthand experience of the fall in question, and in both Evagrius is involved. We may reasonably assume that these are the Stephen and Eucarpios about whose fall Palladius, Evagrius, and Albanus come to question Paphnutius. Draguet refers to these fragments as HL [72] (Stephen's story) and HL [73] (Eucarpios's story).[20] A summary of their stories will serve our purposes here, as with the three previous fallen monks.

---

[17] *In Prov* 11:14 (G 125; P. Géhin, ed., *Scholies aux proverbes,* Sources Chrétiennes 340 [Paris: Cerf, 1987], 222). For the New Testament texts cited by Evagrius, see Eph 4:14 and 1 Tim 1:19.

[18] For example, *Lt* 27:3; 28:1; 52:5–6; 56:5; *Praktikos* 38; *In Prov* 2:5 (G 20), *M* 38–44 with my comments in ACW *Ad Monachos,* 86–89.

[19] For example, *M* 88–92.

[20] R. Draguet, *Les formes syriaques de la matière de l'Histoire Lausiaque,* CSCO Script. syr. 169–70, 173–74 (Louvain, 1978). The Syriac text is found in vol. 173, pp. 365–72; the translation is in vol. 174, pp. 236–41. For Draguet's reasons for considering the material authentically Palladian, see 173:365. For a lengthier discussion of the significance of these fragments, see Bunge, *Quatre ermites égyptiens,* 53–55, 68–69, 76–80.

Whereas the monks Valens, Heron, and Ptolemy were all from the monastery of Cells, the stories of Stephen and Eucarpios unfold in Scete. Thus, it is likely that Paphnutius of Scete would certainly know their stories and, like the other fathers, would have reflected on them. Their stories exhibit the same themes we have already encountered, but each exhibits its own particular version of the same old problem: pride.

At the beginning of Stephen's story, Palladius[21] uses the explicit expression that we are concerned with in this study; namely, Stephen "was abandoned by divine providence on account of his arrogance and a pride beyond all measure" (*LH* 72:1).[22] His problems begin when he separates himself from the brotherhood, even making bold to say, "I am in submission to Macarius and yet my observances are better than his." He eventually heads off to find city life in Alexandria and falls into the standard dynamic of the passions, which moves from gluttony to fornication. Stephen has a habit of rendering explicit in his speech the most shocking attitudes, seemingly unaware of how deluded he sounds. Regarding his fornication, he says, "For the perfect there is no law. I don't do what I do from passion. There is no sin in fornication because"—here he quotes scripture—"after all 'male and female were created by God'" (Gen 1:27) (*LH* 72:2).[23]

It happens that Palladius and "the blessed Evagrius" have to go one day to Alexandria in the company of four other monks. They find that the whole city is alive with talk about the goings-on of Stephen. When Evagrius finds Stephen, he begins to cry and makes the humble gesture of falling at Stephen's feet, begging him to come to his senses; but Stephen does not even incline his head toward the man on the ground at his feet. Eventually they persuade the erring monk to go to the part of the city where they are going, and Evagrius says to him, "Truly, beloved, you have fallen from the elevated occupation with angels to the depths of evil...but even if Satan has been able to bring you low by such a fall, I beg you not to despair of your salvation. Rise, come back to the desert with us, and through the hands of the merciful God, you can reach again your former level" (*LH* 72:3).[24] But Stephen is not moved. He accuses the monks of a useless asceticism and claims at last to have found the truth.

The story does not finish happily. Stephen appears to be living in a place still called a monastery, to which he has taken a young woman who was an orphan, ostensibly to help her in her need but really with a debased view

---

[21] For convenience we shall refer to the author as Palladius, even though this identity cannot be determined with certainty.

[22] Syriac, p. 361; translation, p. 236, lines 29–30.

[23] Syriac, p. 366; translation, p. 237, lines 15–18.

[24] Syriac, p. 367, l; translation, pp. 237–38, lines 32–34.

in mind (*LH* 72:4).[25] Bandits come, tie them up, and at the end set fire to their house. They are burned alive. Palladius comments with the words of Paul: "Since they did not see fit to acknowledge God, God handed them over to their undiscerning mind to do what is improper (Rom 1:28)" (*LH* 72:4).[26] He concludes, "These things happened to Stephen because he separated himself from the brotherhood and was so puffed up in his spirit that he thought himself perfect" (*LH* 72:5).[27]

Eucarpios

Like all the other monks whose falls we have heard about, Eucarpios was first an impressively accomplished monk. He had stayed closed within his cell for eighteen years and had not spoken a word to anyone in fifteen. His diet was sparse. But, "in the end he too was mocked by the demons because of the vain opinion he had of himself" (*LH* 73:1).[28]

Palladius's discussion of his fall lists again the source of his problems: separating himself from contact with other brothers, ceasing to meditate on holy books, restricting his practice to constant prayer. This latter seems at first glance praiseworthy, but the point is that it ought to be submitted to the "checks and balances" of the community and the sacred writings. Instead, pride entered into Eucarpios in such a way that he thought he could constantly see God in his mind (*LH* 73:2).[29]

Satan appears to Eucarpios "under the form of an angel of light" and says to him, "I am Christ" (*LH* 73:3).[30] The deluded monk, of course, worships him and asks for a word. The satanic message that follows is delivered in extremely shrewd terms, and it is not difficult to imagine that they represent a kind of "spirituality" that from time to time someone might try to let fly in the desert. Understanding the message with the focus that Evagrius's theology provides, we could say that Satan, masquerading as Christ, convinces Eucarpios that there is no need for *praktikē* in monastic life, but

---

[25] Such an example is used by Paphnutius in his answer in chapter 47; cf. *LH* 47:7.

[26] Syriac, p. 368; translation, p. 238, lines 28–29. This same text is cited by Paphnutius at *LH* 47:17.

[27] Syriac, p. 368; translation, p. 238, lines 33–35.

[28] Syriac, pp. 368–69; translation, p. 239, lines 10–11.

[29] As Bunge points out, the thought of being able to see God is the background for much of Evagrius's *Chapters on Prayer*. See Bunge, *Quatre ermites égyptiens*, 55. I observed the same concerning Valens above; namely, that Evagrius's work is carved out by his own and other fathers' reflections on this particular kind of delusion among monks they have known.

[30] Syriac, p. 369; translation, p. 239, lines 18–20. The expression "Satan appearing as an angel of light" is taken from 2 Cor 11:14, where the context helps to understand the allusion. Evagrius speaks of this often. See *Prayer* 95, *Lt* 29:4, *In Prov* 20:27 (G 221), *Antirrhetikos* 25, 56.

that monks should pass forthwith to the sweet place of knowledge. "I wish to make my dwelling in you...You have become perfect," says the false Christ to him, "and you are now to go and teach the brothers that they should no longer concern themselves with the reading of the Scriptures or the Office of psalms, nor should they do bodily labors or wear themselves out with hunger, thirst, and fasting. Instead they should be concerned with the labors of the soul so that they can all the more quickly be capable of being introduced to the supreme degree and gaze on me constantly in their understanding. Then can I show them my glory" (*LH* 73:3).[31]

In what follows, this Christ appoints Eucarpios as the new head of Scete, specifying that Macarius is no longer suited to the position. The next day he is sent to make this announcement to the gathered brethren. When Eucarpios arrives at the assembly, he sees the brothers gathered around John listening to his teaching. This most likely is John the Dwarf.[32] Eucarpios launches a vulgar insult at him and announces that he is now the leader in Scete. When asked who has made him the leader, he tells that Christ himself had made him leader the previous night. Then, interestingly, he singles out three teachers for special invective: Evagrius, John, and Macarius. He says of Macarius and Evagrius something that echoes what we heard earlier in the demonically fabricated message suggesting that monks need not linger in *praktikē* but should move on quickly to the higher things. Specifically he says that Macarius does not know how to lead the brethren toward "celestial things." As for Evagrius, he is "a chisler of words who wears out the brethren with his writings and impedes spiritual work in them" (*LH* 73:4).[33] These complaints ring true to what we know of the teaching of Macarius and Evagrius. Each in his own way constantly insists that no monk can go on to higher things without a firmly established *praktikē* that is always maintained.

Thus, as Palladius makes explicit, we have to do here again with a monk "who did not want to meditate on the holy books or on the doctrine of the fathers" (*LH* 73:4).[34] For him, too, the others had no choice but to resort to the famous chains and to prayer. After eleven months in chains, Eucarpios comes to his senses and is healed of his pride. He lives another year, following the commands of the fathers to serve the sick and wash the feet of strangers, that is, very solid exercises in the life of *praktikē* (*LH* 73:5).

---

[31] Syriac, pp. 369–70; translation, p. 239, lines 23–34. It should be noted that here again the temptation is a question of some manner of actually seeing of God.

[32] It was during this time that John the Dwarf was active at Scete and so greatly admired there. Draguet observes in a note that this experience is recounted in a number of manuscripts of the *Apophthegmata Patrum* under the name of John the Dwarf. See Draguet, *Les formes syriaques,* 240 n. 1.

[33] Syriac, p. 371; translation, pp. 240–41, lines 20–23.

[34] Syriac, p. 371; translation, p. 241, lines 6–7.

Five Fallen Monks: A Summary

Granted whatever caveats a modern interpreter may wish to make about these accounts of Palladius, granted *l'esprit d'Évagre,* which marks his telling, granted the didactic purposes of the genre employed, it is clear that these stories have their roots in concrete experiences that troubled the monastic life not only at Cells but also at Scete. These stories give us a detailed sense of what stood behind the question posed to Paphnutius in chapter 47 of the *Lausiac History.* They also give us a picture of the concrete circumstances in which Evagrius himself carved out his own teaching and the reasons for many of the themes that that teaching emphasizes.

All of the fallen monks have in common an overriding pride that exhibits itself in a vanity about outstanding and severe ascetical accomplishments. All of them dared to distance themselves from the established teaching of the fathers as well as from the community of the brothers that is formed around such fathers. In three cases it is mentioned that they no longer felt it necessary to participate in the eucharistic mysteries, so great had their perfection become. They think that they have direct access to Christ, even that they see him in special visions. Yet what is clear to others is that these unfortunate monks have become the playthings of demons, who are only too happy to make sport of them. When such disturbing actions and thoughts occur among monks who are acknowledged as once having been among the best, it is no wonder that other monks would wonder long and hard, and with a certain fear of their own possible fall, about what actually were the causes of such derailments. These are questions to put to the wisest of the fathers; and in posing them to Paphnutius, the monks who ask are very much in need of whatever light he can shed on so dark a mystery. We can turn now to hear what Paphnutius has to say about the matter.

PAPHNUTIUS'S ANSWER EXPRESSED IN ITS OWN RIGHT

After the question is posed and the context described by the mention of the names of the five monks whose stories we have examined, the answer of Paphnutius is solemnly introduced with the words, "Then Paphnutius, the most knowledgeable (ὁ γνωστικώτατος) gave us this answer" (*LH* 47:5, lines 37–38).[35] According to him there are two basic ways in which one ought to understand the fall of a monk: it comes about either by the good

---

[35] This title, as Evagrius's theology makes clear, is reserved for monks who have reached contemplative heights while keeping their *praktikē* intact.

pleasure of God or by his consent (εἴς τε εὐδοκίαν θεοῦ καὶ συγχώρησιν) (*LH* 47:5, lines 39–40). If it comes about by the good pleasure of God, then it is with a view toward somehow glorifying God. If it comes about by his consent, then we have to do with some moral fall. In the framework of this basic starting point, the teaching unfolds.

It can happen, Paphnutius explains, that virtue is sometimes pursued for a perverse purpose: to gain the praise of others or to promote one's own way of thinking. In these cases, "it is God himself who abandons them to a fall for their own good, so that through such abandonment they can feel the difference of the change and correct either their purpose or their actions" (*LH* 47:6, lines 48–15). In this explanation we have for the first time in this chapter the appearance of the technical term that will be the object of our study when we come to Evagrius; namely, abandonment: ἐγκαταλείπω and ἐγκατάλειψις. This teaching is filled out with examples. The error of the monk sometimes occurs with regard to its purpose, at other times with regard to the action itself. Concerning the former, for example, a monk might give alms to a young woman but with a perverse purpose in mind. The action itself is good, but the aim is wrong.[36] Or one might give alms really to help another, but it is done in a stingy way. In this case, the purpose is good but the action is wanting in quality.

Paphnutius is aware that monks have genuine gifts of different kinds. Some have a natural disposition for thought; others are especially fit for asceticism. What becomes important is how these gifts are understood. When those thus gifted ascribe their good qualities to their own capacities, "they are abandoned (ἐγκαταλειφθέντες) and fall prey to sordid actions and passions" (*LH* 47:8, lines 67–69). It is an especially grave problem "when someone puffed up by pride in the excellence of his words, does not ascribe to God this excellence or the wealth of his knowledge (τὴν χορη-γίαν τῆς γνώσεως) but thinks instead that it comes from his own asceticism or nature. Then God withdraws the angel of providence from him" (*LH* 47:9, lines 72–75). Such a one is turned over to the enemy for his own humiliation.

There next follows a very interesting image to describe "the souls of those under the sway of the passions (αἱ τῶν ἐμπαθῶν ψυχαὶ)" (*LH* 47:10, line 85). They resemble various kinds of fountains. As he gives examples, Paphnutius actually lists the passions in a particular order, an order that follows their inner dynamic and interrelation. Such wisdom was common in the desert, and of course Evagrius is famous for his detailed description of the eight principal passions and their interconnections. The monastic practice of drawing up such lists is inspired in part by biblical lists that do the

---

[36] We saw an example of this very thing in the story of Stephen, which ended with him and the woman being burned alive.

same; in part it is refined through particular experiences.[37] Paphnutius's list begins, as is everywhere common, with the passion of gluttony and wine loving. Those enslaved to this passion resemble muddy fountains. Money lovers and the ambitious resemble fountains full of frogs. Finally, the envious and those proud at having the highest aptitude for knowledge (ὑπερήφανοι ἐπιτηδειότητα δὲ γνώσεως ἔχοντες) are said to resemble fountains where serpents breed, fountains from which no one would draw water because of their bitter taste (*LH* 47:10). Having presented this list of vices, Paphnutius ties them together by noting, "For this reason David begged for three things: goodness, instruction, and knowledge (χρηστότητα καὶ παιδείαν καὶ γνῶσιν).[38] For without goodness, knowledge is useless" (*LH* 47:10, lines 91–93).

For our particular purposes, it is important to note that Paphnutius's list ends with those proud about knowledge. This is the crux of the issue for him.

> If such a one corrects himself, laying aside his pride—the cause of abandonment (τὴν αἰτίαν τῆς ἐγκαταλείψεως)—and regains humility, recognizes his limits without exalting himself over others, and gives thanks to God, then knowledge will come back to him again. Spiritual discourses which are not accompanied by a holy life and temperance are ears of corn emptied by the wind. (*LH* 47:11, lines 93–99)[39]

Every sin of whatever kind will result in an abandonment proportionate to the pride involved.

In what follows, Cronius is also involved in the answer to the question that is put by the three visitors. The teaching is introduced with the phrase "Those men also said this to us" (*LH* 47:13, line 108). It continues to develop themes associated with pride and the necessity of conforming one's life to one's words. Then the theme of abandonment is taken up again with a view toward tying the whole conversation together. "Therefore, concerning the causes of divine abandonment," they begin, and further reasons are given. One cause, which may be considered in a positive light, is so that hidden virtue may be made manifest, as in the case of Job. The text of Job 40:3 is cited and then paraphrased to indicate how it is

---

[37] For example, Matt 15:19; Mark 7:21–22; Rom 1:29–31; 13:13; 1 Cor 5:10–11; 2 Cor 12:20–21; Eph 4:31. See S. Wibbing, *Die Tugend- und Lasterkataloge im Neuen Testament und ihre Traditionsgeschichte unter besonderer Berücksichtigung der Qumran-Texte,* Beihefte zur Zeitschrift für die Neutestamentliche Wissenschaft 25 (Berlin: A. Töpelmann, 1959). A. and C. Guillaumont, *Praktikos,* 1:63–84.

[38] The reference is to Ps 118:66.

[39] My translation avoids solving the meaning of the difficult expression ἡ ἐμμάρτυρος γνῶσις, for which, however, one should consult the note by Bartelink, *La Storia Lausiaca,* 384.

meant to apply.[40] Thus, the reason why Job appeared to be abandoned by God is as if God were saying to him, "You were known to me, the One who sees what is hidden. But because you were unknown to men, who suspected that you adored me because of your riches, I changed your riches in order to show them the gratitude that pervades your conduct (τὴν εὐχάριστόν σου φιλοσοφίαν)" (*LH* 47:15, lines 126–30).[41]

Another cause of divine abandonment is with a view toward checking pride. Here the biblical example is Paul. So great were his miracles and his successes that he stood in danger of becoming completely puffed up and falling prey to a diabolical pride. Thus does Paul tell of the remedy in his own words, "For this reason a thorn in the flesh was given me, an angel of Satan, to beat me to keep me from being proud" (2 Cor 12:7, as in *LH* 47:15, lines 133–34). Then other biblical examples of abandonment are mentioned, which shows Paphnutius's knowledge of both testaments, as was mentioned at the beginning of the chapter (*LH* 47:3, lines 18–19). The paralytic is abandoned because of his sins. Judas is abandoned, the reason being expressed in a tight phrase: "because he preferred money to the Logos." Esau is abandoned "because he preferred his filthy stomach to a paternal benediction."[42] Paul is cited to summarize the meaning of these three examples. It is of such as these that he says, "And since they did not see fit to acknowledge God, God handed them over (παρέδωκεν) to their undiscerning mind to do what is improper (Rom 1:28)." And another verse of Paul is cited with this introduction: "Concerning those who seem to have knowledge of God in a corrupt mentality" (*LH* 47:17, lines 145–47). Paul says, "For although they knew God they did not accord him glory as God or give him thanks (Rom 1:21), God handed them over (παρέδωκεν) to degrading passions (Rom 1:26)." The whole teaching (and the chapter) is concluded with these words: "From all this we know that it is impossible to fall into shameful circumstances unless one is abandoned (ἐγκαταλειφθέντα) by the providence of God" (*LH* 47:17, lines 149–51).

A REACTION TO PAPHNUTIUS'S TEACHING FROM THE STANDPOINT OF EVAGRIUS

Before examining Evagrius's own teaching on the reasons for abandonment, a preliminary reaction to Paphnutius's teaching can be useful. There are themes here that catch the eye of one who is familiar with the broad

---

[40] This style of exegesis is common in the desert, that is, first a citation and then a rephrasing of it in such a way that its application to a particular question becomes clear.

[41] For this translation of τὴν εὐχάριστόν σου φιλοσοφίαν, see Bartelink, *La Storia Lausiaca*, 384–85.

[42] For the paralytic, Judas, and Esau, see *LH* 47:16, lines 134–42.

strokes of Evagrius's whole theology. This can, of course, be explained at least in part by the influence of Evagrius on Palladius, by the fact that we have to do here with "une œuvre écrite dans l'esprit d'Évagre." But in the light of the broader interpretation of this evaluation of the material in the *Lausiac History* that I am urging, we can react to the teaching as it is presented here, asking ourselves how such a teaching, if presented to Evagrius by a teacher like Paphnutius, might have struck him and how it might have been part of the foundation for something that Evagrius later developed in a more systematic way.[43]

The two basic reasons that Paphnutius advances for abandonment, whether as expressed in the beginning of the conference or at the end, will form the backbone of Evagrius's teaching. Indeed, Paphnutius's centering the problem in pride is where Evagrius also centers it. Yet Evagrius's teaching is more elaborate, more nuanced than what is found here. It is possible to think that Evagrius receives an initial insight from Paphnutius, which he later develops. Both Paphnutius and Evagrius, when they address the question, sound like men who are speaking from experience. Stories like those of the five fallen monks will be the reason why pride is so consistently warned against.

Something else that catches the attention of one familiar with the general outlines of Evagrius's theology is the way in which Paphnutius divides the possible problems as being concerned either with thought (διανοία) or asceticism (ἄσκησις). This corresponds to Evagrius's more neatly conceived divisions between *praktikē* and knowledge, his preferred terms for speaking about what Paphnutius speaks of here. The division of the whole of monastic life between *praktikē* and knowledge is something for whose clarity we are indebted to Evagrius, but he certainly cannot be considered responsible for inventing it. It is found everywhere in desert teaching, even if with different terminology; and the reason is that it is simply in the nature of things. Monastic life is not an ascetical workout. Its asceticism is employed for reaching some more noble goal, however that goal might be named. The problem with abandonment moves somewhere between the poles of ascetical achievement and reaching the higher goal. When the monk becomes proud about one or the other, he is abandoned.

The vivid image of various passions being compared to different fountains strikes the Evagrian reader both for what it says and for what it leaves unsaid. A list of vices, describing their dynamic interrelation, is found often

---

[43] If "une œuvre écrite dans l'esprit d'Évagre" simply means here that Palladius put Evagrius's teaching in the mouth of Paphnutius, he certainly foreshortened Evagrius's teaching; and he lost several major opportunities to promote Evagrian teaching, as, for example, in the list of vices, which leaves out some of those most significantly developed by Evagrius. The same might be said about some of the terminology, which, as we shall see, does not tend to use some of Evagrius's preferred terms for expressing certain ideas.

in Evagrius's writings. Evagrius's starting point is always gluttony, as is Paphnutius's here, although Evagrius does not usually specify wine loving when it is a question of drawing up a list. For Evagrius, gluttony is always followed by fornication, as was the case with some of the fallen monks whose stories were examined. Paphnutius, however, does not mention this. He passes immediately to love of money and ambition. For Evagrius, love of money follows fornication, and though he speaks of ambition, it does not find its way into his lists. From here Paphnutius passes immediately to envy and pride, the summit of the list, the most pernicious of all the passions. Pride holds the same culminating position in Evagrius, but Paphnutius's teaching leaves out four vices which form a very large part of Evagrius's teaching: sadness, anger, listlessness, and vainglory.[44] At least two of these, anger and vainglory, certainly figured in the stories of the fallen monks. If Palladius's purpose in speaking of the visit to Paphnutius was simply to promote Evagrius's teaching, it is odd not to find "fountains" of anger and vainglory placed in his mouth, not to mention sadness and listlessness. A possible explanation is that we simply have here an account of the real teaching of Paphnutius on the question.

Whether or not the comparison of passions to fountains is original to Paphnutius, Evagrius himself is struck by the idea, either as he may have received it here or elsewhere in the tradition. In commenting on Proverbs 9:18c, he says, "In the same way as there is with God a fountain of life (cf. Ps 35:10), so there is with the devil a fountain of death. And if the fountain of God is the fountain of virtue and knowledge, so the fountain of the devil is a fountain of evils and ignorance. And so should other such words [in the scripture] be interpreted, like *rivers, wells, water,* and *rain*" (*In Prov* 9:18c).[45] To apply this to Paphnutius's teaching, we could say that the devilish fountain of gluttony and love of money are fountains of evils, while the fountain of pride is a fountain of ignorance. Evagrius is neat and clear in his speech; Paphnutius, less so.

If Evagrius really heard from Paphnutius the reference to David's psalm at the end of the fountain discourse, he could not have failed to be struck by the language of David, who prayed for goodness, instruction, and knowledge (χρηστότητα καὶ παιδείαν καὶ γνῶσιν).[46] Evagrius would have noted in this scriptural text, as he found in many others, the divisions of the monastic life into *praktikē* and knowledge. Χρηστότητα καὶ παιδείαν would apply to *praktikē,* and here the scripture uses, as it often does, the specific name, not a symbolic one, for the goal of the monastic quest:

---

[44] For a typical expression of Evagrius's listing of the passions, see *Praktikos* 6, with subsequent descriptions of each in *Praktikos* 7–14.

[45] G 116; Géhin, p. 214.

[46] For χρηστότης, see *In Prov* 25:21 (G 314); 27:25 (G 341). For παιδεία, see *In Prov* 1:2 (G 3).

γνῶσις. Thus, when Paphnutius concludes, "Without goodness, knowledge is useless" (*LH* 47:10, lines 92–93), such a phrase summarizes the whole monastic life as Evagrius conceives it; and it could just as well be found in his mouth. In the end it is probably impossible to decide if Palladius has put this phrase into Paphnutius's mouth or if Evagrius learned such things from fathers such as him. But the latter possibility is not unlikely and cannot be excluded out of hand.

Two other biblical lessons from Paphnutius and Cronius would also have struck Evagrius for their formulation. Judas's story of abandonment is concluded with what I called a tight phrase: "because he preferred money to the Logos." The expression is odd unless one is aware of how often the Egyptian monks move within the framework of the two great divisions of monastic life and find the scripture secretly speaking of it everywhere. On one level the expression should perhaps be translated more simply as "preferring money to a word,"[47] but the double entendre is always operative for the monk who listens carefully. In monastic terminology, Judas was abandoned because he fell from knowledge (his friendship with the Logos) into the passion of money-loving.[48]

Something similar pertains for the forceful formulation about Esau, who was abandoned "because he preferred his filthy stomach to a paternal benediction." Here again the fathers have uncovered in the biblical text the basic patterns that still hold true in the monastic life; namely, that someone subject to a passion (in this case gluttony) cannot hope to enjoy the life of knowledge (here expressed as a paternal benediction). If Palladius represents here a real encounter of Evagrius with monastic teachers, we begin to see how he himself learned such careful and tight reading of the biblical text, expressing his own insights especially in his scholia. However one wants to measure the *Lausiac History* as "une œuvre écrite dans l'esprit d'Évagre," it is certain that Evagrius is not unique in the desert for interpreting the scripture in this way, nor is it a practice reserved to the monks of Cells and Nitria, where it is said Origen was more likely to be read.

EVAGRIUS'S OWN TEACHING ON THE REASONS FOR ABANDONMENT

The foregoing hopefully has shown that if Evagrius is going to develop a teaching on abandonment, it will not be a theory developed in a vacuum

---

[47] ...προτιμήσας λόγου ἀργύριον... (*LH* 47:16, line 139).

[48] Elsewhere Evagrius remarks of Judas, "Judas the traitor received an intelligible richness and spiritual goods, but he did not know how to use them, because for the sake of gain, he betrayed the wisdom and the truth of God" (*In Eccl* 5:17–19 [G 43]; P. Géhin, ed., *Scholies à l'Ecclésiaste*, Sources Chrétiennes 397 [Paris: Cerf, 1993], 138).

or by an intellectual theorist. It will come from his own experience of specific fallen monks with whom he had lived or whose stories he knew. And it will come from his consultation of other fathers, whose own thoughts on the matter would have influenced his own.

Perhaps the single most all-encompassing text of Evagrius on abandonment is found in the *Gnostikos*. Its presence in that particular work shows that understanding the question is the special competence of the gnostic or teacher to whom this work is addressed. Evagrius speaks of it here to indicate that it is part of a father's task to discern the causes of abandonment with a view toward helping the monk who finds himself in such conditions. He says:

> Remember the five causes of abandonment so that you can raise up again the weak souls brought down by this affliction. In fact, abandonment reveals hidden virtue. When virtue has been neglected, it reestablishes it through chastisement. And it becomes the cause of salvation for others. When virtue has reached a high degree, it teaches humility to those who have shared in it. Indeed, the one who has had an experience of evil, hates it; for experience is a flower of abandonment, and such abandonment is the child of passionlessness. (*Gn* 28)[49]

To read this text cold, as if out of a manual, does not offer very much. Against the background of a visit such as the one reported in chapter 47 of the *Lausiac History*, it fairly shimmers with meaning. The text is usefully analyzed by A. and C. Guillaumont in their critical edition of the *Gnostikos*,[50] showing also the widespread influence of this teaching on subsequent authors. They, of course, mention the text's obvious connection with chapter 47 of the *Lausiac History;* and as we have already noted, they are inclined to see Palladius as having put this teaching in the mouth of Paphnutius. In any case, the two basic reasons for abandonment purportedly put forward by Paphnutius are found within—or we might say spread out among—the five reasons that Evagrius gives. One recognizes the idea of hidden virtue being revealed, as well as the other basic idea of chastisement or keeping the virtuous humble.

Evagrius says there are five reasons for abandonment, but it is not easy to know for sure exactly where in his text to place the numbers that divide what he is speaking about.[51] Nonetheless, we can pry open this text and the teaching that is tightly packed therein by commenting on it in

---

[49] A. and C. Guillaumont, *Le Gnostique*, 134–35.

[50] Ibid., 135–43.

[51] This complicated question of numbers both in Evagrius and subsequent authors that rely on him is treated by A. and C. Guillaumont in *Le Gnostique*, 136–39.

reference to other of Evagrius's writings. In the last analysis, after having situated Evagrius with as much clarity as possible in the concrete circumstances in which he taught and wrote, this is always the best method for understanding him.

We can begin with the idea of abandonment revealing hidden virtue. In Paphnutius's teaching, Job was presented as the biblical model for this kind of abandonment. Paphnutius cited Job 40:3 and then paraphrased it to focus his point. Perhaps Evagrius learned this point from him. In any case, Evagrius uses the same scriptural citation to explain a line from the psalms in which he anticipates a legitimate objection. The psalmist says, "I have never seen a just man abandoned (οὐκ εἶδον δίκαιον ἐγκαταλελειμμένον)" (Ps 36:25). But the monks of the desert could say otherwise based on their own experience of fallen brothers. Or one could object with the biblical example of Job. Thus Evagrius explains:

> The just are subjected to abandonment for a while but for the purpose of testing. So said the Lord to Job: "Do not think that I have dealt with you in any other way than that you might appear to be just" (Job 40:3). (*In Ps* 36:25)[52]

Evagrius, and probably many other monks, would have meditated long and hard on the figure of Job.[53] He represents for them the fact that not all abandonment, not every fall, is due to a moral lapse. In Proverbs 22:14 one can read, "The mouth of a transgressor is a deep pit; and he that is hated of the Lord shall fall into it." Evagrius's only comment is to preclude anyone from thinking that Job could be considered an example of such a one. He says, "Job fell into it not because he was hated by the Lord but with a view toward testing him" (*In Prov* 22:14).[54]

There are also other scriptural words to describe this same reality. Ecclesiastes says, "I have seen the just man perishing (ἀπολλύμενος) in his justice (Eccl 7:15)." Evagrius's scholion seizes this vocabulary to explain,

> Abandonment for the sake of testing (ἡ διὰ δοκιμὴν ἐγκατά-λειψις) is also called "perishing" (ἀπώλεια), as we see in the case of Job, who said, "I have perished (ἀπωλόμην) and have become an outcast" (Job 6:18). (*In Eccl* 7:15)[55]

---

[52] J. B. Pitra, *Analecta sacra spicilegio Solesmensi, parata* (Paris, 1883), 3:12.

[53] Chains attest to the fact that Evagrius probably developed scholia on the book of Job that have not come down to us in any single collection. See A. and C. Guillaumont, *Praktikos,* 1:36.

[54] G 243; Géhin, p. 338.

[55] G 61; Géhin, p. 166.

This is a typical exegetical procedure, finding different words in the sacred text to describe the same basic reality. The steps in the logic with which Evagrius constructs his brief scholion are these: Job as an example of abandonment (ἐγκατάλειψις), a text in Job where another word for the same is used (ἀπώλεια), that same word found in the Ecclesiastes text, and accordingly explained. Palladius learned the lesson. Speaking in his own person, he cites the text from Ecclesiastes as his conclusion for the account of the fall of Valens (*LH* 25:6).

If Evagrius knows an abandonment for the sake of testing, far more frequent in his writings is the abandonment that is meant to establish humility, to combat pride. This could be said to be the major theme of all his teaching on abandonment. Pride, for Evagrius, is ultimately a form of madness, a complete misperception of the nature of things, in which the proud one is abandoned to become the plaything of the demons, much as we saw with the fallen monks described in the *Lausiac History.* He can describe it vividly.

> Do not give your soul to pride, and you will not see chilling fantasies. For the soul of the proud is abandoned (ἐγκαταλιμπάνε-ται) by God, and it becomes a source of glee for demons. By night it [the soul] will fantasize about hoards of invading beasts, and by day it will be agitated by thoughts of cowardice. (*Eight Spirits* 17)[56]

In the chapter on pride in the *Praktikos,* Evagrius describes it as the demon that causes the most severe fall. Experience with fallen monks is what probably gives him the details of his description:

> It [pride] persuades the soul to declare that God is not its help and to think that it is the cause of its own good actions, to puff itself up against the brothers, considering them stupid. (*Praktikos* 14)[57]

This sounds like Valens, Heron, or the others, as does the way the finish of the proud one is described:

> Then there follow anger and sadness and then the last evil: losing the wits, and frenzy, and a vision of a crowd of demons in the air. (*Praktikos* 14)[58]

---

[56] PG 79:1161C-D.
[57] A. and C. Guillaumont, *Praktikos,* 2:532–34.
[58] Ibid., 534.

Elsewhere this "frenzy" or "the chilling fantasies" are also described:

> [The proud monk] sees the air around his cell on fire, bolts of
> lightning flashing against the walls. Then voices of pursuers and
> pursued. And chariots with horses etched against the sky and the
> whole house filled with Ethiopians and commotion. (*On Evil
> Thoughts* 23)[59]

In short, for Evagrius pride is a form of madness because it leads away
from the truth. What could be further from truth, Evagrius would ask,
what more insane, than thinking oneself, rather than God, the cause of
one's own good qualities?

Yet in all these cases divine providence is at work. There is a scope of
healing involved. And when a monk returns to his senses after such a fall,
the severe mercy of God can be considered by all with wonder.

> It is a great thing, a man helped by God. He has been abandoned
> (ἐγκαταλίπῃ) and thus come to know the weakness of his nature.
> You possess nothing that you have not received from God...
> Acknowledge the Giver, and do not exalt yourself above him...
> You have ascended to citizenship in the heights, but it is he who
> led you there. Hold converse with the one who raised you so that
> you may remain firm in those heights. Acknowledge your fellows
> as being of the same essence as you. (*Eight Spirits* 18)[60]

Here, in attitudes and practices like these, there is no madness, but a great
equilibrium of spirit.

As we saw, when monks fell into such madness, hard remedies were
applied by the fathers, even chains. And we saw genuine conversion, a
return to the senses. Evagrius must have been encouraged by this and he
makes it part of his teaching, seeing always the hand of God at work.

> The hate we have for the demons helps our salvation a great deal,
> and it favors the practice of virtue. Yet we are not strong enough
> to nourish it in ourselves like a good seed, for spirits that love
> pleasure destroy it and summon the soul back to its old love and
> habits. But the doctor of souls cures this love, or rather this hor-
> rible gangrene, through abandonment (δι᾽ ἐγκαταλείψεως). He
> permits that we suffer some terror caused by them, during the
> night and during the day, and so the soul comes again back to its

---

[59] P. Géhin, ed., *Évagre le Pontique, Sur les pensées,* Sources Chrétiennes 438 (Paris: Cerf,
1998), 234.

[60] PG 79:1164A-B.

original hate, having learning from David to say to the Lord, "With a perfect hatred I have hated them; they have become enemies to me" (Ps 138:22). For this is the one who hates his enemies with a perfect hate, the one who sins neither in act nor in thought. Such is proof of the first and the greatest passionlessness. (*On Evil Thoughts* 10)[61]

It is worth examining with special care some of the vocabulary and expressions used in this text. Evagrius teaches that it is salutary to cultivate a hate for the demons, but such a hate is difficult to maintain. Thus, the doctor of souls "permits" (συγχωρεῖ) an abandonment designed to rekindle hatred for the demons. In using the word συγχωρεῖ Evagrius is conscious of adopting a traditional vocabulary, nuanced in the theological idea it expresses, used in discussions about abandonment. Reading the difficult biblical text, which claims, "God has given to the sons of men an evil occupation with which to occupy themselves" (Eccl 1:13), Evagrius feels obliged to explain, "He who is the source of good is not the cause of evils." Then he seizes on the problematic word in the biblical text and explains what could be its only correct interpretation:

It says "give" here in the sense of "permit," according to the language of abandonment (λέγεται διδόναι ὡς συγχωρῶν κατὰ τὸν τῆς ἐγκαταλείψεως λόγον). (*In Eccl* 1:13)[62]

Such an explanation likely has its roots in an anti-gnostic polemic, as P. Géhin points out in his commentary on this scholion, where the concern would be to avoid verses where the God of the Old Testament seems responsible for evil. Origen had already drawn the distinction. Evagrius uses it elsewhere. Didymus does the same. Such distinctions become regular *topoi*, particularly in monastic contexts.[63] We find this same word in the mouth of Paphnutius as he opens his discourse: "All the things that happen can be divided into two kinds, either according to the good pleasure of God or according to his permitting it (εἴς τε εὐδοκίαν θεοῦ καὶ συγχώρησιν)" (*LH* 47:5, lines 38–40). Indeed, his whole discourse unfolded within this basic distinction.

In discussing the idea of cultivating a hate for the demons, Evagrius's use of Psalm 138:22, "I have hated them with a perfect hatred," is well chosen. In the same spirit of monastic exegesis that would grapple with such a text wondering to whom a Christian might appropriately direct hate, Evagrius applies such words to the demons, and further wonders what

---

[61] Géhin, *Sur les pensées,* 184–86.
[62] G 4; Géhin, p. 62.
[63] For the whole, with relevant texts, see Géhin, *Scholies à l'Ecclésiaste,* 63–65.

"perfect hate" would be. It would be the hate for the demons that one who had been abandoned would have, arising from the experience of the terrors of abandonment. This lends a bit of meat and imagery to what might otherwise strike the reader as rather an abstract statement in the first text of Evagrius from the *Gnostikos* that we examined: "Indeed, the one who has had an experience of evil, hates it; for experience is a flower of abandonment" (*Gn* 28).[64]

Also of interest in the passage from *On Evil Thoughts* is the distinction Evagrius draws at the end, where he speaks of "the one who sins neither in act nor in thought (ὁ μήτε κατ᾽ ἐνέργειαν μήτε κατὰ διάνοιαν ἁμαρτάνων)." Such an expression covers the entire sweep of monastic life, sin in act relating to *praktikē*, sin in thought relating to knowledge. Paphnutius had drawn a similar distinction when he spoke about the different kinds of gifts that souls have, "some for nobility of thought, some with a capacity for asceticism (ἐν ταῖς μὲν εὐφυΐα διανοίας, ἐν ταῖς δὲ ἐπιτηδειότης ἀσκήσεως)" (*LH* 47:5, lines 63–64). Evagrius is speaking about sin according to these categories, as does Paphnutius as well. The one who sins in neither category hates his enemies with a perfect hatred.

Evagrius says that this would be "a proof of passionlessness," indeed, of the greatest passionlessness. The significance of this expression can be measured by seeing its use in an important series of chapters in the *Praktikos*. In chapters 63–70 Evagrius speaks of the superior forms of passionlessness.[65] The series begins with the theme of the mind beginning to pray undistractedly. "Undistracted prayer is the highest activity of the mind" (*Prayer* 18).[66] But a new struggle begins at this point. Again the stories of the fallen monks, all of whom had reached genuine heights, help us to understand in concrete terms the nature of such a struggle. Here Evagrius locates the struggle in the irascible part of the soul. The monk has made progress to the point that the passions of the body have been cut off (cf. *Praktikos* 36); but precisely because the demons feel threatened by this progress, they step up the battle in a more vulnerable part of the soul, the irascible. They work there because, according to one text, the irascible part of the soul is joined in the heart especially closely to the intelligible part, which is now turning itself toward this undistracted prayer (cf. *KG* VI, 84). The demons know that an agitated irascible can blind the mind (cf. *KG* V, 27). Evagrius speaks of this battle as occuring "during the night and during the day," the same expression he used in the chapter from *On Evil Thoughts*.

---

[64] A. and C. Guillaumont, *Le Gnostique*, 134.

[65] The following draws from chapter 1 above, "Spiritual Progress in the Works of Evagrius Ponticus," pp. 24–27.

[66] For this text, see A. and C. Guillaumont, *Praktikos*, 2:646–647.

The expression that interests us here occurs in the next chapter:

> It is a proof of passionlessness when the mind begins to see its own proper light and when it remains still before the visions seen in sleep and when it looks at objects indifferently. (*Praktikos* 64)[67]

Seeing the mind's own light is a sign that the monk is involved in the life of knowledge, but it is here that the demons will begin to try to fool the mind with visions, again as we saw in the stories of the fallen monks. The monk must remain calm before these, paying them no attention, knowing that they come from the demons, hating these with a perfect hatred. That would be the proof of the greatest passionlessness.

The next chapter of the *Praktikos* makes it clear that we are concerned here with questions that concern the highest levels of knowledge and prayer and the sort of delusions to which the monk is so easily subject when he moves in these realms.

> The mind is strong when it does not see as phantasms the things of this world at the hour of prayer. (*Praktikos* 65)[68]

Such a strong mind, unfortunately, did not characterize the prayer of Valens and Eucarpios, both of whom thought they had seen Christ and heard him speaking to them.

The next chapter continues in the same vein, reminding the monk of what must never be forgotten; namely, the help of God. In this chapter the grammatical structure of the sentence is a particularly clear expression of the intricacies of the spiritual life and the right attitudes that must be held in balance within it. The core of the sentence is "a mind hardly senses any more the irrational part of the soul." This is again a τεκμήριον of passionlessness. But this condition is modified by several participial phrases before the core sentence and by a genitive absolute afterwards. Thus, such a mind hardly senses the irrational part of the soul because "with God it has accomplished the life of *praktikē*" and also because it "has drawn near to knowledge." The genitive absolute casts its force over the whole sentence and explains how it is that the mind is now in such a condition: "knowledge catches the mind up on high and withdraws it from all perceptible

---

[67] A. and C. Guillaumont, *Praktikos*, 2:648. "It looks at objects indifferently" (λεῖος βλέπων τὰ πράγματα) should be compared with the expression in *KG* VI, 52, "Many passions are hidden in our souls, which are revealed by the sharpness of the temptations when these passions slip out of us. So, it is necessary 'to keep the heart with the utmost care' (Prov 4:23) lest when the object [for which we have a passion] appears (μήποτε παραφανέντος ἐκείνου τοῦ πράγματος), we be won over to the passion, carried off suddenly by demons and do something abhorrent to God" (translated from the Greek in I. Hausherr, "Nouveaux fragments grecs d'Évagre le Pontique," *Orientalia Christiana Periodica* 5 [1939]: 231).

[68] A. and C. Guillaumont, *Praktikos*, 2:650.

things" (*Praktikos* 66).[69] Thus the "ἀπαθείας τεκμήριον" is something that the monk learns after having been abandoned (as in the text from *On Evil Thoughts*) or something that keeps a monk who comes to the heights of prayer from the pride that would cause him deservedly to be abandoned (as in these chapters from the *Praktikos*).

We can summarize all that we have seen in these texts which collect Evagrius's teaching on abandonment by turning to two final sayings. These, like so many of his short formulations, contain so much for one who is generally familiar with the general lines of his teaching. In the *Chapters on Prayer,* he says,

> Pray first to be cleansed from passions, then to be delivered from ignorance and unawareness, and thirdly to be delivered from all temptation and abandonment. (*Prayer* 38)[70]

Again, the whole sweep of monastic life is expressed here, with special focus on the issue that concerns us in this study. In praying to be cleansed from passions one is praying to reach the goal of *praktikē*. In praying to be delivered from ignorance, one prays for the goal of gnosis or knowledge. The prayer to be delivered from temptation and abandonment is so that one will not be tempted to pride after having reached the goals of *praktikē* and knowledge. For the monk who is well steeped in Evagrius's teaching, such a chapter can serve to summarize it all.

One of the proverbs in *Ad Monachos* captures in just a few lines all the vivid warnings about the demons that Evagrius advances when he teaches about abandonment. When one knows the stories of the fallen monks Valens, Heron, and others, the teaching becomes all the more effective.

> Do not give your heart to pride
> 　　and do not say before the face of God, "Powerful am I,"
> 　　lest the Lord abandon your soul
> 　　and evil demons bring it low.
> For then the enemies will flutter around you through the air
> 　　and fearful nights will follow you, one upon another. (*M* 62)[71]

In light of the foregoing, this proverb needs no comment in itself. However, as is often the case in a text written by Evagrius and as is especially the case in his *Ad Monachos,* the place where this proverb stands within the whole work increases its impact and the range of its possible meditation.[72]

---

[69] Ibid.

[70] PG 79:1176A.

[71] H. Gressmann, ed., "Nonnenspiegel und Mönchsspiegel des Euagrios Pontikos," *Texte und Untersuchungen* 39, no. 4 (1913): 158.

[72] For no. 62 in particular, see ACW *Ad Monachos,* 98–99, 273–84.

Although pride is not mentioned with special frequency in *Ad Monachos,* no. 62 is a powerfully constructed proverb and powerfully placed. It is the last proverb to precede an extended and intricately developed chain that stands at the center of the whole collection (nos. 63–72), a chain that speaks eloquently on the relation between *praktikē* and knowledge. Pride will always be a temptation for a monk whose *praktikē* is firm and who has entered into knowledge. If the monk gives way to it, he will fall from knowledge; the evil demons will bring him low. With this severe warning and its powerful images of abandonment, the reader then comes upon the beautiful proverbs which show the intricate connection between *praktikē* and knowledge.[73]

CONCLUSION

The present chapter has set out to be an exercise in reading together several groups of texts: the chapters from the *Lausiac History* and the many little chapters collected from Evagrius's writings. I have tried to present the material from the *Lausiac History* in such a way as to open wider a possible understanding of the kind of material found in this "œuvre écrite dans l'esprit d'Évagre." It is not possible to establish beyond doubt that Evagrius was influenced by Paphnutius in his teaching on abandonment. Yet it is perhaps too simplistic to think that Palladius's account of his visit with Evagrius and Albanus to Paphnutius is an entirely fictitious construct. If so, Palladius has put in Paphnutius's mouth a less than satisfactory version of Evagrius's teaching, even while writing impressively developed stories of fallen monks which could have provided him with material to develop in the Paphnutius discourse. Instead, it is Evagrius, not the Paphnutius that Palladius presents, who has taken up details of these falls and made something of it in his teaching.[74] Based on what these texts reveal, this much at

---

[73] Within *Ad Monachos,* Evagrius has also hidden a relationship, which he expects the careful reader to discover, between this proverb on pride and the resultant abandonment and the proverb that forms the turning point of the whole text, no. 107, which reads, "Like a morning star in heaven and a palm tree in paradise, so a pure mind in a gentle soul." In brief, this proverb describes the beauty of the one who reaches the heights of knowledge and does not fall from there, because the mind is pure, forming no images or visions when it prays, because the soul is gentle. That is, among other things, one does not think oneself better than others. For the extended discussion of the relationship between these two proverbs, see ACW *Ad Monachos,* 127–28, 283, 308–19.

[74] Of course it is possible to explain these accounts as also simply written "dans l'esprit d'Évagre," but again I want to ask what this means. Are we to think that Evagrius was the only monk of the desert who knew of fallen monks and reflected at depth on what could have brought them to it?

least can be maintained: that Evagrius's own teaching on abandonment did not develop as a theory purely his own; that there were monks throughout the desert, in various traditions, who reached great heights of contemplative prayer and knowledge; that some fell; and that entering such a milieu and seeing all this, Evagrius would have consulted other fathers who represented an already established wisdom on the question.

I hope this study may also have helped to detail the richness of Evagrius's own teaching on the question. As in other of the major themes in his works, what he says on abandonment greatly focuses the concerns of the whole tradition and indeed develops it by its depth and by the precision with which he locates the issue. When a monk is solidly established in ascetical virtues and genuinely begins to touch the heights of prayer and knowledge, should he forget the grace that led him there and say before God, "Powerful am I," he will be abandoned and left to the demons. But there is a providence in this. The doctor of souls will teach him to hate these demons again, to hate them with a perfect hatred.

7

EXEGETICAL PROCEDURES
IN THE DESERT MONK POEMEN

A t the beginning of the last chapter I spoke of opening the focus in
these three final chapters to the wider monastic world of which
Evagrius was a part. Thus, we examined the interface between Evagrius and the great Paphnutius of Scete. Now the focus opens even wider
to examine the much-esteemed Poemen, a monk especially appreciated
and sought out for the skill with which he applied the text of scripture to
monks in concrete situations who were asking his advice. Generally Evagrius and Poemen are not placed together by scholars, but as we shall see,
there are more connections between their monastic traditions than may at
first be suspected. The present chapter will focus almost exclusively on
Poemen, and indeed on the exegetical procedures he employs. This will
enable us to investigate in the final chapter the connection between the
thought of Evagrius and that of Poemen through their common fathers.

If one examines the use of the Bible and exegesis in the lives of the desert
monks, it becomes clear that their way of handling the sacred text is, in
principle, not so very different from the mainline exegetical procedures
that were developed in the church at large, extending from Origen to
Augustine or to, say, Cyril of Alexandria. But there is this difference: the
desert fathers will use that exegetical procedure—we may call it a tradition—not so much for the creation and articulation of theological positions, often developed during particular controversies, but they will use it
to apply a given text immediately to their personal lives and the process of
continual conversion in which they are intensely involved.

The collection of the sayings of the desert Fathers, the *Apophthegmata
Patrum*, bears witness to a rich exegetical and theological world, one perhaps only recently being mined by modern scholars for its theological
depth.[1] In this chapter, I would like to examine this process in a small sampling of texts from the desert father Poemen. Poemen is really the hero of

---

[1] Two fine recent examples would be D. Burton-Christie, *The Word in the Desert: Scripture
and the Quest for Holiness in Early Christian Monasticism* (Oxford, 1993); and G. Gould, *The
Desert Fathers on Monastic Community* (Oxford, 1993).

the *Apophthegmata*. Under his name we find the largest number of stories in the alphabetical collection, and he is likewise among the most frequently cited of the fathers in the systematic collection.[2] Among all the fathers in these collections, Poemen is especially appreciated for his skill in interpreting the scriptures. I would like to distinguish what I hope to do in this brief study from what Douglas Burton-Christie did in his excellent monograph *The Word in the Desert: Scripture and the Quest for Holiness in Early Christian Monasticism*.[3] His study is thematic and ranges across the whole text of the *Apophthegmata* in the various collections. Across this broad range he gathers evidence of many ways and levels in which the scriptures influence the lives of the desert monks. He selects themes that frequently occur in the literature and examines how the biblical text and the way it is interpreted shape these themes and their development. Of course, texts from Poemen are cited frequently. His large study makes my smaller one possible. I will not focus on the Bible in general nor on any particular themes. I will concentrate only on exegetical procedures and these in only one of the fathers, albeit one of the most representative on this issue. What steps and what "logic" are operative for Poemen that permit a given interpretation and application of a scriptural text?

The present study also relies on and can be distinguished from a study nearer to what I hope to do here; namely, J. P. Lemaire's "L'abbé Poemen et la Sainte Écriture."[4] Lemaire's work is a thorough collection of apophthegmata in all the collections where Poemen and the scriptures are somehow at issue. Analysis of the texts is followed by a systematic conclusion grouped around the themes of Bible as book, as authority, as inspiration. I come to his topic some twenty-five years later with the suggestion that the many excellent studies on patristic exegesis in the intervening years, combined with Burton-Christie's recent work, have created a situation in which a more thorough analysis of Poemen's procedures is now possible. Lemaire has collected the relevant texts and offered many useful insights into them. My study hopes to build on his valuable beginning and is no more than another start itself, a start at looking yet more carefully at the very interesting procedures that were operative as the monk Poemen read and interpreted the scriptures.[5]

---

[2] For the statistics on Poemen, see J. C. Guy, *Les Apophtegmes des pères: Collection systématique, chapitres I-IX*, Sources Chrétiennes 387 (Paris: Cerf, 1993), 77–79. The various collections of the apophthegmata present a very complex textual situation. For a description, see Guy, 18–35 or Burton-Christie, *Word in the Desert*, 85–95.

[3] See n. 1 above.

[4] J. P. Lemaire, "L'abbé Poemen et la Sainte Écriture" (Licentiate thesis; University of Fribourg, 1971). This study was done as a license thesis at Fribourg in 1971, but it has not been widely available or known.

[5] Since the present study was first published, W. Harmless has studied Poemen. See W. Harmless, "Remembering Poemen Remembering: The Desert Fathers and the Spirituality of Memory," *Church History, Studies in Christianity and Culture* 69 (2000): 483–518.

I begin this chapter with a brief look at several apophthegmata that give some measure of the skill and swiftness with which Poemen applies the scriptural text. This is followed by a selection of individual stories in which Poemen's exegetical procedure is more carefully analyzed.[6]

"POEMEN HAS THE CHARISM OF THE WORD"

Certainly one of the things that is so attractive about Poemen's scriptural interpretations is the unexpected twist that he gives to a biblical word, the surprising application, the unusual choice of texts to meet a brother's problem or concern. For that very reason, his sayings are remembered and recorded. But a deep mystery is already operative in this fact. Poemen is making a text memorable, that is to say, operative over time in the deepest parts of the consciousness of the one to whom the word is given. The word is re-membered again and again in the monk's heart, and it continues to bear fruit there precisely because the surprise remains and even further unfolds, for eventually, through the continued meditation, one discovers in the interpretation Poemen gives that, though it is unexpected, unusual, and surprising, it is in fact profoundly and mysteriously suited to the situation to which he has applied it.

The following story speaks of Poemen's skill in doing this.

> It was said that when others came to see Abba Poemen, he would send them to Abba Anoub first, because he was older. But Abba Anoub would say to them, "Go to my brother Poemen because he has the charism of the word (τοῦ λόγου τὸ χάρισμα)." (Poemen 108)[7]

Worth noting here is that Poemen's talent is identified by the Pauline word χάρισμα; that is to say, it is specifically identified and qualified as a charism of the Spirit (see 1 Cor 12:4, 8). His gift is extending the scriptural word to the inquiring disciple, and thus his word carries an authority like the scripture itself. "There are diversities of charisms, but the same Spirit" (1 Cor 12:4).[8]

---

[6] The texts of Poemen are found in PG 65:317–68. The translations will be mine.

[7] PG 65:348D. The complete story includes another line whose purpose is to show the humility of Poemen in the presence of his brother: "But if Abba Anoub was seated near Abba Poemen, Abba Poemen would never speak in his presence." I am drawing attention to the story to highlight a different aspect.

[8] For extended discussion of this point see G. Gould, "A Note on the *Apophthegmata Patrum*," *Journal of Theological Studies* n.s. 37 (1986): 133–38. Burton-Christie, *Word in the Desert*, 107–29. J. Driscoll, ACW *Ad Monachos*, 174–95.

We can briefly look at some examples of this "charism of the word" in action in order to catch their spirit and to see how memorable Poemen's interpretation can render a text. For example,

> Abba Joseph told about how Abba Poemen had said, "This is the word written in the Gospel: 'Let him who has a mantle sell it and buy a sword' (Lk 22:36), that is: let him who is at rest give it up and take the narrow way (Matt 7:14)." (Poemen 112)[9]

The method Poemen employs here is that of interpreting scripture with scripture, one word of the Lord with another. The first text from Luke in its original context concerns a teaching of the Lord to his disciples about going into the world. They will have to sell a mantle and buy a sword. The Lord himself is already speaking with images here, and Poemen recognizes that his task as interpreter is to understand them. But he does so by extending the meaning from this original context to his present, and he asks himself the question what would "selling a mantle" mean for a monk and what would "buying a sword" be. Though his answer is delivered in the very next line, we may imagine that he did not arrive at it quickly but only through slow and searching meditation on the scripture. The surprise of his combination of texts requires of his disciples a similar meditation if they are to grasp the profound link that does in fact exist between the two texts.

To have answered the question of the first text's meaning with yet another word of the Lord is to lend a divine authority to the interpretation. This is nothing other than the practice of a procedure already well established in more sophisticated theological circles; namely, that of interpreting one passage of scripture with another, confident that the one Spirit is the author of "the diversity" of texts, just as the one Spirit who gives a "diversity of charisms" gave Poemen the "charism of the word." Thus, "selling a mantle" will have had its own concrete meaning for the apostles, and that meaning extends itself to monks in fifth-century Egypt, seeking to imitate the apostolic life; and there concretely it will mean giving up ease, embracing the asceticism of the desert. The "sword" that the apostles were to buy will have had its own concrete meaning for them. For their imitators, the monks, the sword is their very way of life, "the narrow way" of which Jesus spoke, the way that leads to life.

Certainly a reason why Poemen was so deeply appreciated for his "charism of the word" would have been his ability to bring the ancient texts so immediately and usefully to bear on an inquiring disciple's life. It is an undisputed presupposition for the desert monks that the scriptures are their rule of life,[10] but the problem was just how and to whom a given text

---

[9] PG 65:349D–352A. Poemen's citation of the Lucan text is not exact. His slight alteration lets him emphasize "has a mantle," which is important to the interpretation he will give.

[10] See Burton-Christie, *Word in the Desert*, 107–29.

was to be applied. Monks found it helpful to come to Poemen when they were unsure.

> Abba Poemen was asked for whom is the word written which says, "Do not be anxious about tomorrow"(Matt 6:34). The old man said, "For the man who is tempted and is short of strength, so that he should not be anxious, saying to himself, 'How long will I have this temptation?' He should rather reflect and say to himself every day, 'Today.'" (Poemen 126)[11]

Once again Poemen has immediately transferred the text to the monastic situation but without having betrayed its original meaning. It is rather the extension of that meaning. The disciple is asking, in effect, how the text might apply to monks in general or even to himself. In the original context of the Sermon on the Mount, the Lord's words are meant to apply to worries over material needs. But monastic life is a life that by definition has reduced these to a minimum, and in any case its economy is well enough organized that only comparatively slight attention need be devoted to such concerns. Do the Lord's words then no longer apply to them? They would not if the only legitimate interpretation of a text were its literal one. But Poemen has found a dimension of the text that very squarely suits also the monastic situation. He sees that the text is not only—and perhaps not mainly—about material goods but that it is also a text about worrying and about trusting. What do monks worry about if they do not worry about what they are to eat or how they will be clothed? (see Matt 6:31). Poemen knows that they worry about temptation and about how long it will last. To such a monk—perhaps it is the one asking—Poemen applies what could only be consoling words from the Lord, "Do not be anxious about tomorrow."

The effectiveness of Poemen's interpretation is precisely in his application of words that the Lord uttered about material needs and also to what is the very heart of the monk's spiritual struggle.[12] The surrounding words of the scriptural passage are meant to come to the mind of the monk as he "reflects" (this too is part of Poemen's advice here) on this word: "the Father knows what you need"; "seek first the Kingdom of God," etc. (see Matt 6:30–34). The attitude suggested for the monk can be expressed in just one word, which may be considered a condensed version of the already

---

[11] PG 65:353D.

[12] The fear that temptations may last longer than the monk can endure is actually a dimension of the well-known monastic problem of acedia or listlessness. See the classical description of Evagrius in *Praktikos* 12, where the demon of listlessness is said to depict to the monk "life lasting for a long time and he [the demon] puts before his eyes the drudgery of the ascetical life" (A. and C. Guillaumont, *Évagre le Pontique. Traité pratique ou le moine*. Sources Chrétiennes 171 [Paris: Cerf, 1971], 526).

pithy "Sufficient to the day is the evil thereof" (Matt 6:34). The monk is simply to say "Today." And by requiring that he say "Today" every day, Poemen is assuring that this scriptural word will be ongoingly active and effective in the monk's life. The practice may be a simple one; but if day after day the monk, who is every day subject to temptation, says "Today," he will thereby be following the Lord's counsel, "Do not be anxious about tomorrow." Then this portion of the Sermon on the Mount becomes a word living and effective in fifth-century Egypt too.

With these several stories, I have tried, however briefly, to throw into relief the kind of scriptural teacher we are dealing with in Poemen. We see him true to his name, which means shepherd, in his "pastoral" application of the texts. I would like to turn now to a more direct and careful analysis of actual exegetical procedure, trying to get behind the method and logic that legitimate these kinds of pastoral applications. We shall take a representative sampling.

THE HEAD COOK DESTROYS THE TEMPLE

> Abba Poemen also said, "If Nabuzardan, the head-cook, had not come, the temple of the Lord would not have been burned (2 Kings 25:8f.), that is, if the ease of gluttony had not come into the soul, the mind would not have fallen in the battle with the enemy." (Poemen 16)[13]

Poemen's procedure here is strongly allegorical and even perhaps slightly comical. In any case, it is memorable. On the historical level of the text, a cook destroys the temple of the Lord. In fact, the Septuagint reading is necessary for Poemen's interpretation, for the Greek translators have misunderstood the Hebrew expression for "captain of the guard" and rendered it as "head cook." Poemen will further emphasize a dimension of the text he wishes to highlight by citing the text as "temple of the Lord" (ὁ ναὸς Κυρίου) rather than the Septuagint's "house of the Lord" (τὸν οἶκον Κυρίου). In any case, he does here with the text what the allegorical tradition had by this time so skillfully established; namely, he seizes upon some small detail in a text, a text that at first glance holds little promise of being especially relevant to an audience so far removed from its original historical circumstances, and he finds in that detail some firm insight about a central concern of the spiritual life.

Poemen's brief word presupposes a knowledge of the particular moment of biblical history in question. The word would unfold further in the med-

---

[13] PG 65:323C.

itating disciple's mind while reading or reflecting on the details of the biblical passage. In 2 Kgs 25:8–9 we read, "Nabuzardan, the head cook, came to Jerusalem and stood before the king of Babylon. And he burnt the house of the Lord, and the king's house, and all the houses of Jerusalem. Every house did the head cook burn." Poemen's allegorical reading of this historical moment is brief and to the point, expressed with a standard exegetical expression that signals allegory: "That is," (Τοῦτο δέ ἐστιν). The head cook coming to Jerusalem is gluttony coming to the soul. Monks would recognize in this interpretation more than may first meet the eye of the uninitiated. Gluttony is the first in the classical list of eight evil thoughts that afflict a monk,[14] and so this moment in Israel's history is showing—the scriptures are the divine confirmation of this fact—what the monastic tradition knows to be true also of gluttony: if this first evil thought is allowed into the city, the whole city will be destroyed.

Poemen, whether consciously or not, adds his own emphasis to his remembering this text by speaking of the "temple of the Lord" being burned, rather than the "house of the Lord" as the Septuagint has it. He also interprets this allegorically. This temple is the mind (ὁ νοῦς), a term that the monastic tradition, especially through Evagrius, has favored as expressing the very center of the monk's being, his being made for knowledge of God. And is not his choice of the word *temple* perhaps explained and justified by an only half-conscious memory or echo of the Pauline texts, "Do you not know that your body is a temple of the Holy Spirit, who is within you?" (1 Cor 6:19).[15] Is this what causes Poemen to substitute "temple" for "house" in the biblical text?

Poemen uses another word not found in the biblical text that likewise exposes the theological conceptions that are guiding his allegorical interpretation. He says, "the mind would not have fallen (κατέπιπτεν) in battle with the enemy." This image and this word, καταπίπτω, are commonly used in the Origenic tradition to refer to the fall of the mind, a struggle that is repeated in the life of each monk.[16] Whatever the explanation for this kind of language and theological framework in Poemen, with his straightforward application of the allegorical method he has managed to express in just a few lines an insight that is of fundamental importance in the monastic tradition; namely, the intimate relationship between the

---

[14] Evagrius and Cassian both are responsible for the classic formulations, but the teaching is not peculiar or original to them. For Evagrius, see *Praktikos* 6 and 7. For Cassian, see the *Institutes* V. For the history of this teaching, see A. and C. Guillaumont, *Praktikos*, 1:90–93.

[15] See also 1 Cor 3:16; 2 Cor 6:16; Eph 2:22.

[16] See καταπίπτω in G. W. H. Lampe, *A Patristic Greek Lexicon* (Oxford: Clarendon, 1961), 714–15. Poemen, as well as Evagrius, identifies gluttony as the first of problems to arrive for the monk, but he also specifies that it arrives in the *soul* and causes the *mind* to *fall*. This is a method of exegesis, a style of theological thought and precision typical of Evagrius. See ACW *Ad Monachos*, 181–94.

ascetical practices that monks undertake and their contemplative goals.[17] Allowing gluttony to enter (destroying asceticism) will mean the fall of the mind (destroying contemplation).

We should attempt to gauge the effect of this procedure. If Poemen only wished to speak about gluttony and contemplation, he did not need to talk about Nabuzardan to do so. But allegory is a tool that enables him to discover a deeper mystery; namely, that there is a continuity between the history of Israel—in this case, one particular detail about a head cook burning down a temple—and the struggle of the monk. With such a discovery, the monk's life is taken up into a drama far larger than a personal struggle with gluttony or, for that matter, any other of the principal evil thoughts. The monk is living the very story of the Bible. It is his guide. In carefully understanding its stories, there is wisdom and practical advice.[18]

In the anonymous series of the apophthegmata, this same interpretation of the figure of Nabuzardan is also found; it is not attributed to Poemen. It may be the case that Poemen's name was forgotten in the retelling or that another father, his name also lost, repeats his interpretation. It does not much matter; it shows a tradition being passed along. But that version of the story is interesting for a citation of words of Jesus that accompany the explanation of the figure of the head cook. Jesus' words are presented as making the same point as the figure of Nabuzardan. It is Jesus as teacher who acts as bridge now between this detail of Old Testament history and the monk who here can understand that he not only is living that same story but is doing so in obedience to the words of Jesus, who said, "Take heed lest at any time your hearts be overcharged with surfeiting and drunkenness, and cares of this life" (Luke 21:34).[19] The meditating monk could add to these words of Jesus something like, "Because this causes the mind to fall in battle."

"BUY A TOMB LIKE ABRAHAM"

A brother asked Abba Poemen, "What should I do?" The old man said to him, "Abraham, when he entered the promised land, bought a sepulchre for himself and by means of this tomb, he inherited the land." The brother said to him, "What is a tomb?"

---

[17] In Evagrius this division is classically expressed as *praktikē* and knowledge, or *theōria*. In Cassian it is *actualis scientia* and *contemplatio*.

[18] For example, Cassian shows that the enemy nations of Israel are understood as representing the eight principal vices. See *Conferences* V, 16–19. Or see the principle enunciated by Evagrius in *KG* VI, 71: "In the same way that perceptible nations are opposed to perceptible Israel, so are there spiritual nations opposed to the spiritual Israel." PO 28, 247.

[19] *Apophthegmata Patrum*, Collectio anonyma, ed. F. Nau, 466.

The old man said to him, "A place of tears and compunction."
(Poemen 50)[20]

To the traditional request by a disciple for a word—here specified as
wondering what to do—Poemen responds with a brief summary of a story
told at considerable length in chapter 23 of the Book of Genesis. The disciple is presumed to know the story; only then does Poemen's interpretation appear in its fullest impact. His reading of the biblical chapter is very
condensed; but, interestingly, it is entirely in accord with the literal sense
of the story that is told there. Chapter 23 has all the atmosphere of a well-
told Semitic tale, enjoying the style of Abraham's bargaining for the tomb,
but even more so—this is the point of the story—Abraham's ingenuity in
establishing a later claim to this land in virtue of his purchase of a tomb.
This is the very point that Poemen stresses: "and by means of this tomb
(καί δία τοῦ τάφου) he inherited the land." It is a very sound reading of the
literal sense of the text.

This is Poemen's response to the question, "What should I do?" The disciple asks for an interpretation, and we shall examine that in a moment. But
it is worth noting that a more capable disciple may not have needed to ask
for an interpretation. Very often—and this is true throughout the apophthegmata and not only with Poemen—a father responds to a request for a
word simply by citing a biblical verse or, as in this case, a biblical story. That
should be enough. The disciple then departs to meditate on it. As the story
is told here, the disciple asks immediately for an interpretation. It may have
occurred that way, or the story may collapse into one scene what would
have been a second visit to confirm an interpretation or to be helped
beyond an impasse. In any case, it is worth our observing that in Poemen's
first answer, before the interpretation, he gives an answer that in itself is no
more than a literal statement: Abraham bought a tomb and inherited the
land. But such a statement is obviously no answer to the disciple's question
unless another sense beyond the literal is implied. The disciple is to find it.
He has asked what he should do, and Poemen tells him he is to do what
Abraham did, but certainly not literally. Here allegory becomes the
method that will show the way toward how the disciple can do what Abraham did. I draw attention to this detail because it can help us to sense the
reasons and the spirit with which allegorical exegesis functioned in the
desert. This is not some idle speculation or toying with texts. The operative presupposition for the monks was that the Bible was a divinely inspired
text "given as types" (1 Cor 10:6) for them.[21] Allegory was one way for
them to discover how.

---

[20] PG 65:333B.
[21] See Cassian, *Conferences* V, 16.

The disciple presses for an interpretation of a detail, and not merely for a general interpretation. He has already understood the allegory in part; namely, that he is to see himself in Abraham; he has already understood what inheriting the land refers to. But he does not understand and so asks, "What is a tomb?" Again, we note how straightforwardly the allegorical method is functioning here. He does not expect the answer, "A tomb is where you put dead people." The question "What is a tomb?" means to ask about the allegorical meaning of the tomb. Poemen answers simply, "A place of tears and compunction (Τόπος κλαυθμοῦ καὶ πένθους)."

This is the word, this is the message, that Poemen wishes to give his inquiring disciple. What should a monk do? He should weep and be filled with compunction. Poemen has chosen with skill a biblical story to illustrate this point, a dimension that he considered fundamental to monastic practice.[22] Throughout the whole of chapter 23 of Genesis there is an atmosphere of sorrow and weeping because of the death of Sarah. The text speaks of the mourning of Abraham, using in v. 2 a word so important for monastic spirituality, πενθῆσαι, the word Poemen uses as a noun in his terse interpretation: πένθους. The whole chapter can be—and Poemen knows this—instruction on tears and compunction.

This biblical story is well chosen by Poemen for yet another reason, because a different dimension of the story enables him to suggest—this part of the interpretation is not explicit—the scope of tears and compunction. These are not an end in themselves. Poemen stresses, "*by means of this tomb*, he inherited the land." The promised land obviously functions here in Poemen's implied allegory as an image for the goal of the monastic life, be that called contemplation, prayer, knowledge. So, once again in only a very brief word the two basic stages of the monastic life are expressed as the deepest sense of a biblical text: the asceticism of tears, the promised land of contemplation.[23]

Again we should attempt to gauge the effect of the exegetical procedure that is operative here. The bare content of Poemen's message is something like "weep now and there is hope for later." But expressed like that, such a content moves no one. Instead, this content is delivered as the deepest sense of a biblical scene that involves one of the greatest "types" of the Old Testament, Abraham. And the disciple is invited to work with a strong image: a tomb. His monastic life is his being like Abraham. His monastic life is buying a tomb, which he shall do by tears and compunction, weeping just as Abraham wept; losing a loved one, just as Abraham did; but

---

[22] See Poemen 119: "for weeping is the way that the Scripture and our Fathers have handed down to us" (PG 65:353A).

[23] In one of the apophthegmata Poemen laments that monks are tending to forget the importance of the goal of asceticism. He says, "Many of our Fathers have become valiant in asceticism, but in finesse of thought there are very few" (Poemen 106; PG 65:348C).

thereby also establishing a right to a heavenly inheritance, just as Abraham established his rights to inherit the land. The whole monastic tradition teaches again and again that a monk must cry and be in mourning, and Poemen teaches here that this is the way taught to us by the scriptures. But he also teaches that there is hope in this mourning, for words of Jesus himself sound just like the language of chapter 23 of Genesis and just like Poemen's summary: "Blessed are they who mourn (πενθοῦντες), for they shall be comforted. Blessed are the meek, for they shall inherit the land (κληρουνομήσουσιν τὴν γῆν)" (Matt 5:4–5).

THE CANAANITE WOMAN AND ABIGAIL

> Abba Poemen said, "The reason why we are subject to such great temptations is that we do not guard our name and place, as the Scripture says. Do we not see the Canaanite woman accepting her name and for that reason the Saviour gave her rest? Or again, Abigail, who said to David, "On me be the sin," and he heard her and loved her. Abigail is a figure of the soul, and David a figure of the divinity. If, therefore, the soul accuses herself before the Lord, the Lord loves her. (Poemen 71)[24]

Poemen offers an explanation for why monks are subject to so many temptations, and the explanation would be especially strange were he not expressly to have stated that this is "as the scripture says." Even then the scriptural references are very condensed. Monks are subject to temptations, he says, because they do not guard their name and their place. What can this mean? What name? What place? Scripture will tell us. Poemen makes reference to one scene from the New Testament and one from the Old, and although the placing of these two scenes in tandem is certainly a surprise, a brief analysis of Poemen's logic will reveal that his choice is well made.

First, we should notice the words "Do we not see?" With such an expression he means to evoke well-known episodes from the Gospels and from the Old Testament, but he refers to them only in the most general way. They are to be "seen," that is, remembered, imagined. If one is unfamiliar with these episodes, the explanation of Poemen is too tightly condensed; and the word he gives becomes an incentive to send the inquiring disciple to search for the meaning within the details of the text. This surely is one of the purposes that the desert fathers had in giving words for meditation that are enigmatic and condensed.

---

[24] PG 65:340B.

Of the Canaanite woman Poemen says only that she accepted her name and for that reason the Lord gave her peace. As the monk "sees" this scene, perhaps referring to the text itself to understand Poemen's meaning, he recalls that a Canaanite woman approaches the Lord, crying out for the cure of her possessed daughter (Matt 15:21–28). Her request is eventually answered, and this fact is meant to stand in contrast to the monks, who "are subject to such great temptations," that is, who remain possessed of a demon like the Canaanite's daughter. The Canaanite woman guards her name, and so her daughter is cured. The monks do not and so remain subject. Poemen, understanding the Gospel text on its literal level quite correctly, sees the key to her request being granted in the interchange that takes place between the woman and Jesus. Jesus responds to her request with a rebuff that has surprised generations of readers, and it is directly on this rebuff that Poemen focuses his attention. Jesus gives the woman a name; he all but calls her a dog, perhaps making a pun between the word *Canaanite* (Χαναναία) and *little dogs* (κυνάρια).[25] He says, "It is not fit to take the children's bread and to cast it to dogs." Her answer is her "accepting her name." She says, "Yes, Lord, but even the dogs eat of the crumbs which fall from their masters' tables." She takes the name "dog," but poses her request anyway. She accepts her place, not one of the "house of Israel" (v. 24), but a foreigner conscious that she has no rights before the Lord. Yet she makes her request anyway. Thus, "to guard one's name and one's place" is to know how to accept a humiliation, the humiliation of one's own proper condition, one's own place; namely, not being a member of the chosen house of Israel but only a foreign dog who must beg before the Lord. Poemen has read the Gospel scene correctly and immediately applied it to the monastic situation. If monks could pray like this Canaanite woman, they would not be subject to the temptations from which they in fact continue to suffer.

Although in this lesson Poemen refers to the central point of the Gospel story, he does so without especially close attention to textual details, apart from the name given the woman by Jesus. Indeed, he summarizes the benefit to the woman not with a word that occurs in the text but with a word commonly employed in monastic vocabulary to refer to the goal of the monastic life, a word used to contrast with the beginning of the monastic life in which one is subject to temptations. He says, "and for that reason the Saviour gave her rest (ἀνέπαυσεν)."[26] With this kind of vocabulary, Poemen is able to "see" the scene more than to "read" the text and draw

---

[25] In any case, Poemen seems to see a pun, which enables him to focus on the theme of the "name."

[26] See ἀνάπαυσις, meanings listed under B. 2–4 in Lampe, *Patristic Greek Lexicon*, 115.

his own conclusions with a monastic vocabulary.[27] To accept one's name and one's place like this Canaanite woman would free monks from temptations and bring them to the goal of the monastic life: rest.

The connection with the Old Testament figure of Abigail is that in that story also a name is involved and once again not a very nice one. To understand Poemen's point here it is necessary to know the whole of the long chapter 25 of 1 Samuel, to which Poemen refers, as we have noted, only in a very condensed way. However, with this story he does perform a little more explicit exegesis than he has done previously. The situation of chapter 25 tells of an insult that David has received from Nabal, whose wife Abigail is. Abigail, without telling her husband, takes gifts and hurries with them to placate David. She intends to apologize in the name of her husband, or actually to take his place. It is this particular moment that Poemen cites explicitly: Abigail says to David, "On me be the sin" (1 Sam 25:24).[28] This in itself does not explain the meaning of what Poemen started with; namely, "guarding our name and our place." But Poemen either expects his disciple to know the rest of Abigail's plea or to discover it by recourse to the biblical text. In what follows, what she says to David does involve accepting a name: "Let not my lord, I pray thee, take to heart this pestilent man, for according to his name, so is he; Nabal is his name, and folly is with him." Folly is what the text understands the name Nabal to mean, and, standing in his place, Abigail accepts this name and proposes it as the explanation for his foolish actions. She accepts the name and pleads for mercy. David is moved by this and forgives. When Nabal dies ten days later, David sends for Abigail to make her his wife. Thus Poemen's summary of the story: "he heard her and loved her."

Poemen has done well to bring the Gospel passage of the Canaanite woman together with this story. In both cases he has accurately read the text on the literal level, and on that level alone he has found a deep relation between the two passages. In both stories, women with no rights before a lord—one is a Canaanite, the other the wife of David's enemy—come before that lord and humbly accept a name and a position from

---

[27] Actually Poemen has foreshortened to some extent the final point of the Gospel passage by drawing attention to the benefits to the woman, whereas in the Gospel itself her humble plea has won the cure for another. The choice of the word ἀνέπαυσεν may be inspired in part by Poemen's memory of the story in the Marcan parallel, where, though the woman is identified as Syrophoenician and as such is less suited to the point Poemen wishes to make, the story ends with more elaboration than is found in Matthew's account. In Mark we read, "'the demon has left your daughter.' And she went home, and found the child lying in bed, and the demon gone" (Mark 7:29–30). In Matthew we find: "'O woman, great is your faith! Be it done for you as you desire.' And her daughter was healed instantly" (Matt 15:28).

[28] The Septuagint has ἐν ἐμοὶ κύριέ μου ἡ ἀδικία μου, which Poemen has cited as ἐν ἐμοί ἐστιν ἡ ἁμαρτία.

which the only recourse is to plead for that lord's mercy, granted in both cases because of the humble acceptance of the name and the place.

Poemen sees the two Testaments as speaking the same lesson, and this already, of course, is interesting as an exegetical procedure. The Holy Spirit, author of both Testaments, has hidden the link between the two episodes in a woman's acceptance of a disagreeable name. But even more interesting is the fact that Poemen finds it necessary to use allegory to interpret the Old Testament text before it can be fully understood to be delivering the same lesson. With the story from the Gospel, Poemen expects monks simply to make the application to themselves. He does not feel it necessary to explain—beyond asking, "Do we not see...?"—that the monk is to see himself in the position of the Canaanite. She comes pleading before Jesus, and the monk is to do the same. Strictly speaking there is no allegory involved here; it is simply a case of applying the scene read on its literal level to the monk's own situation. However, such an application is not so obvious when the figures are an Abigail and a David. Thus, the need for allegory. Poemen performs the operation on the text easily and straightforwardly, and he uses a technical term from the tradition of exegesis to do so. He says simply, "Abigail is a figure (πρόσωπον) of the soul, and David a figure of the divinity." It is a simple key of interpretation, but it shifts the level of all the material in the long chapter 25 of 1 Samuel, making it all available as an exposition of what the monk can hope for if he but guard his name and his place.

Poemen is not interested in teaching what we might call a naked content; in the present instance, something like the importance of humility as a means of avoiding temptation. He is interested in conveying a biblical content, for the Bible presents the monk with strong images and figures, key moments from a sacred history, in which are embedded many kinds and levels of wisdom suited for the monastic way of life. A good father directs his disciples to some portion of the sacred text and gives them the key that will let that text become useful to them. With the simple allegorical explanation "Abigail is a figure of the soul, and David a figure of the divinity," one receives from the text not only what one should do but the very words of a prayer: "On me be the sin." And recourse to the whole chapter, where much is said both by Abigail and by David, gives even more words (Abigail's words) for the soul to pray (vv. 26–31) and offers a divine word (David's words) in response to the soul (vv. 32–35).

Poemen expects this further exploration. He expects the monk to rejoice in the blessings that Abigail's (the soul's) action and words elicit from the mouth of David (of the divinity). And when later Nabal dies and David sends for Abigail to make her his wife, the soul knows from the text to "arise and do reverence with her face to the ground and say, 'Behold thy servant is for a handmaid to wash the feet of thy servants'" (v. 41). These are words and scenes that Poemen has summarized with his condensed "If, therefore, the soul accuses herself before the Lord, the Lord loves her."

"It Is the Holy Spirit Who Says That"

One of the Fathers asked Abba Poemen, "Who is it who says, 'I am a companion of all who fear you'" (Ps 118:63), and the old man said, "The Holy Spirit is the one who says that." (Poemen 136)[29]

This extremely pithy word hides a wealth of opportunity for meditation, and behind it lies an exegetical procedure that had been practiced within the mainline traditions already for some centuries. In the biblical text at large, but especially in the Psalter, there is a kind of exegesis that modern scholars have labeled "prosopological" exegesis, that is, the search for the person, the πρόσωπον, who is mysteriously speaking in the biblical text, particularly when the text is cast in the first person.[30] The question posed to Poemen comes from within this tradition. A line from the psalms is cast in the first person, and to understand it at its deepest level, it is necessary to know the "person" who is speaking.

The questioner has taken the verse out of its context, a procedure common in prosopological exegesis, rather like what is done in a scholion, where the genre allows for a deepened understanding of a single verse, not usually by reference to its context but by reading the text against the background of the whole of the Christian mysteries. Poemen does not look to the context of the psalm to discover who is speaking. His reference is larger. His swift and direct answer has all the force of a powerful word from a master interpreter, for he surely surprises the inquirer, and subsequent readers, with his claim that it is the Holy Spirit who says these words. If the verse is given an interpretation by reference to its context in the psalm, or even if it is given the more likely interpretation it would have as a single verse separated from its context, the speaker at first glance would appear to be the psalmist proclaiming that he walks with others who fear the Lord. Even within the framework of prosopological exegesis, one might more readily expect a christological interpretation; namely, that it is Christ who

---

[29] PG 65:356B.

[30] An examination of this exegesis in the Psalter is the subject of the studies by M. J. Rondeau, *Les commentaires patristiques du Psautier (III-V siècles)*, vols. 1–2, Orientalia Christiana Analecta 219, 220 (Rome, 1982,1985). For the basic description of this kind of exegesis and its widespread practice, see 1:18–21.

is companion with others who fear the Lord. Within what sort of theological understanding can Poemen's interpretation that it is the Holy Spirit who says that be grasped?

Poemen is speaking a monastic language, and monks would recognize in the very common biblical expression "fear of the Lord" the sacred text's indication of the beginning of the monastic life, under the influence of "The fear of the Lord is the beginning of wisdom" (as in Ps 110:10; Prov 1:7; 9:10; Sir 1:16). Evagrius, who is often thought to represent a different tradition from Poemen's, is surely representative of the whole desert tradition in the clarity and consistency with which he lays down fear of the Lord as the beginning of monastic life.[31] In this context, Poemen's interpretation of the psalm verse crosses the whole arc of the monastic life, from its beginning in fear to its goal, here described by the sacred text as companionship with the Holy Spirit.[32] This is the gift of Poemen's interpretation. He surprises us by uncovering in just a few words of scripture the whole range of monastic life from beginning to end, and in so doing he renders the text both memorable and fertile. Throughout a monk's whole life he can seek to fear the Lord; and repeating, "I am a companion of all who fear You," he will be strengthened and consoled with the knowledge that "the Holy Spirit is the one who says that." [33]

We perhaps are meant to detect the Holy Spirit in yet another word where Poemen cites Anthony. In any case, the text is interesting as yet another example of prosopological exegesis.

A brother asked Abba Poemen, "Is it good to pray (Καλὸν τὸ προσεύχεσθαι;)?" The old man said to him that Abba Anthony said, "This utterance proceeds (ἐκπορεύεται) from the person of

---

[31] See, e.g., the Prologue of the *Praktikos*, or *Praktikos* 81, *M* 4, *Scholia on Proverbs* 2:5. For my own opinions about drawing too strong a contrast between a Poemen and an Evagrius, see my *'Ad Monachos' of Evagrius Ponticus*, 353–59.

[32] Evagrius also sometimes indicates the Holy Spirit as a goal of the monastic asceticism that fear of the Lord sets in motion. On this theme in his writings, see G. Bunge, "In Geist und Wahrheit," in *Das Geistgebet: Studien zum Traktat "De Oratione" des Evagrios Pontikos* (Cologne, 1987), 88–109, and *Geistliche Vaterschaft: Christliche Gnosis bei Evagrios Pontikos* (Regensburg, 1988), 37–38.

[33] In the *Apophthegmata* under Anthony 32, we also find Anthony completing the Old Testament and the beginner's fear of God by a New Testament text, with the same tight exegesis operating: "Abba Anthony said, 'I no longer fear God, but I love Him. For love casts out fear' (1 John 4:18)" (PG 65:85C). It is difficult not to draw attention to the first half of v. 16 in 1 Cor 3 and wonder if it does not also shed some further light on Poemen's interpretation of Nabuzardan's burning of the temple, which we examined above. Fear of the Lord sets the monk on guard against the attacks of demons like gluttony. In the context of that story we could say that fear of the Lord prevents the temple of the Holy Spirit from being burned.

the Lord (ἐκ προσώπου Κυρίου): 'Comfort (παρακαλεῖτε) my people, says the Lord; comfort (Isa 40:1).'" (Poemen 87)[34]

The question put to Poemen is in some ways an odd one or seems unnecessary. Surely no one would expect the answer, "No, it is not good to pray?" Perhaps the question should be translated something like, "Is prayer beautiful?" or "Is there comfort in prayer?" There are in fact in desert monasticism two kinds of prayer: one kind in which the monk prays short, intense prayers in the midst of temptations and trials and another in which the word is synonymous with the contemplative goal of the monastic life.[35] So the questioner may be asking about this second kind of prayer. In any case, our interest is in the exegetical procedure that Anthony, and now Poemen remembering him, use on the text they cite. The interpreter has identified the person speaking in the Isaiah text and does so by referring to this technical language of exegesis, ἐκ προσώπου Κυρίου. Thus, Anthony and Poemen prepare carefully for the citation of the biblical verse, and in that preparation lies the whole exegetical exercise. It is simple enough to understand who is saying these words, and the disciple's question will thereby be answered. The speaker is identified as the Lord. In fact, to make this distinction of persons clear, Anthony and/or Poemen, in citing the Isaiah text, change the Septuagint's λέγει ὁ Θεός to λέγει Κύριος. The Isaiah text to be cited is called an "utterance which proceeds from the person of the Lord." It is probably too much to claim it with certainty, but it is certainly not too much to wonder if the careful disciple is not meant to uncover a surprise in the formulation of this solemn introduction. Does it mean to indicate that the Holy Spirit, the Comforter, ὁ παράκλητος, comes forth from words of the Lord[36] and that the "comfort" of which the Isaiah text speaks is ultimately found for the monk in the presence of the Holy Spirit? It seems to me that only by pushing the sense of Anthony's and Poemen's words this far do they function as an answer to the question posed. Is prayer good or beautiful? Yes, when the Holy Spirit is the monk's companion, when the Holy Spirit dwells in the monk, when the Holy Spirit comforts.

CONCLUSION

We have examined only a few of the more than two hundred apophthegmata that are found under Poemen's name in the alphabetical

---

[34] PG 65:344A.

[35] This distinction is classically laid out in the prologue to Evagrius's *Chapters on Prayer*.

[36] The Greek says literally "proceeds" (ἐκπορεύεται), probably not in the technical sense of this term, though ἐκπόρευσις is used of the procession of the Holy Spirit from the Father. See Lampe, *Patristic Greek Lexicon*, 436–37.

collection. Many more of them contain examples of very interesting and sophisticated exegesis. I have tried here at least to indicate the kind of wealth that awaits the student of that material. Nonetheless, we have perhaps done enough to allow ourselves some conclusions that I believe would be further borne out in the examination of other texts.

I would not want to claim that Poemen himself is a sophisticated exegete. However, I do wish to suggest that he relies heavily on sophisticated exegetical traditions in order to create what seem in his hands simple but profound interpretations of biblical texts. His exegesis does not unfold or defend the elaborate arguments with which his theological predecessors carved out the case for the legitimacy of allegory, for the reasons why one Testament can speak to another, for the moral application of a text in the reader's present. But his exegesis presumes all that. Its gains are his heritage. And so he uses allegory with ease and yet in ways that bring profound insights to a text. He quickly brings a text from one Testament to speak to the other, making no apologies for it. And he swiftly brings the text to bear on the present, uncovering its moral implications.

It is this last point that is perhaps most characteristic not only of the *how* with which he reads the scriptures but also of the *why*. He reads them as the source of wisdom for his own monastic life and for the life of those who regard him as their father. He knows the exegetical techniques that enable him to bring the text immediately to bear on the existential situation of the monk, whether that be what it means *for the monk* to sell a mantle and buy a sword or what relevance *for monks* there may be in Abraham's buying a tomb, and so forth.

In addition, we have seen that there is a sort of grid operative in Poemen's exegesis which, when layed over the text, often causes the two basic phases of the monastic life to emerge from it; namely, the ascetic life and the life of contemplation and prayer. We moderns tend to view this as no more than a reading of our own concerns into the text, an eisegesis. But I think something deeper than that is operative here. The conception of monastic life according to these two fundamental phases—however they are named and differently exposed within the various monastic traditions— may itself be considered a general summary of a fundamental biblical and Christian insight; namely, that one must suffer so to enter into glory.[37] The monastic way is an arrangement of life according to this insight, not the only possible arrangement but nonetheless a very firm arrangement for all that. Once such a premise is accepted, as it is by the monks, then "Moses and the prophets and the psalms" and the Lord himself (see Luke 24:44) all speak to the mystery. Each particular text can shed new light on this pat-

---

[37] It is superfluous to cite texts, but a sampling from various parts of the biblical text makes the point: Mark 8:31; Luke 9:31; 24:25–26; Acts 17:2–3; 26:22–23; Rom 8:17; Phil 2:5–11 (esp. v. 5); 3:8–11; Jas 1:2–5; 5:10–11; 1 Pet 1:6–8.

tern of cross and glory, and through deep insight into some detail of the history of Israel the monk can learn, for example, that gluttony destroys contemplation, tears bring an inheritance, humiliation before the Lord awakens his love, fear of the Lord causes the indwelling of the Holy Spirit. This kind of attitude about the sacred text and the exegesis it brings in its wake allow monks to understand in their own way what all Christians are meant to understand in reading the scriptures: the story of Israel and the story of Jesus are the story of each one. If that is so, we see why people would approach a father like Poemen, with the Bible either literally or metaphorically in hand, and say, "Father, what should I do? Father, give me a word."

8

THE FATHERS OF POEMEN AND
THE EVAGRIAN CONNECTION

T he exegesis of Poemen examined in the previous chapters forms a
significant part of the larger context in which, among other things,
the works of Evagrius should be read. Unfortunately, an unconta-
minated memory of Evagrius in many monastic sources has not reached us
because of the Origenist crisis at the end of the fourth century, and even
more so because of the second Origenist crisis in the middle of the sixth
century. Often contemporary scholars repeat the prejudices against Evagrius of the ancient texts. Of Poemen, L. Regnault says, "Avec l'abbé Poemen, l'école de spiritualité du désert a vraiment atteint un sommet et c'est
aussi avec lui que le genre apophtegmatique parvient à son apogée."[1] He
represents the continuation of the tradition of the monasticism of Scetis
after the Origenist crisis at the end of the fourth century and consequently,
it has been suggested, may be representing a tradition more likely cautious
about anything tainted with Origenism. Thus, he is sometimes described
as one of those (supposedly simple) Coptic monks (supposedly) not much
interested in what is termed the "speculation" of monks influenced by
Origen. The basis of the collections later grouped under the title *Apophthegmata Patrum* very likely grew up in a circle around Poemen.[2] They are
one of the best sources we have for knowing fourth- and fifth-century
monasticism in Egypt, but in their present redaction they come to us in a
form that is not especially friendly to the memory of Evagrius and to others
who were considered to have suffered the influence of Origen.[3]

---

[1] L. Regnault, *Les sentences des Pères du désert: Collection Alphabétique* (Solesmes, 1981),
220. Cf. W. Bousset, *Apophthegmata: Studien zur Geschichte des ältesten Mönchtums* (Tübingen, 1923), 60–71. Bousset calls Poemen "der eigentlichen Vermittler und Fortpflanzer der
Tradition des sketischen Kreises" (p. 65).

[2] On this possibility with the necessary nuances, see J. C. Guy, *Les Apophtegmes des pères:
Collection systématique, chapitres I-IX,* Sources Chrétiennes 387 (Paris: Cerf, 1993), 83–84.

[3] For the evidence, see A. Guillaumont, *Les 'Képhalaia Gnostica' d'Évagre le Pontique,*
51–59. Also L. Regnault, "La prière continuelle 'monologistos' dans la littérature apophtegmatique," *Irénikon* 47 (1974): 467–93, esp. 477ff.

It is in part this dimension of the text that suggests to me the present investigation. In virtually all of my own studies on Evagrius I have argued both implicitly and explicitly that he ought to be considered more representative of a great deal of what was happening in Egyptian monasticism, that he ought not be considered some oddball, albeit an interesting one, but rather an excellent representative of some of the very best of the whole desert tradition. A comparison between Evagrius and Poemen would be a rather rigorous test of such a suggestion, for Poemen is indisputably a representative of the mainstream. Therefore, if there is anything like Evagrius in Poemen or vice versa, it might require a reassessment of where Evagrius is thought to fit within the whole tradition. I find myself suspicious of an assessment such as the following, which asserts of Evagrius, Cassian, and Palladius that they are authors "qui certes sont intéressants, mais qui ne représentent pas la tradition pure du terroir monastique égyptien. Or l'intérêt propre des Apophtegmes réside dans le fonds primitif qui s'est constitué aux quatrième et cinquième siècles, surtout à Scété, dans l'entourage de l'abbé Poemen."[4] To this it can at least be said that Evagrius, Cassian, and Palladius all three lived for some years in the desert, and their writings consequently reflect firsthand testimony, which, it must be admitted, the hand of the final redactor of the *Apophthegmata Patrum* does not. Surely they can be given some credit for reflecting some part of the tradition. However, this direction of argument is not the one I wish to pursue here. I wish to read the *Apophthegmata* here without solving the problem of how reliable they may or may not be as a historical source. I am reading them more as a witness to a particular vision of monastic spirituality; I will focus on the figure of Poemen and then compare that with Evagrius's vision.[5]

[4] L. Regnault, *Les Sentences, Troisième recueil & tables* (Solesmes, 1976), 8.

[5] Regnault's remark represents a much larger controversy among scholars of ancient monasticism in which positions are taken and evaluations made about the degree of literacy or not among fourth- and fifth-century Egyptian monks. Based largely on the influence of Athanasius's *Life of Anthony* and the final redaction of the *Apophthegmata*, many scholars believe that the purest movement of Egyptian monasticism is represented in illiterate peasant types. K. Heussi (*Der Ursprung des Mönchtums* [Tübingen, 1936], 278) represents an old example: "Die Mehrzahl der Mönche wird aus Analphabeten bestanden haben." In his authoritative work, D. Chitty says as much: "Antony was an illiterate layman, and the majority of the Egyptian monks were much the same" (*The Desert a City: An Introduction to the Study of Egyptian and Palestinian Monasticism under the Christian Empire* [Crestwood, 1966], 86). Many scholars simply repeat these opinions, for example, F. Young, *From Nicaea to Chalcedon: A Guide to the Literature and Its Background* (London, 1983), 47; R. Hanson, *The Search for the Christian Doctrine of God* (Edinburgh, 1988), 268; J. Binns, *Ascetics and Ambassadors of Christ* (Oxford, 1996), 203. However, such views have been strongly challenged in recent years. In Evagrius's regard, see G. Bunge, "Évagre le Pontique et les deux Macaire," *Irenikon* 56 (1983): 215–27, 323–60. For Antony, see S. Rubenson, *The Letters of St. Anthony: Origenist Theology, Monastic Tradition and the Making of a Saint* (Lund, 1990); for specific discussion about the *Apophthegmata*, see pp. 131, 145–62. For a general assessment, see M. Sheridan, "Il mondo spirituale e intellettuale del primo monachesimo

J. C. Guy rightly notes that Poemen appears less as a pioneer of monastic life than as the wise steward of an inheritance that fell to him. Understanding that with the sack of Scetis in 407 a page of monastic history had been turned, Poemen seeks to ensure that the treasures of the previous century not be lost. He distributes this inheritance in two ways. First, he preserves the words and actions of many fathers and passes them on now as his own. Second, by his own words and teaching he passes on the heritage of his forebears.[6] This suggests at least two possible tracks of investigation for comparing Evagrius and Poemen in their respective roles within desert monasticism. One could study the fathers Poemen cites, or one could study his own teaching, in both cases seeking comparisons. It is the first of these tracks, Poemen's fathers, that I wish to follow here.[7]

In both Poemen and Evagrius, reverence for their monastic fathers is notable. To Evagrius actually we owe the oldest of any collections of apophthegmata, as, for example, at the end of the *Praktikos* (nos. 91–100), or at the end of the *Gnostikos* (nos. 44–48), or within the *Chapters on Prayer* (nos. 106–12). He teaches also about the importance of the monk's relationship with a father, as in *Ad Monachos* (nos. 88–92).[8] This is not unusual. The whole of Egyptian monasticism is shot through with this attitude, and it is as close as we come to an institutional means of passing on a tradition. So, it is not surprising to find the same regard for fathers and tradition in Poemen. I propose studying here the actual fathers that Poemen himself cites in giving his own word to disciples. In each case I want to ask the question of how that teaching stands in relationship to Evagrius's teaching. In some instances the connection is strong, in others more meager. But when the teachings are collected together, a picture emerges that shows a Poemen and an Evagrius perhaps not so widely different, as some would have it, in the traditions they represent.[9]

---

egiziano," in *L'Egitto cristiano: Aspetti e problemi in età tardo-antica,* ed. A. Camplani (Rome, 1997), 177–216. Very helpful for providing more concrete historical information and for thus shaping a more nuanced view are the studies of E. Wipszycka, collected in E. Wipszycka, *Études sur le christianisme dans l'Égypte de l'antiquité tardive* (Rome, 1996). These much-needed, balancing reactions should not cause us to forget that we nonetheless have in the *Apophthegmata Patrum* a precious witness to monastic life in fourth- and fifth-century Egypt, even if they cannot be taken at face value and as the only witness. G. Gould, aware of the controversy I have only indicated in this note, speaks of the ways in which the text can in fact provide a historically reliable picture. See G. Gould, *The Desert Fathers on Monastic Community* (Oxford, 1993), 9–25.

[6] Guy, *Apophtegmes des pères,* 78–79.

[7] These are conveniently identified by Guy, *Apophtegmes des pères,* 78.

[8] See my commentary on this in ACW *Ad Monachos,* 114–18.

[9] Bunge offers a model of this sort of comparative study in his "Évagre le Pontique et les deux Macaire" (cited above in n. 5). These studies did much to bring contemporary evaluations of Evagrius to admit his presence much closer to the mainstream of Egyptian monasti-

I would like to begin first with a small word of Poemen himself, in which he is not citing other fathers, but in which I think there is hidden an important key to understanding him correctly.

> Abba Poemen said, "Many of our fathers have become very courageous in asceticism, but in finesse of perception there are very few." (Πολλοὶ τῶν Πατέρων ἡμῶν ἐγένοντο ἀνδρεῖοι εἰς τὴν ἄσκησιν. εἰς δὲ τὴν λεπτότητα, εἶς, εἶς.) (Poemen 106)[10]

A word like this is a trap door that lets us crawl through to what I like to call the world under the text, that is, the actual world in which these monks lived. In this world Evagrius and Poemen begin to sound more alike. When Poemen contrasts asceticism to finesse in perception, Evagrius helps us to understand that this is not much different from something that is a cornerstone of his own thought; namely, the distinction between *praktikē* and knowledge, as well as the importance of always pointing *praktikē* beyond itself to the final goal of knowledge. If anything, in this word Poemen is lamenting in his own time the loss of something among the monks that certainly characterized the time of Evagrius and, before that, the time of the two Marcarii. Of this dimension of monastic experience the *Apophthegmata Patrum* give us few details, but they point to it frequently. As Guy has pointed out many years ago, the *Apophthegmata Patrum* are a collection mainly concerned to present the issues of *praktikē*. That they do not speak of what Evagrius would call the realm of knowledge should not be taken to mean that such was not a part of the monastic spirituality referred to by this text.[11] To imagine desert monasticism, so full of accounts of remarkable asceticism, as existing without also the experience of mystical prayer would be to, as Bunge suggests, "l'exposer au danger du

---

cism. This is the fruit of much of Bunge's work on Evagrius. The investigation I am conducting here is in some ways similar to what Bunge has done with the two Macarii, but it is more fragile because it is not possible to claim direct contact between Evagrius and Poemen. I am not claiming that Evagrius was a father for Poemen, as were the two Macarii for Evagrius. Instead I want to suggest that in both Poemen and Evagrius we find a common monastic tradition and evidence of a more peaceful coexistence and interchange among the learned and unlearned monks, between the centers of Nitria and Scetis. Chronologically with the two Macarii we are more toward the beginning of a tradition. With Poemen we are toward the end. Evagrius shows us some of what we have in the middle; namely, a development of what was in the beginning and—I hope to show here—still present in part toward the end.

[10] PG 65:348C. I have commented already on my understanding of the significance of this text in *'Ad Monachos' of Evagrius Ponticus,* 356–57. The English translations of Poemen and other texts from the alphabetical collection are, unless otherwise stated, by B. Ward in *The Sayings of the Desert Fathers: The Alphabetical Collection* (Kalamazoo, 1984).

[11] J. C. Guy, "Les Apophthegmata Patrum," in *Théologie de la vie monastique* (Paris, 1961), 73–83, here 82, esp. n. 32.

fakirisme."[12] In any case, let us turn now to the fathers whom Poemen cites by name.

ALONIUS

He [Poemen] also said that a brother questioned Abba Alonius saying, "What does it mean to be of 'no account' (ἐξουδέ-νωσις)?" And the old man said, "It means to be lower than irrational creatures and to know that they will not be condemned." (Poemen 41)[13]

This is a question about the meaning of a scriptural word, Greek ἐξουδένωσις, found in Psalm 21:6 (LXX): "I am a worm and not a man, a reproach of men, and scorn of the people (ἐξουθένημα λαοῦ)." Such a question is typical of the sort proposed to fathers, for the monks wanted to fulfill in their own lives the meaning of the various verses and so needed to understand them correctly. Poemen himself was a master at this, and in citing Alonius he shows that his own mastery was developed by noting how other fathers did it. Alonius's answer is given inside the logic of the scriptural verse, where he glosses "worm" with the explanation "irrational creatures" (ἀλόγων). This is perhaps a common enough explanation in the desert for a question like this. Concerning Evagrius, it can be noted that themes such as this are also present in his teaching. I think especially of his urging that the monk remember and even imagine in some detail the day of judgment.[14]

He [Poemen] also said, "As the old men were sitting at a meal one day, Abba Alonius got up to serve and when they saw that, they praised him. But he answered absolutely nothing. So one of them said to him privately, 'Why don't you answer the old men who are complimenting you?' Abba Alonius said to him, 'If I were to reply to them I should be accepting their praises.'" (Poemen 55)[15]

---

[12]Bunge, "Évagre le Pontique," 354. For a general reluctance in monks to speak about their mystical visions, see A. Guillaumont, "Les visions mystiques dans le monachisme oriental chrétien," in *Colloque organisé par le Secrétariat d'Etat à la Culture* (Paris, 1976), 116–27. One should not conclude from such reluctance that this dimension of monastic life was neither present nor important.

[13] PG 65:332C. Translation altered.

[14] *Rerum monachalium rationes* 9. M 54.

[15] PG 65:336A.

Clearly an edifying example of humility. Not much need to be said about it here. Poemen obviously remembers the scene approvingly, and the apophthegmata are full of such edifying examples. For our purposes in this study it is enough to note how central humility is in the teaching of Evagrius, which is sometimes overlooked by those who would draw attention only to his supposedly intellectual tendencies. For Evagrius humility is not merely some sort of monastic decoration that he feels required to give lip service to so that he can go on to discourse on what he really cares about; namely, knowledge. There is no knowledge without humility, humility concretely practiced as in the example of Alonius.[16]

AMMONAS

> Abba Poemen said that Abba Ammonas said, "A man can spend his whole time carrying an axe without succeeding in cutting down the tree; while another, with experience of tree-felling brings the tree down with a few blows. He said that the axe is discernment (διάκρισις)." (Poemen 52)[17]

Ammonas was a disciple of Anthony the Great, and as such he represents the very center of the Egyptian monastic tradition. Poemen passes on a word of his that has evidently come down through several generations. The word is a vivid metaphor for what describes a point of arrival for an accomplished monk; namely, discernment. The message is not unlike Poemen 106, with which I opened this study: asceticism in itself is useless unless it carries its practitioner to a level beyond. Here that level is identified with the key word διάκρισις, discernment.

Ammonas's expression of "a man spending his whole time" can perhaps be connected with another word of his found under his own name: "I have spent fourteen years in Scetis asking God night and day to grant me the victory over anger" (Ammonas 3).[18] Several things are striking about this. If this prayer went on for fourteen years, he must have had some personal experience of sometimes "spending his whole time" in a mistaken way. But the theme itself of the importance of a relentless struggle against anger cannot fail to strike the reader who knows Evagrius. This theme is so pervasive in Evagrius's writings as to render citations unnecessary. Even a

---

[16] I have studied the significance of humility in Evagrius's spiritual theology in ACW *Ad Monachos*, 259–65.

[17] PG 65:334D.

[18] PG 65:120B.

casual reader will notice how frequently it occurs.[19] The monk's time must
be passed in his cell, not failing to confront the evil thoughts with which
he must do battle. Ammonas knew this. "Sit in your cell and eat a little
every day, keeping the word of the publican always in your heart, and you
may be saved" (Ammonas 4).[20] But this staying in the cell was not merely
an ascetical practice. The fourteen letters preserved under his name speak
at length not only of the theme of the fight against temptations but—and
this is the important point—this as the preparation for acquiring the Holy
Spirit.[21]

Evagrius speaks of the importance of remaining in the cell also with the
same double-pronged theme of doing battle and acquiring knowledge:

> If the spirit of listlessness mounts you,
>   do not leave your house;
>   and do not turn aside in that hour from profitable wrestling.
> For like someone making money shine,
>   so will your heart be made to glow.[22]

Several generations later Poemen is still teaching in this way (Poemen
162). And he will use Ammonas again to make the point about the ultimate goal of the ascetical practice.

> He [Poemen] said that Abba Ammonas said, "A man may remain
> for a hundred years in his cell without learning how to live in the
> cell." (Poemen 96)[23]

This is a very pithy call to the inner substance of what staying in the cell
is about. It is not very different from "Many of our fathers have become
very courageous in asceticism, but in finesse of perception there are very
few" (Poemen 106).[24] To come full circle from where we began with
Ammonas, one way of expressing the goal of staying in the cell would be
to speak of the axe of discernment, which can fell a tree in several blows.
Such discernment is also expressed clearly as a goal in Evagrius's monastic
tradition. It is a part of the realm of gnosis, or knowledge. He says:

---

[19] For my own digestion of this theme, see my "Gentleness in the *Ad Monachos* of Evagrius
Ponticus." *Studia Monastica* 32 (1990): 295–321.

[20] PG 65:120C.

[21] Preserved in PO 10:567–616.

[22] *M* 55. H. Gressmann, "Nonnenspiegel und Mönchsspiegel des Euagrios Pontikos,"
Texte und Untersuchungen 39, no. 4 (1913): 157. For a commentary on this text with many
additional references, see ACW *Ad Monachos*, 265–73.

[23] PG 65:345B.

[24] As cited above at p. 145.

If an anchorite wants to receive the knowledge of discernment (γνῶσιν διακρίσεως), then let him first succeed in keeping the commandments eagerly (προθύμως), omitting nothing, then at the hour of prayer, "let him ask" knowledge "from God who gives to all generously and ungrudgingly" (James 1:5–6). (*On Evil Thoughts* 26)[25]

Evagrius is typically consistent in what he says here of discernment. That it belongs in the realm of knowledge is made clear first by the fact that keeping the commandments (*praktikē*) is its prelude. Then we see that he conceives of discernment as a kind of knowledge, and so the expression "knowledge of discernment." "The hour of prayer" is a common Evagrian expression for knowledge, knowledge that comes precisely through a way of praying.[26] Of Evagrius and discernment his disciple Palladius says, "He purified his mind to the highest degree and so was judged worthy of the gifts of knowledge, of wisdom, of discernment of spirits" (*LH* 38).[27]

ANTHONY

[Poemen] said of Abba Pambo that Abba Anthony used to say of him, "Through fearing God, he made the Spirit of God to dwell in him." (...ὅτι ἐκ τοῦ φοβεῖσθαι τὸν Θεὸν ἐποίησε τὸ Πνεῦμα τοῦ Θεοῦ οἰκεῖν ἐν αὐτῷ.) (Poemen 75)[28]

This word makes it clear that Poemen is teaching from an already well established tradition, citing two of the greatest authorities of the desert in Anthony and Pambo, authorities from virtually the first generation. Pambo was a monk from Nitria, Evagrius's own monastic center; and he represents the best of the monastic tradition that Evagrius would inherit. The whole arc of the monastic life is presented in this brief statement of Anthony about Pambo, and Poemen is certainly aware of how much is condensed into this saying. It is Anthony who speaks, describing Pambo as greatly accomplished in the monastic life. Now Poemen simply passes on what he said. But it should be noticed that Anthony's words are drawn from the scriptures and that there is an implicit exegesis operative in them, very tightly packed. The expression "fearing God" may be taken as a general

---

[25] P. Géhin, ed., *Évagre le Pontique, Sur les pensées*, Sources Chrétiennes 438 (Paris: Cerf, 1998), 244.

[26] See Evagrius's *Prayer* 11, 13, 19, 44, 45, 114, 117, 120, 128, 148.

[27] C. Butler, *The Lausiac History of Palladius*, 2 vols. (Cambridge, 1898, 1904), vol. 2, 120.

[28] PG 65:340D.

kind of biblical language, drawn from a number of different places in the Old Testament. But the expression "Spirit of God to dwell in him" is a direct use of the New Testament language of 1 Corinthians 3:16, where it is useful to read the phrase in the context of the whole sentence: "Do you not know that you are the temple of God and that the Spirit of God dwells in you (τὸ πνεῦμα τοῦ Θεοῦ οἰκεῖ ἐν ὑμῖν)?"

Speaking a brief sentence that is completely scriptural, Anthony has in effect shown how the New Testament completes the Old. The first half of his sentence is from the Old Testament and is an expression representing where the monastic life begins, with fear of the Lord. The second half of the sentence is from the New Testament and is Anthony's Christian specification of "The fear of the Lord is the beginning of wisdom." Anthony means to indicate that this wisdom is concretely the Spirit of God dwelling in Pambo. In Evagrian terms, fear of God is *praktikē*, and the Holy Spirit dwelling in the monk describes the realm of knowledge.[29] Or, as he says in one place, "The mind is a temple of the Holy Trinity" (*Skemmata* 34).

The connection between Evagrius and Poemen at this point lies in a style of exegesis. Of course, it is well known that Evagrius is a master exegete of the Alexandrian tradition. Not only do his hundreds of scholia on biblical verses attest to this, but likewise the whole manner of his language in anything that he writes.[30] In these several citations of Anthony by Poemen we can see that Poemen himself functions within the same kind of exegetical scheme, and his citation of Anthony is an indication of his awareness of a whole tradition. In fact, more than anything it is in his own practice of such exegesis that Poemen shows his greatest debt to the tradition and his own skill as a spiritual father.

There is yet another place where Poemen cites Anthony.

> Abba Poemen said that blessed Abba Anthony used to say, "The greatest thing a man can do is to throw his faults before the Lord and to expect temptation (πειρασμόν) to his last breath." (Poemen 125)[31]

Such a thought is common enough in the desert. Perhaps the point for us here is not simply that the tradition passes from Anthony all the way to Poemen but that between these two stands, Evagrius teaches in the same vein. Indeed, characteristically Evagrius does not simply repeat a commonplace of the monastic tradition but penetrates the actual experience of

---

[29] This is standard in Evagrius. For a typical expression of fear of the Lord, see *Praktikos*, Prologue 8. For the Holy Spirit, see *Prayer* 59, 60, 63.

[30] I have presented a longer study on Evagrius's language as scriptural in ACW *Ad Monachos*, 181–94.

[31] PG 65:354C.

temptation with his capacity for analysis. He speaks of why temptation goes on until the end for the monk.

> The more the soul makes progress, more numerous become those who begin to combat against it. I do not think that it is always the same demons that are ranged against it. They who know this best are those who observe their temptations with greater attention and who see the passionlessness which they have acquired being attacked in successive waves. (*Praktikos* 59)[32]

So temptation is connected with progress. The monk must not consider it a sign that something is not working in the life he is trying to lead. "One must not quit the cell at the hour of temptations no matter how plausible seem the excuses. Rather one should stay seated inside and be patient and nobly receive the attackers, every one" (*Praktikos* 28).[33] The reason why the fathers taught the monks to expect temptation to the end was so that they would not mistakenly think that its presence meant that they were making no progress. Evagrius once again renders precise this basic insight by distinguishing between temptation and sin. "The temptation of the monk is a thought that mounts through the passionate part of the soul and darkens the mind. The sin of the monk is consent to the forbidden pleasure which the thought suggests" (*Praktikos* 74, 75).[34] This description, which concerns the passionate part of the soul, makes it clear that Evagrius is here discussing temptation in the life of *praktikē*. But even after the monk has reached the passionlessness at which *praktikē* aims, temptation continues. Now it is temptation for the gnostic or the knower. In the *Gnostikos*, in chapters that parallel these just cited from the *Praktikos*, Evagrius says, "The temptation of the knower is a false opinion which presents itself to the mind....The sin of the knower is false knowledge of things in themselves or their contemplation" (*Gn* 42, 43).[35] So, false ideas are always present and will tempt the monk. But actually to accept them and count them as knowledge is the sin. Since the monk is meant to be always making progress in knowledge, the temptation to false ideas will always be there. Evagrius's teaching on this matter helps us to see that Anthony's and Poemen's phrase "temptation to the last breath" does not simply mean that a monk will always be disturbed by thoughts of things like gluttony, fornication, and love of money. Even after passionlessness is attained over these, a temptation peculiar to the gnostic continues.[36]

---

[32] A. and C. Guillaumont, *Praktikos,* 2:638–40.

[33] Ibid., 2:564.

[34] Ibid., 2:662.

[35] A. and C. Guillaumont, *Le Gnostique,* Sources Chrétiennes 356 (Paris: Cerf, 1989), 170.

[36] Indeed, Evagrius's teaching on temptation is extensive. His numerous discussions of the

BESSARION

Abba Poemen said that a brother who lived with some other brothers asked Abba Bessarion, "What ought I to do?" The old man said to him, "Keep silence and do not measure yourself." (Poemen 79)[37]

There are two pieces of advice here. Let us begin with the idea of not measuring oneself. What Poemen attributes to Bessarion he also taught in his own name (Poemen 36, 73).[38] The sense certainly is not that the monk should not examine himself before God but rather more that he should not be turned in on himself, attributing an importance to his own self assessment. As the context shows—"a brother who lived with some other brothers"—it means not comparing oneself to others. By citing Bessarion, Poemen refers himself to one of the greatest monks of Scetis. And the greatness of Bessarion was not merely in his ascetical practice but precisely in his ability to combine this with a very high form of mystical prayer. The apophthegmata gathered under his own name show him standing in prayer for fourteen days and then paying a visit to the great mystic John of Lycopolis, to consult with him about a vision (Bessarion 4). At the point of death he is reported to have said, "The monk ought to be as the Cherubim and the Seraphim: all eye" (Bessarion 11).[39]

A major reason for the advice to keep silence, widespread in the desert, was to avoid sinning with one's tongue. Again, the context of brothers living together indicates this dimension. But certainly another dimension of the command to silence is to keep quiet about one's visions. Bessarion's humility about his own spiritual powers is one of the things best remembered about him (Bessarion 5). As has been mentioned, reluctance of this sort is a widespread theme among the fathers.[40] But lack of talk about such things should not be construed to mean that a deep mystical life is something peculiar only to a supposedly out-of-the-mainstream type of Evagrian monasticism. Furthermore, it is striking to remember, as we see

---

eight principal evil thoughts are about temptations and how they move in the monk. It is difficult to imagine that on this score either Evagrius or Poemen should not be considered in the mainstream of the Egyptian tradition. Thus, Poemen: "The distinctive mark of the monk is made clear through temptations" (Poemen 13; PG 65:325B). Evagrius would not have said otherwise.

[37] PG 65:341C. Translation mine.

[38] The same word reported of Bessarion in Poemen 79 is found at Bessarion 10.

[39] PG 65:141D.

[40] Guillaumont, "Les visions mystiques."

Poemen citing a father who had visited John of Lycopolis, that Evagrius too visited John to speak about profound questions concerning knowledge and the state of the mind during prayer (see *Antirrhetikos* VI, 16). And likewise from Evagrius issues the command, "Let the ineffable [Trinity] be worshipped in silence" (*Gn* 41).[41] Or again Poemen, who said, "If you have visions or hear voices do not tell your neighbour about it, for it is a delusion in the battle" (Poemen 139).[42] Or again Evagrius, getting at the issue a little more theologically and psychologically: "The beginning of deception in the mind is vainglory: it is this that stirs the mind to attempt to circumscribe the divine in some shape and form" (*Prayer* 116).[43]

ISIDORE OF SCETIS

He [Poemen] also said that Abba Isidore, the priest of Scetis, spoke to the people one day saying, "Brothers, is it not in order to endure affliction (κόπος) that we have come to this place? But now there is no affliction for us here. So I am getting my sheep-skin ready to go where there is some affliction and there I shall find rest (ἀνάπαυσιν)." (Poemen 44)[44]

With his reporting of this word, Poemen is using a classic monastic vocabulary, contrasting affliction (κόπος) and (ἀνάπαυσις) rest. Actually it is Evagrius who helps us to get to the deepest sense of what Isidore and now Poemen are saying. In the *Praktikos* Evagrius explains, "Rest (ἀνάπαυσις) is wisdom's, but affliction (κόπος) is yoked to prudence" (*Praktikos* 73).[45] As he does so often, Evagrius thus signals the two major realms of monastic life, *praktikē* and knowledge. Isidore's paradoxical expression—where there is affliction, there is rest—is thus a way of saying that the labors of *praktikē* result in knowledge, here indicated with the word ἀνάπαυσις and all its scriptural overtones from Matthew 11:28–29: "Come to me, all who labor and are heavy laden, and I will give you rest." Evagrius uses this vocabulary extensively for expressing the basic two-pronged

---

[41] A. and C. Guillaumont, *Le Gnostique,* 166. For the influence of Neoplatonism and Gregory of Nyssa on Evagrius here, see ibid., 169.

[42] PG 65:355D–357A. For other advice to silence, see Poemen 42, 45.

[43] PG 79:1193A. See also *Prayer* 73, 74 for further discussion of these kinds of questions, which may in fact represent some of the fruit of Evagrius's visit to John. Such, in fact, is the suggestion of I. Hausherr, *Les leçons d'un contemplatif: Le Traité de l'Oraison d'Évagre le Pontique* (Paris, 1960), 106.

[44] PG 65:332D.

[45] A. and C. Guillaumont, *Praktikos,* 2:660.

structure of the monk's journey,[46] and here we see also the mainstream Isidore and Poemen doing the same.

Isidore is one of the most admired monks of Scetis, cited by many other monastic sources.[47] In this present chapter, in which possible links are being gathered between the fathers that Poemen admired and the monastic tradition represented in Evagrius, it is worth looking for a moment at Isidore helping Abba Moses in his struggle with the temptation of fornication. When Moses came to see Isidore, Isidore exhorted him to return to his cell; but Moses said that he could not, evidently feeling himself too fragile to face the temptation in solitude. So Isidore took him outside and revealed to him in a vision a host of demons in the west and a host of angels in the east. The angels were an innumerable multitude, much outweighing the force of the demons, and Isidore said to him, "See they are sent by the Lord to the saints to bring them help, while those in the west fight against them. Those who are with us are more in number than they are" (Moses 1).[48] Angels and demons similarly ranged against each other around the monk is an image that occurs again and again in Evagrius. "The souls of the just, angels guide; the souls of the wicked, demons will snatch up" (*M 23*).[49]

JOHN THE DWARF

A brother asked Abba Poemen saying, "Can a man put his trust in one single work?" The old man said to him that Abba John the Dwarf said, "I would rather have a bit of all the virtues" (Poemen 46)[50]

Poemen's citation of John here gives us an opportunity to draw many connections with Evagrius. A longer word under John's own name in the Alphabetical Collection and in the Systematic Collection under the chapter titled "Spiritual Progress" gives us a fuller sense of John's teaching on this matter. He begins by saying, "I think it best that a man should have a

---

[46] I examine many of the relevant texts in ACW *Ad Monachos*, 249–59. See also A. and C. Guillaumont, *Praktikos*, 2:661–63.

[47] For analysis of references to Isidore by Cassian, Palladius, Rufinus, and elsewhere in the *Apophthegmata*, see Guy, *Apophtegmes des pères*, 57–58. Poemen's memory is the source for what is remembered about Isidore in three of the apophthegmata collected under his name, at Isidore 5, 6, 10.

[48] PG 65:281D. Isidore is also featured as helping Moses in the chapter on Moses in the *Lausiac History*, 19.

[49] Gressmann, "Nonnenspiegel," 155. For this theme in desert literature in general, see Guillaumont, "Les visions mystiques," 120–21. For the theme in Evagrius's *Scholia on Proverbs*, see P. Géhin, SCh 340, pp. 45–48.

[50] PG 65:333A.

little bit of all the virtues. Therefore, get up early every day and acquire the beginning of every virtue and every commandment of God" (John the Dwarf 34).[51] After this he mentions many virtues and practices: patience, long-suffering, humility, vigils, avoiding anger, poverty both material and spiritual, not measuring oneself, "hunger and thirst, cold and nakedness" (citing 1 Cor 11:27), and many more.[52]

Virtually all these practices are spoken of by Evagrius and make up his own conception of the life of *praktikē*. It is not necessary to document this connection one by one, but it is worth examining at least one of the kinds of practice of which John is speaking to indicate how Evagrius finds himself in the same stream of tradition. From the beginning John mentions long-suffering (μακροθυμία) and avoiding anger. This is the very center of Evagrius's teaching on the virtues.[53] In a letter Evagrius says, "Let no one, I beg you, devote himself only to temperance. For not with only one stone is a house built, nor with only one brick is a house constructed. An irascible temperate person is a dried up tree, fruitless, twice dead, uprooted" (*Lt* 27:13).[54] This would be Evagrius's answer to the question put to Poemen, "Can a man put his trust in one single work?" His answer is characteristically more structured, which is his peculiar contribution to the already existing tradition; but it is essentially the same as John's and now Poemen's. Evagrius is concerned to show that a quieting of the irascible part of the soul must accompany temperance, a virtue generically describing the concupiscible part of the soul. One or the other would not be enough.[55] But in this same context Evagrius characteristically connects what he is saying about the virtues with the goal of monastic life in the realm of knowledge. After the passage of the letter just cited, he continues, "An irascible person will not see the morning star rising, but will go to a place from

---

[51] PG 65:216B. The same in the Systematic Collection at I, 13.

[52] To see how John himself is teaching within a tradition in offering a word like this, one can compare this with Anthony 33. Both words are a mosaic of biblical verses. For an analysis of this not only in Anthony and John but also in other fathers as well, see L. Mortari, *Vita e detti dei padri del deserto* (Rome, 1971), 16–18.

[53] G. Bunge, *Vino dei draghi e pane degli angeli, l'insegnamento di Evagrio Pontico sull'ira e la mitezza* (Magmano, 1999); Driscoll, "Gentleness in the *Ad Monachos* of Evagrius Ponticus."

[54] Translated from a Greek fragment found in C. Guillaumont, "Fragments grecs inédits d'Évagre le Pontique," *Texte und Untersuchungen* 133 (1987): here 220, lines 65–67.

[55] Many of Evagrius's letters deal with this theme, a sign that it is of concern throughout the desert: in those to whom he wrote, in those to whom John spoke, still in Poemen as already in Anthony. For examples in Evagrius, see *Lt* 28:1, which speaks of temperance together with long-suffering and love. Letter 52:5–6 speaks of how fasting alone is not sufficient to reach the knowledge that is the monk's goal. He goes on to speak of concentrating on ridding the soul of a number of other evil thoughts, including memory of injury and anger. Letter 56:5 is quite strong: "Accept no temperance that chases away gentleness." C. Guillaumont, "Fragments," 218, lines 11–12. See also *Praktikos* 38 for the importance of temperance and love going together.

which he will not return, into a land dark and gloomy, into a land of eternal darkness" (*Lt* 27:3).[56] The morning star rising is Evagrius's biblical image for knowledge. This is the goal: having a little of all the virtues so as to see the morning star rising. "Like a morning star in heaven and a palm tree in paradise, so a pure mind in a gentle soul" (*M* 107).[57]

It could not be legitimately argued that Evagrius's concern to move on from *praktikē* to the realm of knowledge or prayer is peculiar to his way of treating the virtues but not to either John's or Poemen's. In the same way that Evagrius refers to what he had learned from John of Lycopolis, as we saw above, thereby linking Bessarion, Poemen, and Evagrius, so Evagrius cites John the Dwarf in his *Chapters on Prayer*. As he introduces him, he calls him "John the Small, I mean, or rather John the supremely great." Then he reports, "He remained unmoved from his communion (συνουσίας) with God while the demon wrapped himself round him in the form of a serpent, chewed on his flesh, and then spit it out in his face" (*Prayer* 107).[58] John could remain wrapt in prayer precisely because he had a "little of all the virtues." But it is such prayer that is the goal of the monastic life, not the virtues alone or in themselves.

Certainly there are differences in the various fathers we have studied thus far, and it is not my intention to overlook them in a simplistic way. But I am undertaking the present exercise as a means of overcoming what I consider the artificial placing of Evagrius, Cassian, Palladius, and others as outside the mainstream. Perhaps it is John and Poemen themselves who help us best to evaluate what differences we find.

> Abba Poemen said that Abba John said that the saints are like a group of trees, each bearing different fruit, but watered from the same source. The practices of one saint differ from those of another, but it is the same Spirit that works in all of them. (John the Dwarf 43)[59]

Poemen speaks of Abba John in still several other places. Key practices of monastic life are recommended by John through Poemen.

> He [Poemen] said that when a brother went to see Abba John the Dwarf, he offered him that charity of which the apostle

---

[56] C. Guillaumont, "Fragments," 220, lines 66–69.

[57] Gressmann, "Nonnenspiegel," 162. This cryptic and tightly packed proverb condenses practically all of how Evagrius understands the relation of having all the virtues to the goal of knowledge. Each word must be deciphered scripturally and also as used within the Evagrian corpus. See ACW *Ad Monachos*, 308–19.

[58] PG 79:1192A. Translation Tugwell.

[59] Text found in J. C. Guy *Recherches sur la tradition grecque des Apophthegmata Patrum* (Brussels, 1962), 24.

speaks, "Charity suffers long and is kind (ἡ ἀγάπη μακροθυμεῖ, χρηστεύεται)." (1 Cor 13:4) (Poemen 74)[60]

John is indeed remembered for demonstrative charity. One can recall the story of the great kindness and patience he showed to the monk who kept forgetting the word that he had given him to ponder (John the Dwarf 18). Or another, when a young girl who had once been very kind to the monks got into trouble with prostitution, all the brethren came to John knowing that he would know what to do for her. John goes into the city, straight into her chambers and, sitting on the bed beside her, wins her back for Christ (John the Dwarf 40). John used to say that a house was not built from the top down but beginning with the foundations. And then, "The foundation is our neighbour, whom we must win, and that is the place to begin. For all the commandments of Christ depend on this one" (John the Dwarf 39).[61] Poemen remembers this kind of charity in John and summarizes it with an interpretation of his own by identifying it with what St. Paul was speaking of in 1 Corinthians. This is typical of Poemen, always quick to find the short, incisive biblical word that summarizes the deepest sense of a story or of a piece of advice.

Of course, it is not difficult to locate Evagrius in this same stream. He is equally well remembered for his great charity; and he made love (ἀγάπη), long-suffering (μακροθυμία), and gentleness (πραΰτης) cornerstones of his own teaching and practice.[62] In the same way that for John such love is a foundation, so also in the teaching of Evagrius it points beyond itself to the kind of intense prayer for which, as we have seen, Evagrius cites John as a preeminent example. Evagrius marvelously condenses the main structural beams of the house of which John speaks of building from the bottom up: "Faith: the beginning of love. The end of love: knowledge of God" (*M* 3).[63]

John the Dwarf is also Poemen's authority for another monastic practice which he strongly recommends.

> A brother asked Abba Poemen, "why should I not be free to do without manifesting my thoughts to the old men?" The old man replied, "Abba John the Dwarf said, 'the enemy rejoices over nothing so much as over those who do not manifest their thoughts (λογισμοὺς αὐτῶν).'" (Poemen 101)[64]

---

[60] PG 65:340D.
[61] PG 65:217A.
[62] See G. Bunge, *Evagrios Pontikos: Briefe aus der Wüste* (Trier, 1986), 126ff. For my attempt at a summary, see "Gentleness in the *Ad Monachos* of Evagrius Ponticus."
[63] Gressmann, "Nonnenspiegel," 153.
[64] PG 65:345D.

Here we have the technical term λογισμός, the evil thoughts with which every monk must do battle. And it is an evil thought itself to think that one can win this battle without the help of spiritual elders. So teaches Poemen, so John, so also Evagrius and virtually all the fathers. For the purposes of the present study, a simple reminder might serve to make the point I am hoping to establish by this slow gathering of bits of evidence. It is this: that we know of no father in the desert who has left us a greater heritage of analysis of the evil thoughts than Evagrius. In this it is obvious that he had imbibed a tradition from his own elders and that he was writing about it because others were now—to use John's phrase—"manifesting their thoughts" to him. Evagrius went out of his way to make it easier for brothers who were hesitant to talk about their thoughts to speak with him. It is remembered of him that when he would speak to the whole gathering of brothers on Saturday nights, at the end he would thoughtfully invite any brother who had a particularly troublesome thought to discuss it with him afterwards in private (*Coptic Life* 114–15).[65] And speaking to others who might find themselves consulted, he advised, "It is necessary for the knower to be neither sullen nor hard to approach. For sullenness comes from ignorance of the reasons of created things, and being hard to approach comes from not wanting 'all men to be saved and to come to knowledge of the truth (1 Tim 2:4)'" (*Gn 22*).[66] In fact, Evagrius's work the *Gnostikos,* from which I am quoting here, is a kind of handbook for those who will find themselves in the role of spiritual guide for others. It shows us the other side of the coin of the same practice of which Poemen is speaking; namely, manifesting one's thoughts to the father. Evagrius for his part advises the fathers, "Become acquainted with the reasons and the laws of times, lifestyles and occupations so that you can easily have something profitable to say to everyone" (*Gn* 15).[67]

PAMBO

We have already examined a word in which Poemen refers to Abba Pambo, reporting a very condensed saying that Abba Anthony spoke in his regard.[68] In two other places Poemen refers to Pambo. We can read them together.

---

[65] In Bunge and de Vogüé, *Quatre ermites égyptiens,* 161–62.

[66] A. and C. Guillaumont, *Le Gnostique,* 122. *Gnostikos* 46 speaks of "eagerly nourishing those who present themselves" to the father for help (p. 182).

[67] A. and C. Guillaumont, *Le Gnostique,* 122. Many other chapters speak about the importance of adapting teaching to the capacity of those to be instructed: *Gn* 6, 23, 25, 31, 35, 36, 40.

[68] See Poemen 75 above, p. 149.

The old man [Poemen] said that a brother asked Abba Pambo if it is good to praise one's neighbour and that the old man said to him, "It is better to be silent." (Poemen 47)[69]

Abba Poemen said, "In Abba Pambo we see three bodily activities; abstinence from food until the evening every day, silence, and much manual work." (Poemen 150)[70]

There is nothing out of the ordinary in these words for what is found in general among the desert monks. Within the scope of the present study, however, it is worth noting that Poemen has cited three times a monk from Nitria, the monastic center in which Evagrius passed most of his monastic life. Pambo was from the early generation, known by Anthony himself, as we saw above. He is one of the best remembered of all the monks of the desert, and in this fact we see a clear example of the peaceful coexistence of different kinds of monks within a broad tradition of which Bunge speaks. It is this picture that has been altered in later accounts of monastic life after the Origenist crisis, including in the final redaction of the material in the *Apophthegmata Patrum*.

Memories about Pambo illustrate the tendencies of such alteration. A. Guillaumont observed many years ago the difference between the account of Pambo's death in the *Apophthegmata Patrum* and the same in the *Lausiac History* of Palladius, which is more favorable to Evagrius. The account in the *Apophthegmata* suppresses the names of the disciples present around Pambo, who would have been considered by the redactor to have had "Origenist" tendencies, especially that of Ammonias, one of the famous Tall Brothers.[71] Pambo was the master of these and many others. He was known to Melania, who was also present at his death. The relation of Evagrius to all these is well known.

Poemen refers to Pambo three times. In the two texts just cited he refers to Pambo's "bodily activities" and the advice to keep silence. Both of these words could be referred to what Evagrius would call *praktikē*. We examined above the way in which Pambo was said to represent in himself the goal of monastic life in that "he made the Spirit of God to dwell in him," what Evagrius would call knowledge. This dimension is part of the memory about Pambo. "God glorified him so that one could not gaze steadfastly at him because of the glory of his countenance" (Pambo 1).[72] "They said of Abba Pambo that he was like Moses, who received the image of the glory of Adam when his face shone. His face shone like lightening

---

[69] PG 65:333A.

[70] PG 65:360A.

[71] Pambo 8 compared with *LH* 10. See A. Guillaumont, *'Képhalaia Gnostica' d'Évagre le Pontique*, 57–58, n. 41.

[72] PG 65:368C.

and he was like a king sitting on his throne. It was the same with Abba Silvanus and Abba Sisoes" (Pambo 12).[73] In short, it can be said that Pambo's *praktikē* took him to the highest levels of knowledge. He himself, like Evagrius after him, knew how to condense into a short word both these dimensions of the monastic life. "Abba Theodore of Pherme asked Abba Pambo, 'Give me a word.' With much difficulty he said to him, 'Theodore, go and have pity on all, for through pity, one finds freedom of speech (παρρησία) before God'" (Pambo 14).[74] "Pity on all" (τὸ ἔλεος σου ἔχε ἐπὶ πάντας) functions here as summary of the love that is the goal of all *praktikē*. It opens the door to παρρησία. Evagrius too understands that one reaches παρρησία through *praktikē*. This is the meaning for him of Proverbs 1:20, translating literally from the Septuagint, "Wisdom is celebrated in exoduses, she leads with freedom of speech (παρρησία) into large places." Evagrius explains: "He [Solomon] calls the going out of a soul from evil and ignorance an 'exodus'... and it is by a soul which has accomplished such a going out that 'wisdom is celebrated.' It is in a soul that has been enlarged by the virtues that 'she leads with freedom of speech'" (*InProv* 1:20-21; G 12).[75] How he conceives such freedom in the presence of God is described in another text, where he advises, "Picture all the good things that await the just: freedom of speech with God the Father and with his Christ, with angels, archangels, powers, and with all the saints" (*Rerum monachalium ratione* 9).[76] Such, for him, is the goal of *praktikē*, the main subject of the work from which this text is cited.

PAPHNUTIUS

Abba Poemen said that Abba Paphnutius was great and he had recourse to short prayers. (Poemen "190")[77]

---

[73] PG 65:372A.

[74] PG 65:372B. The difficulty with which Pambo is said to have spoken is probably to be explained by what is said of him in *LH* 10:6, that he had the "virtue of precision with the word." For useful comments on Pambo 14 with the probable allusion to Heb 4:16, see Mortari, *Vita e detti*, 137, n. 162.

[75] P. Géhin, ed., *Scholies aux proverbes*, Sources Chrétiennes 340 (Paris: Cerf, 1987), 102–4.

[76] PG 40:1261C. In speaking of what awaits the "just," Evagrius uses a term that he always understands to signify "virtue in all the parts of the soul." See *Praktikos* 89. "Freedom of speech with God the Father" can be usefully compared to the expression for prayer, conceived as the final goal of monastic life, in *Prayer*: "Prayer is an intercourse of the mind with God... without intermediary" (ἡ προσευχὴ, ὁμιλία ἐστὶ νοῦ πρὸς θεόν...μηδενὸς μεσιτεύοντος) (PG 79:1168D).

[77] Or Supplement 3 found in Guy, *Recherches sur la tradition grecque des Apophthegmata Patrum*, 30.

We have here yet another father evidently much admired by Poemen. For the purposes of the present study it is significant that the connections between Evagrius and the widely admired Paphnutius are strong indeed. We know that Paphnutius was another of the fathers whom Evagrius consulted personally, and it is possible to show the influence of Paphnutius on Evagrius's own teaching about the relationship between pride and the providential abandonment by God which can return a proud monk to his senses.[78] Paphnutius was one of the strongest and most influential monks in the history of Scetis, and it is to this influence that Poemen is referring when he says, "Paphnutius was great."[79] One can perhaps hear a sense of nostalgia in this statement, almost as if to say that the likes of him are no longer known. Other statements of Poemen permit such an interpretation.[80] In any case, the fact that Evagrius and others of his company go to consult Paphnutius in Scetis is yet another piece of evidence of a more peaceful sort of interchange between the monks of Scetis and Nitria before the Origenist crisis. This is not merely a question of friendly relations, but a capacity to talk the same kind of theological talk concerning dimensions of the spiritual life shared in common. The consultation with Paphnutius concerned no less sophisticated a question than why spiritually advanced monks sometimes fall.[81]

MOSES

What Poemen says of Moses can draw this chapter to a close.[82]

> Abba Poemen said, "Since Abba Moses and the third generation in Scetis, the brothers do not make progress any more." (Poemen 166)[83]

---

[78] See the previous chapter.

[79] For a useful summary of the role of Paphnutius at Scetis, see Guy, *Apophtegmes des pères,* 59–61.

[80] See above, as we began, with Poemen 106 (p. 145), and below the discussion of Moses in Poemen 166.

[81] The consultation with Paphnutius is reported in *LH* 47. Interestingly, Guy notes that this consultation sometimes had an autonomous existence in the manuscripts (*Apophtegmes des pères,* 60 n. 5). The practice of short prayers which Poemen mentions is a common dimension of *praktikē,* found also in Evagrius. For example, "At the time of such temptations, make use of a short and intense prayer" (*Prayer* 98; PG 79; 1189A). For Evagrius's practice of a hundred such prayers a day, see *LH* 38.

[82] I have chosen not to take into account here others to whom Poemen makes reference. He refers to a Sisoes in 82, 89, and 187; but a secure definition of this figure makes it difficult to draw the kinds of conclusions I am searching for in this study. For the difficulties with Sisoes, see Guy, *Apophtegmes des pères,* 49. Nor do I discuss Pior (Poemen 85), Theonas (Poemen 151) or Timothy (Poemen 70). As far as I can tell, these add nothing of further significance to the present discussion.

[83] PG 65:361C.

Once again, so much is said so briefly. In some ways this word embodies the whole spirit of Poemen's teaching. He wanted nothing else than to pass on the teachings of those who had preceded him. He did this, as we have seen, by making frequent reference to them by name. Moreover, his own teaching represents what is already found in those who came before him. But in referring to Moses and the third generation of Scetis, he is referring to a strong time of the monastic tradition which Poemen and his contemporaries no longer enjoy. This, of course, was the Scetis that endured to its first sacking in 407, the Scetis that knew John the Dwarf and others like him, the Scetis made possible by Macarius and Isidore and Paphnutius, the Scetis that Evagrius would have known. Poemen would that monks could be in his time as they had been then, and he expresses his wish in terms of "making progress."

One can gain some sense of how much Poemen is saying here by referring to Evagrius, in whom the word *progress* functions as a summary of so much of the tradition that he himself had learned from the fathers.[84] In many of the fathers that have been examined in this study, "progress in contemplation" would have been a natural concern and indeed the constantly renewed goal of the monastic journey. Poemen feels this dimension slipping and wants to counteract it. We have come full circle from where this chapter began: "Many of our fathers have become very courageous in asceticism, but in finesse of perception there are very few" (Poemen 106).[85]

CONCLUSION

I said in introducing this investigation that it was more "fragile" than the sort of material that G. Bunge considered in his studies on the relation between Evagrius and the two Macarii. In Bunge's studies, solid historical links could be established between the figures examined and between their teachings. We do not have the same kind of evidence to connect Evagrius and Poemen. Nonetheless, I think that the texts examined here do show that there is something that links the two figures; namely, a tradition of fathers, a tradition from which both of them imbibed and which in the end each came to represent in his own way. I think we read both of them more accurately if we see them not as contrasting figures but as fathers who lived a same tradition, albeit at different times, in different historical circumstances, and according to their different personal characteristics. We have seen Poemen citing many of the fathers who likewise influenced Evagrius,

---

[84] See chapter 1 above, "Spiritual Progress in the Works of Evagrius Ponticus."
[85] PG 65:348C.

teaching the same kinds of basic themes. All of the fathers taught these themes with a touch particular to each, but it was a common human nature they were all dealing with, desirous of a same kind of progress in the interior life.[86]

In the cases of Evagrius and Poemen we are dealing with two of the greatest and most widely consulted of them all. Both knew that a demanding ascetical regime was necessary to achieving the goal of monastic life, but that it was not the goal itself. Both knew that a monk entered the depths and heights of prayer only by means of love. With their own gentleness they led their disciples toward love. Both knew that a little of all the virtues would lead toward love. Both were skilled interpreters of scripture, not hesitating to employ allegory to get immediately to an existential application of the text in the monastic situation. Both knew the importance of manifesting thoughts, and each had learned from the tradition and from personal experience how to help monks troubled by certain evil thoughts. In the end both knew that union with God—or call it "finesse of perception" or "knowledge" or "progress" or "discernment" or "the Spirit of God" or "rest" or "prayer" or "freedom of speech before God"—was the ultimate goal of any monastic asceticism, of any interpretation of the scripture.

---

[86] M. Sheridan concludes the study cited in n. 5 above suggesting something similar: "Invece di ipotizzare l'esistenza di tipi di monachesimo radicalmente diversi in Egitto, con diverse fonti di ispirazione e diverse impostazioni spirituali, sarebbe meglio prendere come ipotesi di lavoro la supposizione di una tradizione comune rispetto alla natura fondamentale della vita spirituale/interiore" ("Il mondo spirituale e intellettuale del primo monachesimo egiziano," 215).

CONCLUSION

The fruit of sowing is sheaves,
and the fruit of the virtues is knowledge.
And as tears accompany sowing,
so joy accompanies reaping.
—Evagrius Ponticus, *Praktikos* 90

Seeds have been planted here in the work of reading, and a spiritual crop has sprouted and grown. What can we reap from it at the end of this labor? The reader who has followed my indications—they are Evagrius's indications actually—to practice the master's "words" by relating *discourse* to *life* will have already begun a reaping that joy accompanies. Each chapter had its lessons; each led us further along the way. In this final chapter I would like to gather the fruits into a storehouse, as it were. This should be conceived as a first gleaning. There is still more in the "words" we have studied than what I will gather here. Each reader is free to and, indeed, should gather the crop in his or her own way. But perhaps here I can show a way how it might be done.

A storehouse. I think of what I will suggest here as indications for a spiritual practice. The lessons of the various chapters can be kept in storage, pulled out at different times, and used along the way of life. Each lesson is a major piece of the spiritual tradition that has brought so many others to holiness, leading them past the intermediate guideposts and around the pitfalls and keeping their minds fixed on the final goal. If I formulate the lessons with comparative brevity, it is not because there is little to say or because it is of scant importance. It is because this too is in the form of *discourse* about *life*. We have seen that the discourse is brief so that its content can be ready to hand for the tasks of practice in life.

I want to come into the place of prayer where the Logos manifests himself to me. I want to be snatched up on high by a supreme love. I want the light of the Holy Trinity to shine on my mind, making it comparable to the color of the sky. I am far from such spiritual loveliness. Yet the talk of Evagrius and the other spiritual masters has given me courage to set out toward that distant land. What must I remember as I go?

• *Spiritual progress.* There is an order of progress in the spiritual life that follows the nature of things. From the start I know the goal toward which

164

my whole being tends: knowledge of the Holy Trinity, pure prayer. But I must come to such a goal by an arduous path of practice, which purifies my wayward thoughts, teaching me to love others, to understand myself, other human beings, and the world. For every stage of this journey Evagrius offers a teaching. Taking up any one of his works without reference to where it can be useful along the scale of progress is tantamount to misunderstanding from the start. To fail to practice the words with patience over time would amount to the same misunderstanding. But now I see the territory and have studied it in advance. I know I must begin by setting out along the path of the virtues, and I know which part of the library can accompany me for that. I know where I want to go: to the place of pure prayer. I know where to find the teaching that helps me find the way.

• *Spousal images.* The journey of spiritual progress is guided by many images taken from the scriptures, which, because they are given by the Holy Spirit, have the power to direct me toward the goal that the Spirit intends. Such images are more than just an imaginative jump-start that sets in motion a more left-brain oriented spirituality. When they are pondered at length with the contemplative respect that this tradition teaches, they become the divinely crafted vessels that deliver a more-than-human help to the human seeker. Spousal images conceive the whole journey as driven forward by love. The mind that shines with the light of the Holy Trinity is a bride who has made herself pure, whose lamp of love is burning bright as she is presented before the One whom she desires. I cleave to this image with all the force of my spiritual longing, letting it slowly transform me into that of which it speaks.

• *Penthos and tears.* I set out on a path that must be begun with compunction of heart and tears. I have learned that I have reason to weep because the beautiful goal is seen from the start and yet it lies so far beyond me. Still, weeping prepares my soul and gives me energy to move. All who have ever made progress have yielded to the gift of tears. This is not a self-centered weeping that vaguely sort of makes me feel like a sinner for a while, before I enjoy the emotional counterpart of feeling "I'm okay" again. Such weeping tames the irascible me. It does battle against the evil thought of listlessness. It saves me from pride. It makes my prayer pleasing to God. I really must come into the place of these authentic tears, and then I can pray the words that the Holy Spirit gives me in the psalms: "Why are you depressed, my soul, why do you disturb me? Hope in God, because I will praise him, the Saviour of my person, my God."

• *Love of money.* Along the way countless evil thoughts threaten to derail me. I must understand their insidious ways of moving within me and of confusing me. "Love of money is the root of all evil." To do battle with one evil thought is to be entangled with them all. Victory over one is the basis of victory over them all. I must therefore free myself from love of riches and all excess in creature comforts, equipping myself for a practical charity toward others. Then I can pursue the true and lasting wealth: knowledge of the Holy Trinity.

• *Apatheia and purity of heart.* The knowledge of the Holy Trinity is a high and distant goal, for in my fallen condition I am necessarily far removed from it. Yet my struggle to rid myself from the tyranny of the passions, to be pure of heart, gives me hope that "the pure of heart are blessed, for they shall see God." If the knowledge of the Holy Trinity far exceeds anything I can even begin to represent in my mind, I do at least have the concrete goal of passionlessness. And, "in front of love passionless marches;/ in front of knowledge, love."

• *Abandonment by God.* A great peace comes into the soul after the battle to reach purity of heart. And yet at this point I must beware of a new kind of danger: the tendency toward vainglory and pride. If I should think that I deserve the praise of others for the progress made or imagine that the new vigor of my inner life is due to my own strength, then God will teach me a harsh lesson. He will (in his mercy!) abandon the fool I have become until I return to my senses. I have learned here that vainglory and pride are wayward thoughts, ever so subtly leading me astray even after I may have made real progress along the spiritual way. I have been warned. Rather than quietly hating those who fail to give me the praise I think my due, I can learn to hate such thoughts "with a perfect hatred." If I do, a new, humble, hidden hope is kindled in me for reaching my goal.

• *Poemen and exegesis.* At every point along this whole way the scriptures are my surest guide. The story of Israel and the story of Jesus about which I read in the thousands of verses of the sacred text are the story of my soul seeking knowledge of the Holy Trinity. Here indeed I can grasp the significance of every scriptural citation and echo that I hear in the words of Evagrius or in any of the other fathers, all of whom delivered their wisdom in this code. For the pure of heart, the words of scripture become more than the human words that they obviously are. They are likewise a divine word, the Spirit's masterpiece, which leads infallibly both to and beyond the sense at which it aims. So I need a guide who will "give me a word" in every moment of my life, making sense of each piece of it, showing me how in this moment I can follow in the footsteps of my Lord, "who had to suffer so to enter into glory." I must never cease to scrutinize the scriptures, to stay ever close to their spiritual grammar, to advance each step only under the force of their guidance.

• *Fathers of Poemen and the Evagrian connection.* In this chapter I learned the happy story of the genealogy of some of the greatest guides of the desert wisdom tradition. Seeing the love and respect with which they cited one another and passed on to others what they themselves had received, I learn an important lesson about the dynamic of spiritual direction. Directing and receiving direction is not a question of looking for and coming up with some new insight that will at last make us feel better. It is a question of listening to the holy ones who have gone before us. The rugged terrain over which I must pass has already been charted. It is I myself who must make the journey, but it would be foolish to set out into such territory without first studying a map, the knowledge of which can save me from many a pitfall and keep high my hopes that I am in fact making progress toward my destination, even while engaged in tremendous battles. I am learning to pray!

Prayer is a conversation of the mind with God. So what condition is required if the mind is to be able to reach out unswervingly towards its own Lord and to converse with him without any intermediary?
　　　　　　　　　　—Evagrius Ponticus, *Chapters on Prayer* 3.

ABBREVIATIONS AND EDITIONS
OF PRIMARY SOURCES

Ant *Antirrhetikos.* W. Frankenberg, ed. *Evagrius Ponticus.* Abhandlungen der königlichen Gesellschaft der Wissenschaften zu Göttingen. Phil.-hist. Klasse. n.F. 13, 2. Berlin, 1912.

Bases *Rerum monachalium rationes* or *The Bases of the Monastic Life.* PG 40:1252–64.

Coptic Life
> The Coptic fragment of the life of Evagrius in E. Amélineau, *De Historia Lausiaca*, 104–24, and cited according to page numbers. Paris, 1887.

CSCO Corpus scriptorum christianorum orientalium. Edited by I. B. Chabot et al. Paris, 1903ff.

CSEL Corpus scriptorum ecclesiasticorum latinorum

Eight Spirits
> *Tractatus de octo spiritibus malitiae* or *The Eight Spirits of Evil.* PG 79:1145–64.

Ep Fid *Epistula Fidei.* J. Gribomont, ed. *Basilio di Cesarea. Le lettre, vol 1.* Turin, 1983. Letter 8 (pp. 84–113) = Evagrius's *Epistula Fidei,* and cited with the line numbers of this edition.

Ep Mel *Epistula ad Melaniam* or *The Letter to Melania.* W. Frankenberg, ed. *Evagrius Ponticus.* Abhandlungen der königlichen Gesellschaft der Wissenschaften zu Göttingen. Phil.-hist. Klasse. n.F. 13, 2. Berlin, 1912; and G. Vitestam, "Seconde partie du Traité, qui passe sous le nom de 'La grande lettre d'Évagre le Pontique à Mélanie l'Ancienne,'" *Scripta Minora Regiae Societatis Humaniorum Litterarum Lundensis* 1963–1964: no. 3, 3–29. Lund, 1964. English cited according to M. Parmentier, "Evagrius of Pontus and the 'Letter to Melania.'" *Bijdragen, tijdschrift voor filosofie en theologie* 46 (1985): 2–38, with his line numbers.

Eulog *Tractatus ad Eulogium Monachum.* PG 79:1093–1140.

GCS Die griechische christliche Schriftsteller der ersten [drei] Jahrhunderte

Gn *The Gnostikos.* A. and C. Guillaumont, eds. *Évagre le Pontique. Le Gnostique ou a celui qui est devenu digne de la science.* Sources Chrétiennes 356. Paris: Cerf, 1989.

In Eccl The Scholia on Ecclesiastes. P. Géhin, ed. *Évagre le Pontique. Scholies a l'ecclésiaste.* Sources Chrétiennes 397. Paris: Cerf, 1993. In the citations, (G, standing for Géhin, with a number) thus, for example (G 1) refers to the numbers given to the scholia in the Géhin edition.

In Prov The Scholia on Proverbs. P. Géhin, ed. *Évagre le Pontique. Scholies aux proverbes.* Sources Chrétiennes 340. Paris: Cerf, 1987. In the citations, (G, standing for Géhin, with a number) thus, for example (G 1) refers to the numbers given to the scholia in the Géhin edition.

In Ps The Scholia on Psalms, cited according to the key of Rondeau in "Le commentaire sur les Psaumes d'Évagre le Pontique." PG 12; PG 27. J. B. Pitra, *Analecta sacra spicilegio Solesmensi, parata,* v. 2, Frascati, 1884; v. 3, Paris, 1883.

Inst ad mon
   Institutio ad monachos or *The Instruction to Monks.* PG 79:1236–40, with supplement by J. Muyldermans, *Le Muséon* 51, 198–204.

KG   The Kephalaia Gnostica. A. Guillaumont, ed. *Les six centuries des "Kephalaia Gnostica."* Patrologia Orientalis 28, fasc. 1. Paris: Firmin-Didot, 1958.

LH   The Lausiac History. G. J. M. Bartelink, ed. *Palladio. La Storia Lausiaca.* Milan: Fondazione Lorenza Valla, 1974. And C. Butler, ed. *The Lausiac History of Palladius.* 2 vols. Cambridge, 1898, 1904.

Lt   Letters. W. Frankenberg, ed. *Evagrius Ponticus.* Abhandlungen der königlichen Gesellschaft der Wissenschaften zu Göttingen. Phil.-hist. Klasse. n.F. 13, 2. Berlin, 1912. With Greek fragments in C. Guillaumont, "Fragments grecs inédits d'Évagre le Pontique." *Texte und Untersuchungen* 133 (1987): 209–21. Paragraph numbers according to G. Bunge, *Evagrios Pontikos: Briefe aus der Wüste. Eingeleitet, übersetzt und kommentiert von Gabriel Bunge.* Trier, 1986.

M   Ad Monachos. H. Gressmann, ed. "Nonnenspiegel und Mönchsspiegel des Euagrios Pontikos." *Texte und Untersuchungen* 39, 4 (1913): 143–65.

Masters and Disciples
   Masters and Disciples. P. Van den Ven, ed. "Un opuscule inédit attribué à S. Nil." In *Mélanges Godefroy Kurth,* v. 2, 73–81. Liège, 1908.

On Evil Thoughts
   De Diversis Malignis Cogitationibus or *The Treatise on Evil Thoughts.* P. Géhin, ed. *Évagre le Pontique. Sur les pensées.* Sources Chrétiennes 438. Paris: Cerf, 1998.

PG   *Patrologiae cursus completus.* Series graeca. Edited by J.-P. Migne. Paris, 1857ff.

PO   Patrologia Orientalis

Praktikos

The Praktikos. A. and C. Guillaumont, eds. *Évagre le Pontique. Traité pratique; ou le moine.* Sources Chrétiennes 170, 171. Paris: Cerf, 1971.

Prayer *De Oratione capitula* or *The Chapters on Prayer.* PG 79:1165–1200, with the edition of S. Tugwell, *Evagrius Ponticus: Practikos and On Prayer, translated by Simon Tugwell.* Published privately by the Faculty of Theology, Oxford, 1987.

Skemmata

Skemmata. J. Muyldermans, ed. *Evagriana.* Extrait de la revue *Le Muséon*, v. 42, augmenté de *Nouveaux fragments grecs inédits*, 38–44. Paris, 1931.

V   *Ad Virginem.* H. Gressmann, ed. "Nonnenspiegel und Mönchsspiegel des Euagrios Pontikos." *Texte und Untersuchungen* 39, 4 (1913): 143–65.

Vices *De vitiis que opposita sunt virtutibus* or *On Virtues Opposed to Vices.* PG 79:1140–44.

SELECT BIBLIOGRAPHY AND WORKS CONSULTED

Amélineau, E. *Histoire des monastères de la Basse-Égypte*. Annales du Musée Guimet 25. Paris, 1894.

———. *De Historia Lausiaca*. Paris, 1887.

Balthasar, H. U. von. "Die Hiera des Evagrius."*Zeitschrift für katholische Theologie* 63 (1939): 86–106, 181– 206.

———. "Metaphysik und Mystik des Evagrius Ponticus." *Zeitschrift für Aszese und Mystik* 14 (1939): 31–47.

Bamberger, J. E. "Desert Calm, Evagrius Ponticus: The Theologian as Spiritual Guide." *Cistercian Studies* 27 (1992): 185–98.

———. *Evagrius Ponticus. The Praktikos: Chapters on Prayer*. Cistercian Studies 4. Kalamazoo: Cistercian Publications, 1981.

Bartelink, G. J. M. *Palladio, La Storia Lausiaca*. Milan: Fondazione Lorenza Valla, 1974.

———. "Les rapports entre le monachisme égyptien et l'épiscopat d'Alexandrie." In *ΑΛΕΞΑΝΔΡΙΝΑ, mélanges offerts à Claude Mondésert S.J.* Paris, 1987.

Battifol, M. "Theologia, Théologie." *Ephemerides Theologicae Lovanienses* 5 (1928): 205–20.

Bernini, G. *Proverbi, versione, introduzione, note*. Rome, 1984.

Berthold, G. "History and Exegesis in Evagrius and Maximus." In *Origeniana Quarta, Die Referate des 4. Internationalen Origeneskongresses (Innsbruck, 2.-6. September 1985)*, edited by Lothar Lies, 390–404. Innsbruck and Vienna, 1987.

Bertocchi, P. "Evagrio Pontico." In *Biblioteca Sanctorum*. Vol. 5, 356–63. Rome, 1964.

Bettiolo, P. *Evagrio Pontico: Per conoscere lui, Exortazione a una vergine. Ai monaci. Ragioni delle osservanze monastiche. Lettera ad Anatolio. Practico. Gnostico. Introduzione, traduzione e note a cura di Paolo Bettiolo*. Bose, 1996.

Bianchi, V. "L'anima in Origene e la questione della metensomatosi." *Augustinianum* 26 (1986): 33–50.

Bostock, G. "The Sources of Origen's Doctrine of Pre-Existence." In *Origeniana Quarta, Die Referate des 4. Internationalen*

Origeneskongresses (Innsbruck, 2.-6. September 1985), edited by Lothar Lies, 259–64. Innsbruck and Vienna, 1987.

Bouillet, M. E. "Le vrai 'Codex regularum' de saint Benoît d'Aniane." *Revue Bénédictine* 75 (1965): 345–49.

Bousset, W. *Apophthegmata: Studien zur Geschichte des ältesten Mönchtums.* Tübingen, 1923.

Bouyer, L. *La spiritualité du Nouveau Testament et des pères.* Paris, 1960.

Büchler, B. *Die Armut der Armen: Ueber den unsprünglichen Sinn der mönchischen Armut.* Munich, 1980.

Bunge, G. *Akedia: Die geistliche Lehre des Evagrios Pontikos vom überdruß.* Cologne, 1989.

———. "<Créé pour être> une citation scripturaire inaperçue dan le <Peri Archon> d'Origène." *Bulletin de litterature ecclesiastique* 98 (1997): 21–29.

———. *Drachenwein und Engelsbrot: Die Lehre des Evagrios Pontikos von Zorn und Sanftmut.* Würzburg, 1999.

———. "Erschaffen und erneuert nach dem Bilde Gottes: Zu den biblisch-theologischen und sakramentalen Grundlagen der evagrianischen Mystik." In *Homo Medietas*, edited by Claudia Brinker-von-der-Heyde and Niklaus Largier. Bern, 1999.

———. "Évagre le Pontique et les deux Macaire." *Irénikon* 56 (1983): 215–27, 323–60.

———. *Evagrio Pontico: Lettere dal deserto, introduzione e note a cura di Gabriel Bunge.* Bose, 1995.

———. *Evagrios Pontikos: Briefe aus der Wüste, Eingeleitet, übersetzt und kommentiert von Gabriel Bunge.* Trier, 1986.

———. *Evagrios Pontikos: Praktikos oder der Mönch, Hundert Kapitel über das geistliche Leben.* Cologne, 1989.

———. "Evagrios Pontikos: Der Prolog des Antirrhetikos." *Studia Monastica* 39 (1997): 77–105.

———. *Das Geistgebet: Studien zum Traktat "De Oratione" des Evagrios Pontikos.* Cologne, 1987.

———. *Geistliche Vaterschaft: Christliche Gnosis bei Evagrios Pontikos.* Regensburg, 1988.

———. "Hénade ou Monade? Au sujet de deux notions centrales de la terminologie évagrienne." *Le Muséon* 102 (1989): 69–91.

———. "Introduction aux fragments coptes de l'Histoire Lausiaque." *Studia Monastica* 32 (1990): 79–129.

———. "Mysterium Unitatis: Der Gedanke der Einheit von Schöpfer und Geschöpf in der evagrianischen Mystik." *Freiburger Zeitschrift für Philosophie und Theologie* 36 (1989): 449–69.

———. "Der Mystische Sinn der Schrift. Anlasslich der Veroffentlichung der Scholien zum Ecclesiasten des Evagrios Pontikos." *Studia Monastica* 36 (1994): 135–46.

―――. "'Nach dem Intellekt Leben': Zum sog. 'Intellektualismus' der evagrianischen Spiritualität." In *Simandron: Festschrift K. Gamber,* edited by W. Nyssen. Cologne, 1989.

―――. "Origenismus-Gnostizismus: Zum geistesgeschichtlichen Standort des Evagrios Pontikos." *Vigiliae Christianae* 40 (1986): 24–54.

―――. "Praktike, Physike und Theologike als Stufen der Erkenntnis bei Evagrios Pontikos." In *Kirche aus Ost und West: Gedenschrift für Wilhelm Nyssen,* edited by M. Schneider and W. Berschin, 59–72. Cologne, 1995.

―――. "The 'Spiritual Prayer': On the Trinitarian Mysticism of Evagrius of Pontus." *Monastic Studies* 17 (1987): 191–208.

―――. *Vasi di argilla, la prassi della preghiera personale secondo la tradizione dei santi padri.* Magnano, 1996.

―――, and Adalbert de Vogüé. *Quatre ermites égyptiens, d'après les fragments coptes de l'Histoire Lausiaque / Présentés par Gabriel Bunge; traduits par Adalbert De Vogüé.* Spiritualité Orientale 60. Bégrolles-en-Mauges (Maine-&-Loire): Abbaye de Bellefontaine, 1994.

Burton-Christie, D. *The Word and the Desert: Scripture and the Quest for Holiness in Early Christian Monasticism.* Oxford, 1993.

Butler, C. *The Lausiac History of Palladius.* 2 vols. Cambridge, 1898, 1904.

Chadwick, H. "Origen, Celsus, and the Resurrection of the Body." *Harvard Theological Review* 49 (1948): 83–102.

―――. *The Sentences of Sextus: A Contribution to the History of Early Christian Ethics.* Cambridge, 1959.

Chitty, D. J. *The Desert a City.* Oxford, 1966.

Clark, E. *The Origenist Controversy: The Cultural Construction of an Early Christian Debate.* Princeton, N.J., 1992.

Colombas, G. *El Monacato Primitivo.* 2 vols. Madrid, 1974.

―――. *La Tradición Benedictina: Ensayo histórico.* Vol. 1. Zamora, 1989.

Comello, F. *Evagrio Pontico: Gli otto spiriti malvagi, a cura di Felice Comello.* Parma, 1990.

Congourdeau, M. H. et al. *Évagre le Pontique, de la prière à la perfection: Au moine Euloge, Sur la Prière.* Paris, 1992.

Conio, C. "Theory and Practice in Evagrius Ponticus." In *Philosophy Theory and Practice: Proceedings of the Internatinal Seminar on World Philosophy,* edited by T. M. P. Mahadevan. Madras, 1974.

Contreras, E. "Evagrio Pontico en los catalogos de varones ilustres." *Salmanticensis* 33 (1986): 333–42.

―――. "Evagrio Pontico: Su vida, su obra, su doctrina." *Cuadernos Monasticos* 11 (1976): 83–95.

Courtonne, Y. *Saint Basile. Lettres.* Vol. 1. Paris, 1957.

Crouzel, H. *Origène.* Paris, 1985.

————. "Origène a-t-il tenu que le Règne du Christ prendrait fin?" *Augustinianum* 26 (1986): 51–62.

————. "Origène, précurseur du monachisme." In *Théologie de la vie monastique*. Théologie 49: 15–38. Paris, 1961.

————. "Recherches sur Origène et son influence." *Bulletin de Littérature Ecclésiastique* 62 (1961): 3–15, 105–13.

————. *Théologie de l'image de Dieu chez Origène*. Théologie 34. Paris, 1956.

Dalmais, I. H. "L'héritage évagrien dans la synthèse de saint Maxime le Confesseur." *Texte und Untersuchungen* 93 (1966): 356–62.

Dattrino, L. *Trattato pratico sulla vita monastica, introduzione, traduzione e note*. Rome, 1992.

Davril, A. "La Psalmodie chez les pères du désert." *Collectanea Cisterciensia* 49 (1987): 132–39.

Dechow, J. F. *Dogma and Mysticism in Early Christianity: Epiphanius of Cyprus and the Legacy of Origen*. Macon, Ga., 1988.

————. "The Heresy Charges against Origen." In *Origeniana Quarta, Die Referate des 4. Internationalen Origeneskongresses (Innsbruck, 2.- 6. September 1985)*, edited by Lothar Lies, 112–22. Innsbruck and Vienna, 1987.

————. "Origen's 'Heresy' from Eustathius to Epiphanius." In *Origeniana Quarta, Die Referate des 4. Internationalen Origeneskongresses (Innsbruck, 2.-6. September 1985)*, edited by Lothar Lies, 405–9. Innsbruck and Vienna, 1987.

Dekkers, E. "ΜΟΝΑΧΟΣ, solitaire, unanime, recueilli." In *Fructus Centesimus: Mélanges offerts à Gerard J. M. Bartelink à l'occasion de son soixante-cinquième anniversaire*, edited by A. A. R. Bastiaensen, A. Hilhorst, and C. H. Kneepkens, 91–104. Steenbrugis, 1989.

Dempt, A. "Evagrios Pontikos als Metaphysiker und Mystiker." *Philosophisches Jahrbuch der Görresgesellschaft* 77 (1970): 297–319.

Desprez, V. "Des diverses mauvaises pensées (2 partie), traduction V. Desprez." In *Lettre de Ligugé* 274 (1995): 24–36.

————. "Évagre le Pontique: Pratique, contemplation, prière." In *Lettre de Ligugé* 274 (1995): 8–23.

————. "Protreptique, Parénéntique, traduction V. Desprez." In *Lettre de Ligugé* 278 (1996): 8–17.

Dorival, G. "Origène et la résurrection de la chair." In *Origeniana Quarta, Die Referate des 4. Internationalen Origeneskongresses (Innsbruck, 2.- 6. September 1985)*, edited by Lothar Lies, 291–321. Innsbruck and Vienna, 1987.

Dornseiff, F. *Das Alphabet in Mystik und Magie*. Leipzig, 1922.

Draguet, R. "L'Histoire Lausiaque, une œuvre écrite dans l'esprit d'Évagre." *Revue d'Histoire Ecclésiastique* 41 (1946): 321–64; 42 (1947): 5–49.

Driscoll, J. *The 'Ad Monachos' of Evagrius Ponticus: Its Structure and a Select Commentary.* Rome, 1991.

———. *Apatheia* and Purity of Heart in Evagrius Ponticus." In *Purity of Heart in Early Ascetic and Monastic Literature*, edited by H. A. Luckman and L. Kulzer, 141–59. Collegeville, Minn., 1999.

———. "The 'Circle of Evagrius': Then and Now." *Studia Monastica* 45 (2003): 7–18.

———. "Evagrius and Paphnutius on the Causes for Abandonment by God." *Studia Monastica* 39 (1997): 259–86.

———. *Evagrius Ponticus: Ad Monachos.* Translation and commentary by Jeremy Driscoll, OSB. Ancient Christian Writers 59. New York/Mahwah, NJ, 2003.

———. "Exegetical Procedures in the Desert Monk Poemen." In *Mysterium Christi: Symbolgegenwart und theologische Bedeutung. Festschrift für Basil Studer*, edited by M. Löhrer and E. Salmann, 155–78. Rome 1995.

———. "The Fathers of Poemen and the Evagrian Connection." *Studia Monastica* 42 (2000): 27–51.

———. "Gentleness in the *Ad Monachos* of Evagrius Ponticus." *Studia Monastica* 32 (1990): 295–321.

———. "A Key for Reading the *Ad Monachos* of Evagrius Ponticus." *Augustinianum* 30 (1990): 361–92.

———. "Listlessness in *The Mirror for Monks* of Evagrius Ponticus." *Cistercian Studies* 24 (1989): 206–14.

———. "'Love of Money' in Evagrius Ponticus." *Studia Monastica* 43 (2001): 21–30.

———. *The Mind's Long Journey to the Holy Trinity: The 'Ad Monachos' of Evagrius Ponticus.* Collegeville, Minn., 1993.

———. "Il pensiero malvagio dell'avarizia, o 'Amore del denaro' in Evagrio Pontico." *Parola, Spirito e Vita* 42 (2001): 219–32.

———. "Penthos and Tears in Evagrius Ponticus." *Studia Monastica* 36 (1994): 147–63.

———. "Spiritual Progress in the Works of Evagrius Ponticus." In *Spiritual Progress, Studies in the Spirituality of Late Antiquity and Early Monasticism*, edited by J. Driscoll and M. Sheridan, 47–84. Rome, 1994.

———. "Spousal Images in Evagrius Ponticus." *Studia Monastica* 38 (1996): 243–56.

Duesberg, H. *Les scribes inspirés.* Paris, 1938.

Durand, M.-G. de. "Évagre le Pontique et le 'Dialogue sur la vie de saint Jean Chrysostome.'" *Bulletin de Littérature Ecclésiastique* 77 (1976): 191–206.

Dysinger, L. "The Significance of Psalmody in the Mystical Theology of Evagrius of Pontus." *Studia Patristica* 30: 176–82. Louvain, 1997.

Elm, S. "Evagrius Ponticus' *Sententiae ad Virginem.*" *Dumbarton Oaks Papers* 45 (1991): 97–120.

————. "The *Sententiae ad Virginem* by Evagrius Ponticus and the Problem of Early Monastic Rules." *Augustinianum* 30 (1990): 393–404.

————. *Virgins of God: The Making of Asceticism in Late Antiquity.* Oxford, 1994.

Evelyn White, H. G. *The Monasteries of the Wâdi 'N Natrûn. Part II: The History of the Monasteries of Nitria and of Scetis.* New York, 1932.

Festugiére, A. J. *Hermes Trismégiste, III.* Paris, 1954.

————. *Historia Monachorum in Aegypto.* Subsidia Hagiographica 53. Brussels, 1971.

Frank, S. *ΑΓΓΕΛΙΚΟΣ ΒΙΟΣ: Begriffsanalytische und begriffsgeschichtliche Untersuchung zum "Engelgleichen Leben" im frühen Mönchtum.* Münster, 1964.

Frankenberg, W. *Evagrius Ponticus.* Abhandlungen der königlichen Gesellschaft der Wissenschaften zu Göttingen. Phil.-hist. Klasse n.F. 13, no. 2. Berlin, 1912.

Géhin, P. "Un nouvel inédit d'Évagre le Pontique: Son commentaire de l'Ecclésiaste." *Byzantion* 49 (1979): 188–98.

————, ed. *Évagre le Pontique, Scholies a l'Ecclésiaste.* Sources Chrétiennes 397. Paris, 1993.

————, ed. *Évagre le Pontique, Scholies aux proverbes.* Sources Chrétiennes 340. Paris, 1987.

————, ed. *Évagre le Pontique, Sur les pensées.* Sources Chrétiennes 438. Paris, 1998.

Gould, G. *The Desert Fathers on Monastic Community.* Oxford, 1993.

————. "A Note on the *Apophthegmata Patrum.*" *Journal of Theological Studies* n.s. 37 (1986): 133–38.

Grébaut, S. "Sentences d'Évagre." *Revue de l'Orient Chrétien* 20 (1915–1917): 211–14, 435–39; 22 (1920–1921): 206–11.

Gregg, R. C. *Athanasius: The Life of Antony and the Letter to Marcellinus, Translation and Introduction.* New York, 1980.

Gressmann, H. "Nonnenspiegel und Mönchsspiegel des Euagrios Pontikos." *Texte und Untersuchungen* 39, no. 4 (1913): 143–65.

Gribomont, J., ed. *Basilio di Cesarea: Le lettere.* Vol 1. Turin, 1983. Letter 8 (pp. 84–113) = Evagrius's *Epistula Fidei.*

Guillaumont, A. *Aux origines du monachisme chrétien: Pour une phénoménologie du monachisme.* Spiritualité Orientale 30. Bellefontaine, 1979.

————. "La conception du désert chez les moines d'Égypte." *Revue de l'Histoire des Religions* 188 (1975): 3–21.

————. "Démon, 2. Évagre le Pontique." *Dictionnaire de spiritualité, ascétique et mystique* 3:196–205.

————. "Évagre et les anathématismes antiorigénistes de 553." *Texte und Untersuchungen* 78 (1961): 219–26.

————. "Evagrius Ponticus." *Theologische Realenzyklopädie* 10:565–70.

————. "Gnose et Monachisme." In *Gnosticisme et monde hellénistique: Les objectifs du colloque de Louvain-la Neuve (11–14 mars 1980),* 97–100. Louvain-la-Neuve, 1980.

————. "Le gnostique chez Clément d'Alexandrie et chez Évagre le Pontique." In *ΑΛΕΞΑΝΔΡΙΝΑ, mélanges offerts à Claude Mondésert S.J.,* 195–201. Paris: Cerf, 1987.

————. "Histoire des moines aux Kellia." *Orientalia Lovaniensia Periodica* 8 (1977): 187–203.

————. "Une inscription copte sur la 'Prière de Jésus.'" *Orientalia Christiana Periodica* 34 (1968): 310–25.

————. "Un philosophe au désert: Évagre le Pontique." *Revue de l'Histoire des Religions* 181 (1972): 29–56.

————. "La 'preghiera pura' di Evagrio e l'influsso del Neoplatonismo." *Dizionario degli Istituti di Perfezione* 7:591–95. Rome, 1983.

————. "La prière de Jésus chez les moines d'Égypte." *Eastern Churches Review* 6 (1974): 66–71.

————. "Le problème des deux Macaire dans les Apophthegmata Patrum." *Irénikon* 48 (1975): 41–59.

————. *Les six centuries des "Kephalaia Gnostica" d'Évagre le Pontique.* Patrologia Orientalis 28, fasc. 1, no. 134. Paris: Firmin-Didot, 1958.

————. "Le travail manuel dans le monachisme ancien. Contestation et valorisation." In *Aux origines du monachisme chrétien: Pour une phénoménologie du monachisme.* Spiritualité Orientale 30, 118–26. Bellefontaine, 1979.

————. "La vision de l'intellect par lui-même dans la mystique évagrienne." *Mélanges de l'Université Saint Joseph,* (1984): 255–62.

————. "Les visions mystiques dans le monachisme oriental chrétien." In *Colloque organisé par le Secrétariat d'État à la Culture,* 116–27. Paris, 1976.

————, ed. *Les 'Képhalaia Gnostica' d'Évagre le Pontique et l'histoire de l'origénisme chez les Syriens.* Patristica Sorbonensia 5. Paris, 1962.

Guillaumont, A. and C. "Évagre le Pontique." *Dictionnaire de spiritualité, ascétique et mystique* 4:1731–44.

————. "Evagrius Ponticus." *Reallexikon für Antike und Christentum* 6:1088–1107.

————. "Le texte véritable des 'Gnostica' d'Évagre le Pontique." *Revue de l'Histoire des Religions* 142 (1952): 156–205.

————, eds. *Évagre le Pontique. Le Gnostique ou a celui qui est devenu digne de la science.* Sources Chrétiennes 356. Paris: Cerf, 1989.

————, eds. *Évagre le Pontique. Traité pratique ou le moine.* Sources Chrétiennes 170, 171. Paris: Cerf, 1971.

Guillaumont, C. "Fragments grecs inédits d'Évagre le Pontique." *Texte und Untersuchungen* 133 (1987): 209–21.

Guy, J. C. "Les Apophthegmata Patrum." In *Théologie de la vie monastique*, 73–83. Paris, 1961.

———. "Un dialogue monastique inédit." *Revue d'ascetique et mystique* 33 (1957): 171–88.

———. "Écriture Sainte et vie spirituelle." *Dictionnaire de spiritualité, ascétique et mystique*, 4:159–64.

———. "Educational Innovation in the Desert Fathers." *Eastern Churches Review* 6 (1974): 44–51.

———. "Note sur l'évolution du genre apophthegmatique." *Revue d'ascetique et mystique* 32 (1956): 63–68.

———. *Recherches sur la tradition grecque des Apophthegmata Patrum.*" Subsidia Hagiographica 36. Brussels, 1962.

———. "Remarques sur le texte des *Apophthegmata Patrum*." *Recherches de Science Religieuse* 43 (1955): 252–58.

Hadot, I. *Arts libéraux et philosophie dans la pensée antique.* Paris, 1984.

Hadot, P. *Exercices spirituels et philosophie antique.* 2d ed. Paris, 1987.

———. *Philosophy as a Way of Life, Edited and with an Introduction by Arnold I. Davidson.* Oxford: Blackwell, 1997.

———. "Théologie, exégèse, révélation, écriture, dans la philosophie grecque." In *Les règles de l'interprétation*, edited by M. Tardieu, 13–34. Paris, 1987.

Hammond, C. P. "The Last Ten Years of Rufinus' Life and the Date of his Move South from Aquileia." *Journal of Theological Studies* 28 (1977): 372–429.

Harl, M. "La préexistence des âmes dans l'oeuvre d'Origène." In *Origeniana Quarta, Die Referate des 4. Internationalen Origeneskongresses (Innsbruck, 2.-6. September 1985)*, edited by Lothar Lies, 238–58. Innsbruck and Vienna, 1987.

———. "Y a-t-il une influence du 'grec biblique' sur la langue spirituelle des chrétiens? Exemples tirés du psaume 118 et de ses commentateurs d'Origène à Théodoret." In *La Bible et les pères*, 243–62. Paris.

Harmless, W. *Desert Christians, An Introduction to the Literature of Early Monasticism.* Oxford, 2004.

———. "Remembering Poemen Remembering: The Desert Fathers and the Spirituality of Memory." *Church History, Studies in Christianity and Culture.* (2000): 483–518.

———, and R. R. Fitzgerald. "The Sapphire Light of the Mind: The *Skemmata* of Evagrius Ponticus." *Theological Studies* 62 (2001): 498–529.

Hausherr, I. "Centuries." *Dictionnaire de spiritualité, ascétique et mystique*, 2:416–18.

———. "Contemplation: Évagre le Pontique." *Dictionnaire de spiritualité, ascétique et mystique,* 2:1775–85.

———. "Les grands courants de la spiritualité orientale." *Orientalia Christiana Periodica* 1 (1935): 114–38.

———. "Ignorance infinie." *Orientalia Christiana Periodica* 2 (1936): 351–62.

———. "Ignorance infinie ou science infinie?" *Orientalia Christiana Periodica* 25 (1959): 44–52.

———. *Les leçons d'un contemplatif: Le Traité de l'Oraison d'Évagre le Pontique.* Paris, 1960.

———. "Nouveaux fragments grecs d'Évagre le Pontique." *Orientalia Christiana Periodica* 5 (1939): 229–33.

———. "L'origine de la théorie orientale des huit péchés capitaux." *Orientalia Christiana* 30 (1933): 164–75.

———. "Par delà l'oraison pure grâce à une coquille. A propos d'un texte d'Évagre." *Revue d'ascétique et de mystique* 13 (1932): 184–88.

———. "Le Traité de l'Oraison d'Évagre le Pontique (Pseudo Nil)." *Revue d'ascétique et de mystique* 15 (1934): 34–93, 113–70.

Hombergen, D. *The Second Origenist Controversy: A New Perspective on Cyril of Scythopolis' Monastic Biographies as Historical Sources for Sixth-Century Origenism.* Rome, 2001.

Hunt, E. D. "Palladius of Helenopolis: A Party and Its Supporters in the Church of the Late Fourth Century." *Journal of Theological Studies* 24 (1973): 456–80.

Ivánka, E. von. "ΚΕΦΑΛΙΑ: Eine byzantinische Literaturform und ihre antiken Wurzeln." *Byzantinische Zeitschrift* 47 (1954): 285–91.

Jaeger, W. *Early Christianity and Greek Paideia.* Cambridge, Mass., 1961.

Joest, C. "Die Bedeutung von Akedia und Apatheia bei Evagrios Pontikos." *Studia Monastica* 35, no. 1 (1993): 48–53.

Jones, C., G. Wainwright, and E. Yarnold, eds. *The Study of Spirituality.* New York, 1986.

Kelly, J. N. D. *Jerome: His Life, Writings and Controversies.* London, 1975.

Klausner, T. "Apophthegma." In *Reallexikon für Antike und Christentum,* 1:545–50.

Kline, F. "The Christology of Evagrius and the Parent System of Origen." *Cistercian Studies* (1985): 155–83.

———. "Regula Benedicti 73:8: A Rule for Beginners." In *Erudition at God's Service,* 97–108. Kalamazoo: Cistercian Publications, 1987.

Labate, A. "L'esegese di Evagrio al libro dell'Ecclesiaste." In *Festschrift A. Ardizzoni,* vol. 1, 485–90. Rome, 1978.

Lackner, W. "Zur profanen Bildung des Euagrios Pontikos." In *Festschrift H. Gerstinger,* 17–29. Graz, 1966.

Langer, S. *Feeling and Form.* New York, 1953.

Le Boulluec, A. "Controverses au sujet de la doctrine d'Origène sur l'âme du Christ." In *Origeniana Quarta, Die Referate des 4. Internationalen Origeneskongresses (Innsbruck, 2.-6. September 1985),* edited by Lothar Lies, 223–38. Innsbruck and Vienna, 1987.

Leclercq, J. "L'ancienne version latine des Sentences d'Évagre pour les moines." *Scriptorium* 5 (1951): 195–213.

———. *The Love of Learning and the Desire for God,* translated by C. Misrahi. New York, 1961.

Lefort, L. T. "A propos d'un aphorisme d'Evagrius Ponticus." *Académie Royale de Belgique. Bulletin de la classe des lettres et des sciences morales et politiques,* 5 série, vol. 36 (1950): 70–79.

Lemaire, J. P. "L'abbé Poemen et la sainte écriture." Licentiate thesis, University of Friburg, 1971.

Levasti, A. "Il più grande mistico del deserto: Evagrio Il Pontico (399)." *Rivista di Ascetica e Mistica* 13 (1968): 242–64.

Lienhard, J. "On Discernment of Spirits in the Early Church." *Theological Studies* 41 (1980): 505–29.

Lilla, S. *Clement of Alexandria.* Oxford, 1971.

Linge, D. E. "Leading the Life of Angels: Ascetic Practice and Reflection in the Writings of Evagrius of Pontus." *Journal of the American Academy of Religion* 68 (2000): 537–68.

Louf, A. "L'acédie chez Évagre le Pontique." *Concilium* 99 (1974): 113–17.

———."Spiritual Fatherhood in the Literature of the Desert." In *Abba: Guides to Wholeness and Holiness East and West,* edited by J. R. Sommerfeldt, 37–63. Kalamazoo: Cistercian Publications, 1982.

Louth, A. *Discerning the Mystery: An Essay on the Nature of Theology.* Oxford, 1983.

———. *The Origins of the Christian Mystical Tradition: From Plato to Denys.* Oxford, 1981.

Luibheid, C. *John Cassian, Conferences: Translation and Preface by Colm Luibheid.* New York, 1985.

Marsili, S. *Giovanni Cassiano ed Evagrio Pontico: Dottrina sulla carità e contemplazione.* Studia Anselmiana 6. Rome, 1936.

Méhat, A. *Étude sur les 'Stromates' de Clément d'Alexandrie.* Paris, 1966.

Melcher, R. *Der 8. Brief des hl. Basilius, ein Werk des Evagrius Pontikus.* Münster, 1923.

Messana, V. "La Chiesa orante nella catechesi spirituale di Evagrio Pontico." In *Biblioteca di science religiose* 46:173–86. Rome, 1982.

———. *Evagrio Pontico: La Preghiera. Introduzione, traduzione e note a cura di Vencenzo Messana.* Rome, 1994.

Miquel, P. *Lexique du désert: Étude de quelques mots-clés du vocabulaire monastique grec ancien.* Bellefontaine, 1986.

Moine, N. "Melaniana." *Recherches Augustiniennes* 15 (1980): 3–79.

Mondésert, C. *Clément d'Alexandrie, Introduction à l'étude de sa pensée à partir de l'Écriture.* Paris, 1944.

Mortari, L. *I padri del deserto: Detti.* Rome, 1980.

———. *Vita e detti dei padri del deserto.* Rome, 1975.

Moscatelli, F. *Gli otto spiriti della malvagità, sui diversi pensieri della malvagità, traduzione, introduzione e note di Francesca Moscatelli.* Milan, 1996.

Mühmelt, M. "Zu der neuen lateinischen Übersetzung des Mönchsspiegels des Euagrius." *Vigiliae Christianae* 7 (1953): 101–3.

Murphy, F. X. "Evagrius Ponticus and Origenism." In *Origeniana Tertia,* edited by R. P. C. Hanson and H. Crouzel, 253–69. Rome, 1985.

———. *Rufinus of Aquileia (345–411): His Life and Works.* Washington, D.C., 1945.

Muyldermans, J. *Evagriana.* Extrait de la revue *Le Muséon,* vol. 42, augmenté de *Nouveaux fragments grecs inédits.* Paris, 1931.

———. *Evagriana.* Extrait de la revue *Le Muséon,* vol. 51. Paris, 1938.

———. *Evagriana Syriaca,* Bibliothèque du Muséon 31. Louvain, 1952.

———. *A travers la tradition manuscrite d'Évagre le Pontique.* Bibliothèque du Muséon 3. Louvain, 1932.

Neumann, G., ed. *Der Aphorismus: Zur Geschichte, zu den Formen und Möglichkeiten einer literarischen Gattung.* Darmstadt, 1976.

Niescior, L. *Anachoreza w Pismach Ewagriusza z Pontu.* Cracow, 1997.

Norris, F. "The Authenticity of Gregory Nazianzen's Five Theological Orations." *Vigiliae Christianae* 39 (1985): 331–39.

O'Cleirigh, P. "Knowledge of This World in Origen." In *Origeniana Quarta, Die Referate des 4. Internationalen Origeneskongresses (Innsbruck, 2.-6. September 1985),* edited by Lothar Lies, 349–51. Innsbruck and Vienna, 1987.

O'Laughlin, M. "The Bible, the Demons, and the Desert: Evaluating the *Antirrheticus* of Evagrius Ponticus." *Studia Monastica* 34 (1992): 201–15.

———. "Evagrius Ponticus in Spiritual Perspective." In *Studia Patristica* 30 (1997): 224–30.

———. *Origenism in the Desert: Anthropology and Integration in Evagrius Ponticus.* Ann Arbor, Mich., 1987.

Parmentier, M. "Evagrius of Pontus and the 'Letter to Melania.'" *Bijdragen, tijdschrift voor filosofie en theologie* 46 (1985): 2–38.

Peterson, E. "Zu griechischen Asketikern. I. Zu Euagrius Ponticus." *Byzantinisch-Neugriechische Jahrbücher* 4 (1923): 5–8.

———. "Zu griechischen Asketikern. II. Noch einmal zu Euagrius Ponticus." *Byzantinisch-Neugriechische Jahrbücher* 5 (1926/27): 412–14.

———. "Zu griechischen Asketikern. III. Zu Euagrius." *Byzantinisch-Neugriechische Jahrbücher* 9 (1930–1932): 51–54.

Pitra, J. B. *Analecta sacra spicilego Solesmensi, parat,* vol. 2, Frascati, 1884; vol. 3, Paris, 1883.

Ramsey, B. *John Cassian: The Conferences, Translated and Annotated by Boniface Ramsey,* O.P. New York, 1997.

Refoulé, F. "La Christologie d'Évagre et l'Origénisme." *Orientalia Christiana Periodica* 27 (1961): 221–66.

———. "Évagre fut-il origéniste?" *Recherches de Science Philosophiques et Théologiques* 47 (1963): 398–402.

———. "La mystique d'Évagre et l'Origénisme." *Vie Spirituelle, Supplément* 64 (1963): 453–72.

———. "Rêves et vie spirituelle d'aprés Évagre le Pontique." *Vie Spirituelle, Supplement* 56 (1961): 470–516.

Regnault, L. "Les apophthegmes et l'idéal du désert." In *Commandements du seigneur et libération évangélique,* edited by J. Gribomont, 47–79. Studia Anselmiana 70. Rome, 1977.

———. *Immerwährendes Gebet bein den Vätern.* Cologne, 1993.

———. "La priere continuelle 'monologistos' dan la littérature apophthegmatique." *Irénikon* 47 (1974): 467–93.

———. *Les sentences des pères du désert.* 4 vols. Solesmes, 1966–1981.

———. *Les sentences des pères du désert: Troisième recueil & tables.* Solesmes, 1987.

———. *La vie quotidienne des pères du désert en Égypte au IV siècle.* Hachette, 1990.

Rondeau, M. J. "Le commentaire sur les Psaumes d'Évagre le Pontique." *Orientalia Christiana Periodica* 26 (1960): 307–48.

———. *Les commentaires patristiques du Psautier (III-V siècles).* Vol. 1. Orientalia Christiana Analecta 219. Rome, 1982.

Rousseau, P. *Ascetics, Authority, and the Church in the Age of Jerome and Cassian.* Oxford, 1978.

Rubenson, S. "Evagrios Pontikos und die Theologie der Wüste." In *Logos. Festschrift für Luise Abramowski zum 8. Juli 1993,* edited by H. C. Brennecke, E. L. Grasmück, and C. Markshies, 384–401. Berlin and New York, 1993.

———. *The Letters of St. Anthony: Origenist Theology, Monastic Tradition and the Making of a Saint.* Lund, 1990.

Rutherford, R. B. *The Meditations of Marcus Aurelius.* Oxford, 1989.

Sheridan, Mark. "The Controversy over ἀπάθεια: Cassian's Sources and His Use of Them." *Studia Monastica* 39 (1997): 287–310.

———. "Il mondo spirituale e intellettuale del primo monachesimo egiziano," in *L'Egitto cristiano: aspetti e problemi in età tardo-antico,* ed. A. Camplani, 177–216. Rome, 1997.

Sinkewicz, R. E. *Evagrius of Pontus, The Greek Ascetic Corpus, Translated with Introduction and Commnentary.* Oxford, 2003.

Skehan, P. "Wisdom's House." In *Studies in Israelite Poetry and Wisdom*, 27–45. Washington, D.C., 1971.

Spoerri, W. "Gnome." In *Der Kleine Pauly* 2:822–29.

Stewart, C. *Cassian the Monk*. Oxford, 1998.

———. "From λογος to *verbum:* John Cassian's Use of Greek in the Development of a Latin Monastic Vocabulary." In *The Joy of Learning and the Love of God: Essays in Honor of Jean Leclercq*, 5–31. Kalamazoo: Cistercian Publications, 1995.

———. "Imageless Prayer and the Theological Vision of Evagrius Ponticus." *Journal of Early Christian Studies* 9 (2001): 173–204.

———. "Radical Honesty about the Self: The Practice of the Desert Fathers." *Sobornost*, 12 (1990): 25–39.

Stroumsa, G. G. "Ascèse et gnose: Aux origines de la spiritualité monastique." *Revue Thomiste* 89 (1981): 557–73.

———. "The Manichaean Challenge to Egyptian Christianity." In *The Roots of Egyptian Christianity*, edited by B. A. Pearson and J. E. Goehring, 307–19. Philadelphia, 1986.

Szymusiak, I. *Elements de théologie de l'homme selon Saint Grégoire de Nazianze*. Rome, 1963.

Taft, R. "The Egyptian Monastic Office in the Fourth Century." Part 1, chapter 4 of *The Liturgy of the Hours in East and West*. Collegeville, Minn., 1986.

Tamburini, M. E. "Espejo de Monjes." In *Evagrio Pontico: Tratado de la Oracion, Tratado Practico, Espejo de Monjes, Espejo de Monjas*, 21–31. Publicación de Cuadernos Monásticos, 1976.

Thompson, J. *The Form and Function of Provebs in Ancient Israel*. The Hague, 1974.

Torjesen, K. J. "Pedagogical Soteriology from Clement to Origen." In *Origeniana Quarta, Die Referate des 4. Internationalen Origeneskongresses (Innsbruck, 2.-6. September 1985)*, edited by Lothar Lies, 370–78. Innsbruck and Vienna, 1987.

Tugwell, S. *Evagrius Ponticus: Practikos and On Prayer*, translated by Simon Tugwell. Published privately by the Faculty of Theology, Oxford, 1987.

Van Den Ven, P. "Un opuscule inédit attribué à S. Nil." In *Mélanges Godefroy Kurth* 2:73–81. Liège, 1908.

Veilleux, A. "Monasticism and Gnosis in Egypt." In *The Roots of Egyptian Christianity*, edited by B. A. Pearson and J. E. Goehring, 271–306. Philadelphia, 1986.

Viller, M. "Aux sources de la spiritualité de S. Maxime le Confesseur: Les oeuvres d'Évagre le Pontique." *Revue d'ascétique et de mystique* 11 (1930): 156–84, 239–68, 331–36.

Vitestam, G. "Seconde partie du Traité, qui passe sous le nom de 'La grande lettre d'Évagre le Pontique à Mélanie l'Ancienne.'" *Scripta Minora Regiae Societatis Humaniorum Litterarum Lundensis* 1963–1964: no. 3, 3–29. Lund, 1964.

Vivian, T. "Coptic Palladiana II: The Life of Evagrius (Lausiac History 38)." *Coptic Church Review* 21 (2000): 8–23.

Vogüé, A. de. "La lecture du Matin dans les Sentences d'Évagre et le *De Virginitate* attribué à saint Athanase." *Studia Monastic* 26 (1984): 7–11.

———. "Un morceau célèbre de Cassien parmi des estraits d'Évagre." *Studia Monastica* 27 (1985): 7–12.

———. "Psalmodier n'est pas prier." *Ecclesia Orans* 6 (1989): 7–32.

———. *Les règles monastiques anciennes (400–700)*. Turnhout, 1985.

Von Rad, G. *Old Testament Theology*. Vol. 1, translated by D. M. J. Stalker. New York, 1962.

———. *Weisheit in Israel*. Neukirchen-Vluyn, 1970.

Waddell, H. *The Desert Fathers*. London, 1936.

Ward, B. *The Sayings of the Desert Fathers: The Alphabetical Collection*. Kalamazoo: Cistercian Publications, 1975.

Williams, J. G. *Those Who Ponder Proverbs: Aphoristic Thinking and Biblical Literature*. Sheffield, 1981.

Wilmart, A. "Les versions latines des Sentences d'Évagre pour les vierges." *Revue Bénédictine* 28 (1911): 143–53.

Wipszycka, E., *Études sur le christianisme dans l'Égypte de l'antiquité tardive*. Rome, 1996.

Wisse, F. "Die Sextus-Spruche und das Problem der gnostischen Ethik." In *Zum Hellenismus in den Schriften von Nag Hammadi,* edited by A. Böhlig and F. Wisse, 55–86. Wiesbaden, 1975.

Young, R. D. "Evagrius the Iconographer: Monastic Pedagogy in the *Gnostikos*." *Journal of Early Christian Studies* 9 (2001): 53–71.

Zandee, J. "Les enseignements de Silvanos et Philon d'Alexandrie." In *Mélanges d'histoire des religions offerts à H.-Ch. Puech*, 337–45. Paris, 1974.

———. "God and Man in 'The Teachings of Silvanus' (Nag Hammadi Codex VII, 4)." In *Proceedings of the XIIth International Congress of the International Association for the History of Religions*. Studies in the History of Religions (Supplements to Numen) 31, edited by C. J. Bleeker, G. Widengren, and J. Sharpe, 209–20. Leiden, 1975.

———. "Die Lehren des Silvanus: Stoischer Rationalismus und Christentum im Zeitalter der Frühkatholischen Kirche." In *Essays on the Nag Hammadi Texts in Honour of A. Böhlig,* edited by M. Krause, 144–55. Nag Hammadi Studies 3. Leiden, 1972.

———. *"The Teachings of Silvanus" and Clement of Alexandria: A New Document of Alexandrian Theology*. Leiden, 1977.

Zandee, J., and M. Peel. "The Teachings of Silvanus from the Library of Nag Hammadi." *Novum Testamentum* 14 (1972): 294–311.

————. "The Teachings of Silvanus (VII, 4), Introduced and translated by Malcolm L. Peel and Jan Zandee, edited by Frederik Wisse." In *The Nag Hammadi Library in English,* edited by J. M. Robinson. Leiden, 1977.

Other books in The Newman Press series: